AS
economics

Peter Smith

OCR

AS
economics

Peter Smith

philip allan
UPDATES

Philip Allan Updates, an imprint of Hodder Education, part of Hachette Livre UK, Market Place, Deddington, Oxfordshire OX15 0SE

Orders

Bookpoint Ltd, 130 Milton Park, Abingdon, Oxfordshire, OX14 4SB
tel: (44) 01235 827720
fax: (44) 01235 400454
e-mail: uk.orders@bookpoint.co.uk
Lines are open 9.00 a.m.–5.00 p.m., Monday to Saturday, with a 24-hour message answering service. You can also order through the Philip Allan Updates website: www.philipallan.co.uk

ISBN: 978-0-340-94807-1

First printed 2008
Impression number   5   4   3   2
Year   2013   2012   2011   2010   2009   2008

This textbook has been written specifically to support students studying OCR AS Economics. The content has been neither approved nor endorsed by OCR and remains the sole responsibility of the author.

All website addresses included in this book are correct at the time of going to press but may subsequently change.

All photographs are reproduced by permission of TopFoto, except where otherwise specified.

Design and artwork by Juha Sorsa and Dianne Shaw
Printed in Italy

Hachette Livre UK's policy is to use papers that are natural, renewable and recyclable products and made from wood grown in sustainable forests. The logging and manufacturing processes are expected to conform to the environmental regulations of the country of origin.

Contents

Introduction.. vi

Part 1   Markets in action

Chapter 1   Introducing economics 2
Chapter 2   The nature of demand 16
Chapter 3   The nature of supply 25
Chapter 4   Using the demand and supply model 31
Chapter 5   Prices, resource allocation and market failure 49
Chapter 6   Externalities 64
Chapter 7   Other forms of market failure 81
Chapter 8   Government intervention and government failure 92
Review section 103

Part 2   The national and international economy

Chapter 9   Measuring economic performance 110
Chapter 10   Aggregate demand 126
Chapter 11   Aggregate supply and macroeconomic equilibrium 136
Chapter 12   The balance of payments and the exchange rate 142
Chapter 13   Macroeconomic policy objectives 155
Chapter 14   Economic growth 168
Chapter 15   Macroeconomic policy instruments 183
Chapter 16   The international economy 196
Review section 211

Index... 217

Introduction

This textbook provides an introduction to economics. It has been tailored explicitly to cover the content of the OCR specification for AS economics. The book is divided into two parts, each covering one of the modules that make up the AS programme of study.

The text provides the foundation for studying OCR economics, but you will no doubt wish to keep up to date by referring to additional topical sources of information about economic events. This can be done by reading the serious newspapers, visiting key sites on the internet, and by reading such magazines as *Economic Review*.

The text features the following:
➤ a statement of the intended learning outcomes for each chapter
➤ clear and concise but comprehensive explanation and analysis of economic terms and concepts
➤ definitions of key terms
➤ examples to show these concepts applied to real-world situations
➤ exercises to provide active engagement with economic analysis

A separate Teacher Guide is available that provides complete answers to all exercises, plus additional material for use in the classroom.

Assessment objectives

In common with other economics specifications, OCR economics entails four assessment objectives. Candidates will thus be expected to:
➤ demonstrate knowledge and understanding of the specified content
➤ apply this knowledge and critical understanding to problems and issues arising from both familiar and unfamiliar situations
➤ analyse economic problems and issues
➤ evaluate economic arguments and evidence, making informed judgements

In the overall assessment of the A-level, the four assessment objectives count equally. However, there is a greater weighting given to the first two objectives in AS, and a greater weighting to the final two objectives in A2.

*(See the OCR AS/A-level GCE Economics specification at **www.ocr.org.uk**.)*

Economics

Economics is different from some other AS subjects in that relatively few students will have studied it before embarking on the AS course. The text thus begins from the beginning, and provides a thorough foundation in the subject and its applications. By studying this book, you should develop an awareness of the economist's approach to issues and problems, and the economist's way of thinking about the world.

The study of economics also requires a familiarity with recent economic events in the UK and elsewhere, and candidates will be expected to show familiarity with 'recent historical data' — broadly defined as the last 7 to 10 years. The following websites will help you to keep up to date with recent trends and events.

Recent and historical data about the UK economy can be found at the website of the Office for National Statistics (ONS) at:
www.statistics.gov.uk/

Also helpful is the site of HM Treasury at:
www.hm-treasury.gov.uk/

The Bank of England site is well worth a visit, especially the *Inflation Report* and the Minutes of the Monetary Policy Committee:
www.bankofengland.co.uk/

The Institute for Fiscal Studies offers an independent view of a range of economic topics:
www.ifs.org.uk

For information about other countries, visit the following:
www.oecd.org/home/
http://europa.eu.int/
www.worldbank.org/
www.undp.org/

Another way of keeping up to date with economic topics and events is to read *Economic Review*, a magazine specifically written for A-level economics students, also published by Philip Allan Updates.

How to study economics

There are two crucial aspects of studying economics. The first stage is to study the theory, which helps us to explain economic behaviour. However, in studying AS economics it is equally important to be able to apply the theories and concepts that you meet, and to see just how these relate to the real world.

If you are to become competent at this, it is vital that you get plenty of practice. In part, this means carrying out the exercises that you will find in this text. However, it also means thinking about how economics helps us to explain news items and data that appear in the newspapers and on the television. Make sure that you practise as much as you can.

In economics, it is also important to be able to produce examples of economic phenomena. In reading this text, you will find some examples that help to illustrate ideas and concepts. Do not rely solely on the examples provided here, but look around the world to find your own examples, and keep a note of these ready for use in essays and exams. This will help to convince the examiners that you have understood economics. It will also help you to understand the theories.

Enjoy economics

Most important of all, I hope you will enjoy your study of economics. I have always been fascinated by the subject, and hope that you will capture something of the excitement and challenge of learning about how markets and the economy operate. I also wish you every success with your AS studies.

Acknowledgements

I would like to express my deep gratitude to Mark Russell, whose thorough reading of the book's precursor and insightful and helpful comments were invaluable in improving the scope and focus of this book. I would also like to thank everyone at Philip Allan Updates, especially Penny Fisher, David Cross and Rachel Furse, for their efficiency in production of this book, and for their support and encouragement.

Many of the data series shown in figures in this book were drawn from the data obtained from the National Statistics website: **www.statistics.gov.uk** Crown copyright material is reproduced with the permission of the Controller of HMSO (PSI licence number C2007001851).

Other data were from various sources, including OECD, World Bank, United Nations Development Programme and other sources as specified.

While every effort has been made to trace the owners of copyright material, I would like to apologise to any copyright holders whose rights may have unwittingly been infringed.

Peter Smith

Markets in action

Part 1

Chapter 1
Introducing economics

Welcome to economics. Many of you opening this book will be meeting economics for the first time, and you will want to know what is in store for you as you set out to study the subject. This opening chapter sets the scene by introducing you to some key ideas and identifying the scope of economic analysis. As you learn more of the subject, you will find that economics is a way of thinking that will broaden your perspective on the world around you.

Learning outcomes

This chapter will introduce you to:
➤ the nature and scope of economic analysis
➤ the concept of opportunity cost
➤ market, centrally planned and mixed economies
➤ the distinction between microeconomics and macroeconomics
➤ the notion of factors of production
➤ the role of models and assumptions in economics
➤ the production possibility curve
➤ the concept of the division of labour
➤ how specialisation can improve productivity
➤ the role of markets
➤ the importance of money and exchange in an economy
➤ positive and normative statements

The economic problem

For any society in the world, the fundamental economic problem faced is that of **scarcity**. You might think that this is obvious for some societies in the less developed world, where poverty and hunger are rife. But it is also true for relatively prosperous economies such as those of Switzerland, the USA or the UK.

 term

scarcity: a situation that arises because people have unlimited wants in the face of limited resources

It is true in the sense that all societies have *finite resources*, but people have *unlimited wants*. A big claim? Not really. There is no country in the world in which all wants can be met, and this is clearly true at the global level.

Talking about *scarcity* in this sense is not the same as talking about *poverty*. Poverty might be seen as an extreme form of scarcity, in which individuals lack the basic necessities of life — whereas even relatively prosperous people face scarcity because resources are limited.

Scarcity and choice

The key issue that arises from the existence of scarcity is that it forces people to make choices. Each individual must choose which goods and services to consume. In other words, everyone needs to prioritise the consumption of whatever commodities they need or would like to have, as they cannot satisfy all their wants. Similarly, at the national level, governments have to make choices between alternative uses of resources.

It is this need to choose that underlies the subject matter of economics. Economic analysis is about analysing those choices made by individual people, firms or governments.

Opportunity cost

This raises one of the most important concepts in all of economic analysis — the notion of **opportunity cost**. When an individual chooses to consume one good, she does so at the cost of the item that would have been next in her list of priorities. For example, suppose you are on a strict diet and at the end of the day you can 'afford' either one chocolate or a piece of cheese. If you choose the cheese, the opportunity cost of the cheese is the chocolate that you could have had instead. In other words, the opportunity cost is the value of the next-best alternative forgone.

Key term

opportunity cost: in decision making, the value of the next-best alternative forgone

This important notion can be applied in many different contexts because, whenever you make a decision, you reject an alternative in favour of your chosen option. You have chosen to read this book — when instead you could be watching television or meeting friends.

Exercise 1.1

Andrew has just started his AS courses, and has chosen to take economics, mathematics, geography and French. Although he was certain about the first three, it was a close call between French and English. What is Andrew's opportunity cost of choosing French?

As you move further into studying economics, you will encounter this notion of opportunity cost again and again. For example, firms take decisions about the sort of economic activity in which to engage. A market gardener with limited land available has to decide whether to plant onions or potatoes; if he decides to grow onions, he has to forgo the opportunity to grow potatoes. From the government's point of view, if it decides to devote more resources to the National Health Service, it will have fewer resources available for, say, defence.

The coordination problem

With so many different individuals and organisations (consumers, firms, governments) all taking decisions, a major question is how it all comes together. How are all these separate decisions coordinated so that the overall allocation of resources in a society is coherent? In other words, how can it be ensured that firms produce the commodities that consumers wish to consume? And how can the distribution of these products be organised? These are some of the basic questions that economics sets out to answer.

Key terms

market economy: market forces are allowed to guide the allocation of resources within a society

centrally planned economy: decisions on resource allocation are guided by the state

mixed economy: resources are allocated partly through price signals and partly on the basis of direction by government

A **market economy** is one in which market forces are allowed to guide the allocation of resources within a society. Prices play a key role in this sort of system, providing signals and incentives to producers and consumers.

In contrast, a **centrally planned economy** is one in which the government undertakes the coordination role, planning and directing the allocation of resources. Such micromanagement has proved costly to implement administratively. The collapse of the Soviet bloc in the 1990s largely discredited this approach, although a small number of countries (such as North Korea and Cuba) continue to stick with central planning.

Most economies operate a **mixed economy** system, in which market forces are complemented by some state intervention. It has been argued that any such state intervention should be *market-friendly*: in other words, when governments do intervene in the economy, they should do so in a way that helps markets to work, rather than trying to have the government replace market forces.

Another important concept that is at the heart of economic analysis is the notion that individuals respond to *incentives*. The difference in the way in which the coordination problem is handled in different forms of economy is through different forms of incentives that influence decision making. In a market economy, prices and profits provide incentives, whereas these incentives are replaced by state directives in a centrally planned economy.

Factors of production

People in a society play two quite different roles. On the one hand, they are the consumers, the ultimate beneficiaries of the process of production. On the other, they are a key part of the production process in that they are instrumental in producing goods and services.

More generally, it is clear that both *human resources* and *physical resources* are required as part of the production process. These productive resources are known as the **factors of production**.

Key *term*

factors of production: resources used in the production process; *inputs* into production, including labour, capital, land and entrepreneurship

The most obvious human resource is *labour*. Labour is a key input into production. Of course, there are many different types of labour, encompassing different skill levels and working in different ways. *Entrepreneurship* is another human resource. An entrepreneur is someone who organises production and identifies projects to be undertaken, bearing the risk of the activity. *Management* is also sometimes classified as a human resource, although it might be seen as a particular form of labour. *Natural resources* are also inputs into the production process. In particular, all economic activities require some use of *land*, and most use some raw materials. An important distinction here is between *renewable resources* such as forests, and *non-renewable resources* such as oil or coal.

There are also *produced resources* — inputs that are the product of a previous manufacturing process. If you like, these can be regarded as a stock of past production used to aid current production. For example, machines are used in the production process; they are resources manufactured for the purpose of producing other goods. These inputs are referred to as *capital*, which includes things like factory buildings and transport equipment as well as plant and machinery.

Factors of production — labour (workers), capital (buildings) and land

The way in which these inputs are combined in order to produce output is another important part of the allocation of resources. Firms need to take decisions about the mix of inputs used in order to produce their output. Such decisions are required in whatever form of economic activity a firm is engaged.

Exercise 1.2

Classify each of the following as human, natural (renewable or non-renewable) or produced resources:

a timber

b services of a window cleaner

c natural gas

d solar energy

e a combine harvester

f a computer programmer who sets up a company to market his software

g a computer

By now you should be getting some idea of the subject matter of economics. The US economist Paul Samuelson (who won the Nobel Prize for Economic Sciences in 1970) identified three key questions that economics sets out to investigate:

1 *What?* What goods and services should be produced in a society from its scarce resources? In other words, how should resources be allocated among producing DVD players, potatoes, banking services and so on?
2 *How?* How should the productive resources of the economy be used to produce these various goods and services?
3 *For whom?* Having produced a range of goods and services, how should these be allocated among the population for consumption?

Exercise 1.3

With which of Samuelson's three questions (what, how, for whom) would you associate the following?

a A firm chooses to switch from producing CD players in order to increase its output of DVD recorders.

b The government reduces the highest rate of income tax.

c Faced with increased labour costs, a firm introduces labour-saving machinery.

d There is an increase in social security benefits.

e The owner of a fish-and-chip shop decides to close down and take a job in a local factory.

Summary

➤ The fundamental problem faced by any society is scarcity, because resources are finite but wants are unlimited. As a result, choices need to be made.

➤ Each choice has an opportunity cost — the value of the next-best alternative.

➤ Decisions need to be coordinated within a society, either by market forces or by state intervention, or a mixture of the two.

➤ The amount of output produced in a period depends upon the inputs of factors of production.

➤ Economics deals with the questions of what should be produced, how it should be produced, and for whom.

Models and assumptions

Economics sets out to tackle some complex issues concerning what is a very complex real world. This complexity is such that it is essential to simplify reality in some way; otherwise the task would be overwhelming. Economists thus work with **models**. These are simplified versions of reality that are more tractable for analysis, allowing economists to focus on some key aspects of the world.

 Key *term*

model: a simplified representation of reality used to provide insight into economic decisions and events

Often this works by allowing them to focus on one thing at a time. A model almost always begins with assumptions that help economists to simplify their questions. These assumptions can then be gradually relaxed so that the effect of each one of them can be observed. In this way, economists can gradually move towards a more complicated version of reality.

In evaluating a model, it is not a requirement that it be totally realistic. The model's desired objectives may be to predict future behaviour, or test empirical evidence collected from the real world. If a model provides insights into how individuals take decisions or helps to explain economic events, then it has some value, even if it seems remote from reality.

However, it is always important to examine the assumptions that are made, and to ask what happens if these assumptions do not hold.

Opportunity cost and the production possibility curve

Economists rely heavily on diagrams to help in their analysis. In exploring the notion of opportunity cost, a helpful diagram is the **production possibility curve (PPC)**, also known as the production possibility frontier. This shows the maximum combinations of goods that can be produced with a given set of resources.

Key *term*

production possibility curve: a curve showing the maximum combinations of goods or services that can be produced in a set period of time given available resources

First consider a simple example. In Exercise 1.1, Andrew was studying for his AS. Suppose now that he has got behind with his homework. He has limited time available, and has five economics questions to answer and five maths exercises to do. An economics question takes the same time to answer as a maths exercise.

What are the options? Suppose he knows that in the time available he can either tackle all of the maths and none of the economics, or all of the economics and none of the maths. Alternatively, he can try to keep both teachers happy by doing some of each. Figure 1.1 shows his options. He can devote all of his efforts to maths, and leave the economics for another day. He will then be at point *A* in the figure. Alternatively, he can do all the economics exercises and no maths, and be at point *B*. The line joining these two extreme points shows the intermediate possibilities. For example, at *C* he does 2 economics exercises and 3 maths problems.

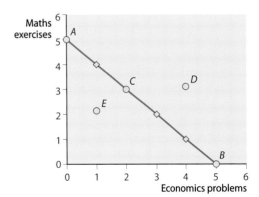

Figure 1.1 *The production possibility curve*

The line shows the maximum combinations that Andrew can tackle — which is why it is sometimes called a 'frontier'. There is no way he can manage to be beyond the frontier (for example, at point *D*), as he does not have the time

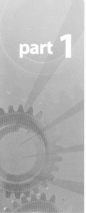

(i.e. resources) to do so. However, he could end up *inside* the frontier, at a point such as E. This could happen if he gives up, and squanders his time by watching television; that would be an inefficient use of his resources – at least in terms of tackling his homework.

As Andrew moves down the line from left to right, he is spending more time on economics and less on maths. The opportunity cost of tackling an additional economics question is an additional maths exercise forgone.

Figure 1.2 shows how the *PPC* provides information about opportunity cost. Suppose we have a farmer with 10 hectares of land who is choosing between growing potatoes and onions. The *PPC* shows the combinations of the two crops that could be produced. For example, if the farmer produces 300 tonnes of onions on part of the land, then 180 tonnes of potatoes could be produced from the remaining land. In order to increase production of potatoes by 70 tonnes from 180 to 250, 50 tonnes of onions must be given up. Thus, the opportunity cost of 70 extra tonnes of potatoes is seen to be 50 tonnes of onions.

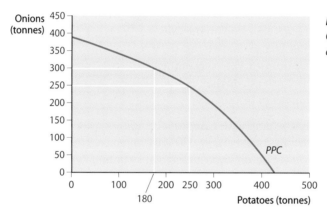

Figure 1.2
Opportunity cost and the PPC

Consumption and investment

To move from thinking about an individual to thinking about an economy as a whole, it is first necessary to simplify reality. Assume an economy that produces just two types of good: capital goods and consumer goods. Consumer goods are for present use, whereas the capital goods are to be used to increase the future capacity of the economy – in other words, for investment.

Figure 1.3 illustrates society's options in a particular period. Given the resources available, society can produce any combination of capital and consumer goods along the *PPC*. Thus, point A represents one possible combination of outputs, in which the economy produces C_1 consumer goods and K_1 capital goods.

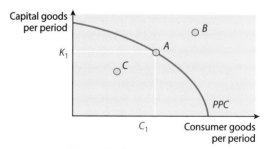

Figure 1.3 *Capital and consumer goods*

As with the simpler examples, if society were to move to the right along the *PPC*, it would produce more consumer goods — but at the expense of capital goods. Thus, it can be seen that the opportunity cost of producing consumer goods is in terms of forgone opportunities to produce capital goods. Notice that the *PPC* has been drawn as a curve instead of a straight line. This is because not all factors of production are equally suited to the production of both sorts of good. When the economy is well balanced, as at *A*, the factors can be allocated to the uses for which they are best equipped. However, as the economy moves towards complete specialisation in one of the types of good, factors are no longer being best used, and the opportunity cost changes. For example, if nearly all of the workers are engaged in producing consumer goods, it becomes more difficult to produce still more of these, whereas those workers producing machinery find they have too few resources with which to work. In other words, the more consumer goods are being produced, the higher is their opportunity cost.

It is now possible to interpret points *B* and *C*. Point *B* is unreachable given present resources, so the economy cannot produce that combination of goods. This applies to any point outside the *PPC*. On the other hand, at point *C* society is not using its resources efficiently. In this position there is *unemployment* of some resources in the economy. By making better use of the resources available, the economy can move towards the frontier, reducing unemployment in the process.

Economic growth

Figure 1.3 focused on a single period. However, if the economy is producing capital goods, then in the following period its capacity to produce should increase, as it will have more resources available for production. How can this be shown on the diagram? An expansion in the available inputs suggests that in the next period the economy should be able to produce more of both goods. This is shown in Figure 1.4.

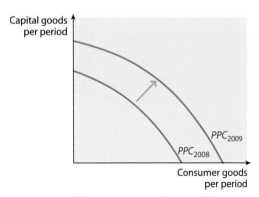

Figure 1.4 Economic growth

Suppose that in the year 2008 the production possibility curve was at PPC_{2008}. However, in the following year the increased availability of resources enables greater produc-

Key term

economic growth: an expansion in the productive capacity of the economy

tion, and the frontier moves to PPC_{2009}. This is a process of **economic growth**, an expansion of the economy's productive capacity through the increased availability of inputs. Notice that the decision to produce more capital goods today means that fewer consumer goods will be produced today. People must choose between 'more jam today' or 'more jam tomorrow'.

part 1

Total output in an economy

Remember that the *PPC* is a model: a much simplified version of reality. In a real economy there are many different goods and services produced by a wide range of different factors of production – but it is not possible to draw diagrams to show all of them. The total output of an economy like the UK is measured by its **gross domestic product (GDP)**.

 term

gross domestic product (GDP): a measure of the economic activity carried out in an economy during a period

Exercise 1.4

Beverly has been cast away on a desert island, and has to survive by spending her time either fishing or climbing trees to get coconuts. The *PPC* in Figure 1.5 shows the maximum combinations of fish and coconuts that she can gather during a day. Which of the points *A* to *E* represent each of the following?

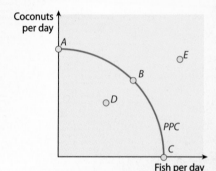

Figure 1.5 *Fish and coconuts*

a   a situation where Beverly spends all her time fishing

b   an unreachable position

c   a day when Beverly goes for a balanced diet — a mixture of coconuts and fish

d   a day when Beverly does not fancy fish, and spends all day collecting coconuts

e   a day when Beverly spends some of the time trying to attract the attention of a passing ship

Summary

➤ The production possibility curve shows the maximum combinations of goods or services that can be produced in a period by a given set of resources.

➤ At any point on the *PPC*, society is making full use of all resources.

➤ At any point inside the *PPC*, there is unemployment of some resources.

➤ Points beyond the *PPC* are unattainable.

➤ In a simple society producing two goods (consumer goods and capital goods), the choice is between consumption and investment for the future.

➤ As society increases its stock of capital goods, the productive capacity of the economy increases, and the production possibility curve moves outwards: this may be termed 'economic growth'.

Specialisation

How many workers does it take to make a pin? The eighteenth-century economist Adam Smith figured that 10 was about the right number. He argued that when a worker was producing pins on his own, carrying out all the various stages involved in the production process, the maximum number of pins that could be produced in one day was 20 — given the technology of his day, of course. This would imply that 10 workers could produce about 200 pins if they worked in the same way as the lone worker. However, if the pin production process were broken into 10 separate stages, with one worker specialising in each stage, the maximum production for a day's work would be a staggering 48,000. This is known as **division of labour**.

Key term

division of labour: a process whereby the production procedure is broken down into a sequence of stages, and workers are assigned to particular stages

The division of labour is effective because individual workers become skilled at performing specialised tasks. By focusing on a particular stage, they can become highly adept, and thus more efficient, at carrying out that task. In any case, people are not all the same, so some are better at certain activities. Furthermore, this specialisation is more efficient because workers do not spend time moving from one activity to another. Specialisation may also enable firms to operate on a larger scale of production. You will see later that this may be advantageous.

This can be seen in practice in many businesses today, where there is considerable specialisation of functions. Workers are hired for particular tasks and activities. You do not see Michael Owen pulling on the goalkeeper's jersey at half time because he fancies a change. Earlier in the chapter, it was argued that 'labour' is considered a factor of production. This idea will now be developed further by arguing that there are different types of labour, having different skills and functions. At another level, firms and even nations specialise in particular kinds of activity.

The benefits from specialisation

Everyone is different. Individuals have different natural talents and abilities that make them good at different things. Indeed, there are some lucky people who seem to be good at everything.

Consider this example. Colin and Debbie try to supplement their incomes by working at weekends. They have both been to evening classes and have attended pottery and jewellery-making classes. At weekends they make pots and bracelets. Depending on how they divide their time, they can make differing combinations of these goods; some of the possibilities are shown in Table 1.1.

Colin		Debbie	
Pots	**Bracelets**	**Pots**	**Bracelets**
12	0	18	0
9	3	12	12
6	6	6	24
3	9	3	30
0	12	0	36

Table 1.1
Colin and Debbie's production

The first point to notice is that Debbie is much better at both activities than Colin. If they each devote all their time to producing pots, Colin produces only 12 to Debbie's 18. If they each produce only bracelets, Colin produces 12 and Debbie, 36. There is another significant feature of this table. Although Debbie is better at producing both goods, the difference is much more marked in the case of bracelet production than pot production. So Debbie is relatively more proficient in bracelet production: in other words, she faces a lower opportunity cost in making bracelets. If Debbie switches from producing pots to producing bracelets, she gives up 6 pots for every 12 additional bracelets that she makes. The opportunity cost of an additional bracelet is thus 6/12 = 0.5 pots. For Colin, there is a one-to-one trade-off between the two, so his opportunity cost of a bracelet is 1 pot.

More interesting is what happens if the same calculation is made for Colin and pot making. Although Debbie is absolutely better at making pots, if Colin increases his production of pots, his opportunity cost in terms of bracelets is still 1. But for Debbie the opportunity cost of making pots in terms of bracelets is 12/6 = 2, so Colin has the lower opportunity cost.

Why does this matter? It illustrates the potential benefits to be gained from specialisation. Suppose that both Colin and Debbie divide their time between the two activities in such a way that Colin produces 6 pots and 6 bracelets, and Debbie produces 6 pots and 24 bracelets. Between them, they will have produced 12 pots and 30 bracelets. However, if they each specialise in the product in which they face the lower opportunity cost, their joint production will increase. If Colin devotes all his time to pottery, he produces 12 pots, while Debbie, focusing only on bracelets, produces 36. So between them they will have produced the same number of pots as before — but 6 extra bracelets.

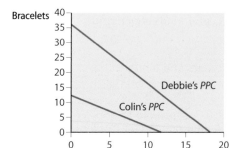

Bracelets

Figure 1.6 Colin and Debbie's production possibilities

One final point before leaving Colin and Debbie. Figure 1.6 shows their respective production possibility curves. You can check this by graphing the points in Table 1.1 and joining them up. In this case the *PPC*s are straight lines. You can see that because Debbie is better at both activities, her *PPC* lies entirely above Colin's. The differences in opportunity cost are shown by the fact that the two *PPC*s have different slopes, as the opportunity cost element is related to the slope of the *PPC* — the rate at which one good is sacrificed for more of the other.

Summary

➤ Adam Smith introduced the notion of division of labour, which suggests that workers can become more productive by specialising in stages of the production process.

➤ Specialisation opens up the possibility of trade.

➤ The gains from specialisation and trade result from differences in opportunity cost.

Markets

You will find that in economics the term **market** is used frequently, so it is important to be absolutely clear about what is meant by it.

A market need not be a physical location (although it could be − you might regard the local farmers' market as an example of 'a set of arrangements that allows transactions to take place'). With the growth of the internet, everyone is becoming accustomed to ways of buying and selling that do not involve direct physical contact between buyer and seller, so the notion of an abstract market should not be too alien a concept.

 Key *term*

market: a set of arrangements that allows transactions to take place

In relation to a particular product, a market brings together potential buyers and sellers. This will be explored in the next chapters.

Markets are very important in the process of resource allocation, with prices acting as a key signal to potential buyers and sellers. If a firm finds that it cannot sell its output at the price it has chosen, this is a signal about the way that buyers perceive the product. Price is one way that firms find out about consumers and their willingness to pay for a particular product. This will be explored more fully in Chapter 5.

Money and exchange

Imagine a world without money. It is lunchtime, and you fancy a banana. In your bag you have an apple. Perhaps you can find someone with a banana who fancies an apple? But the only person with a banana available fancies an ice cream. The problem with such a *barter economy* is that you need to find someone who wants what you have and who has what you want − a *double coincidence of wants*. If this problem were to be faced by a whole economic system, undertaking transactions would be so inefficient as to be impossible. Hence the importance of *money* as a *medium of exchange*.

In order to fulfil this role, money must be something that is acceptable to both buyers and sellers. Nobody would accept money in payment for goods or services if they did not trust that they could proceed to use money for further transactions. Money must thus also act as a *store of value*: it must be possible to use it for future transactions. This quality of money means that it can be used as one way of storing wealth for future purchases. Money also allows the value of goods, services and other assets to be compared − it provides a *unit of account*. In this sense, prices of goods reflect the value that society places on them, and must be expressed in money terms.

A further role for money is that it acts as a *standard of deferred payment*. For example, a firm may wish to agree a contract for the future delivery of a good, or may wish to hire a worker to be paid at the end of the month. Such contracts are typically agreed in terms of a money value.

All of these *functions of money* are important to the smooth operation of markets, and are crucial if prices are to fulfil their role in allocating resources within society. This will become apparent as you learn more about economics.

Microeconomics and macroeconomics

The discussion so far has focused sometimes on individual decisions, and sometimes on the decisions of governments, or of 'society' as a whole. Economic thinking is applied in different ways, depending on whether the focus is on the decisions taken by individual agents in the economy or on the interaction between economic variables at the level of the whole economy.

Key terms

microeconomics: the study of economic decisions taken by individual economic agents, including households and firms

macroeconomics: the study of the interrelationships between economic variables at an aggregate (economy-wide) level

Microeconomics deals with individual decisions taken by households or firms, or in particular markets.

Macroeconomics examines the interactions between economic variables at the level of the aggregate economy. For example, it might examine the effect of a change in income taxes on the level of unemployment, or of the interest rate on total demand and the rate of inflation.

In some ways the division between the two types of analysis is artificial. The same sort of economic reasoning is applied in both types, but the focus is different.

Exercise 1.5

Think about the following, and see whether you think each represents a macroeconomic or microeconomic phenomenon:
a The overall level of prices in an economy.
b The price of ice cream.
c The overall rate of unemployment in the UK.
d The unemployment rate among catering workers in Aberdeen.
e The average wage paid to construction workers in Southampton.

Positive and normative statements

Economics tries to be objective in analysis. However, some of its subject matter requires careful attention in order to retain an objective distance. In this connection, it is important to be clear about the difference between **positive** and **normative statements**.

In short, a positive statement is about *facts.* In contrast, a normative statement is about *what ought to be.* Another way of looking at this is that a statement becomes normative when it involves a *value judgement.*

Key terms

positive statement: a statement about what *is*, i.e. about *facts*

normative statement: a statement about what *ought to be*

Suppose the government is considering raising the tax on cigarettes. It may legitimately consult economists to discover what effect a higher tobacco tax will have on the consumption of cigarettes and on government revenues. This would be a *positive* investigation, in that the economists are being asked to use economic analysis to forecast what will happen when the tax is increased.

A very different situation will arise if the government asks whether it *should* raise the tax on cigarettes. This moves the economists beyond positive analysis because it entails a value judgement — so it is now a *normative* analysis. There are some words that betray normative statements, such as 'should' or 'ought to' — watch for these.

Increasing taxes on tobacco affects consumption of cigarettes and government revenue

Most of this book is about positive economics. However, you should be aware that positive analysis is often called upon to inform normative judgements. If the aim of a policy is to stop people from smoking (which reflects a normative judgement about what *ought* to happen), then economic analysis may be used to highlight the strengths and weaknesses of alternative policy measures in a purely positive fashion.

Critics of economics often joke that economists always disagree with one another: for example, it has been said that if you put five economists in a room together, they will come up with at least six conflicting opinions. However, although economists may arrive at different value judgements, and thus have differences when it comes to normative issues, there is much greater agreement when it comes to positive analysis.

Summary

➤ A market is a set of arrangements that allows transactions to take place.

➤ A barter economy is a highly inefficient way of conducting transactions, hence the importance of money in enabling exchange to take place.

➤ Money plays key roles as a medium of exchange, a store of value, a unit of account, and a standard of deferred payment.

➤ By fulfilling these various roles, money enables the smooth operation of markets, and allows prices to act as a guide in allocating resources.

➤ Microeconomics deals with individual decisions made by consumers and producers, whereas macroeconomics analyses the interactions between economic variables in the aggregate — but both use similar ways of thinking.

➤ Positive statements are about *what is*, whereas normative statements are about *what ought to be*.

part **1**

Chapter 2
The nature of demand

The demand and supply model is perhaps the most famous of all pieces of economic analysis; it is also one of the most useful. It has many applications that help explain the way markets work in the real world. It is thus central to understanding economics. This chapter introduces the demand side of the model. Chapter 3 will introduce supply.

Learning outcomes

After studying this chapter, you should:
➤ be familiar with the notion of the demand for a good or service
➤ be aware of the relationship between the demand for a good and its price
➤ be familiar with the demand curve and the law of demand
➤ understand the distinction between a movement along the demand curve and a shift in its position
➤ be aware of the distinction between normal and inferior goods
➤ understand the other influences that affect the position of the demand curve

Demand

Consider an individual consumer. Think of yourself, and a product that you consume regularly. What factors influence your **demand** for that product? Put another way, what factors influence how much of the product you choose to buy?

When thinking about the factors that influence your demand for your chosen product, common sense will probably mean that you focus on a range of different points. You may think about why you enjoy consuming the product. You may focus on how much it will cost to buy the product, and whether you can afford it. You may decide that you have consumed a product so much that you are ready for a change; or perhaps you will decide to try something advertised on television, or being bought by a friend.

 Key term

demand: the quantity of a good or service that consumers choose to buy at any possible price in a given period

Whatever the influences you come up with, they can probably be categorised under four headings that ultimately determine your demand for a good. First, the *price* of the good is an important influence on your demand for it, and will affect the quantity of it that you choose to buy. Second, the *price of other goods* may be significant. Third, your *income* will determine how much of the good you can afford to purchase. Finally, almost any other factors that you may have thought of can be listed as part of your *preferences.*

This commonsense reasoning provides the basis for the economic analysis of demand. You will find that a lot of economic analysis begins in this way, by finding a way to construct a model that is rooted in how we expect people or firms to behave.

Individual and market demand

A similar line of argument may apply if we think in terms of the demand for a particular product — say, DVDs. The market for DVDs can thus be seen as bringing together all the potential buyers (and sellers) of the product, and market demand can be analysed in terms of the factors that influence all potential buyers of that good or service. In other words, market demand can be seen as the total quantity of a good or service that all potential buyers would choose to buy at any given price. The same four factors that influence your own individual decision to buy will also influence the total market demand for a product. In addition, the number of potential buyers in the market will clearly influence the size of total demand at any price.

R. Parkes/Ontanet

Demand and the price of a good

Assume for the moment that the influences mentioned above, other than the price of the good, are held constant, so that the focus is only on the extent to which the price of a good influences the demand for it. This is a common assumption in economics, which is sometimes expressed by the Latin phrase **ceteris paribus**, meaning 'other things being equal'. Given the complexity of the real world, it is often helpful to focus on one thing at a time.

This ceteris paribus assumption is used a lot in economics, and is a powerful tool. Focusing on one influence at a time is a way of coping with the complexities of the real world and makes the analysis of economic issues much clearer than if we try to analyse everything at once. You will see many instances of it as the course proceeds.

So how is the demand for DVDs influenced by their price? Other things being equal (ceteris paribus), you would expect the demand for DVDs to be higher when the price

 term

ceteris paribus: a Latin phrase meaning 'other things being equal'; it is used in economics when we focus on changes in one variable while holding other influences constant

is low and lower when the price is high. In other words, you would expect an inverse relationship between the price and the quantity demanded. This is such a strong phenomenon that it is referred to as the **law of demand**.

If you were to compile a list that showed how many DVDs would be bought at any possible price and plot these on a diagram, this would be called the **demand curve**. Figure 2.1 shows what this might look like. As it is an inverse relationship, the demand curve slopes downwards. Notice that this need not be a straight line: its shape depends upon how consumers react at different prices. According to this curve, if price were to be set at £40, the quantity demanded would be 20,000 per period. However, if the price were only £20, the demand would be higher, at 60,000.

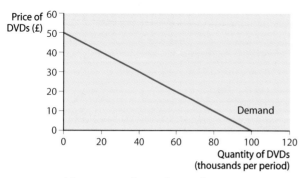

Figure 2.1 *A demand curve for DVDs*

Key terms

law of demand: a law that states that there is an inverse relationship between quantity demanded and the price of a good or service, ceteris paribus

demand curve: a graph showing how much of a good will be demanded by consumers at any given price

Exercise 2.1

Table 2.1 shows how the demand for oojits varies with their price. Draw the demand curve.

Price	Quantity
100	0
90	3
80	7
70	15
60	25
50	40
40	60
30	85
20	120

Table 2.1
The demand for oojits

Extension point

An analysis of why the demand curve should be downward sloping would reveal that there are two important forces at work. At a higher price, a consumer buying a DVD has less income left over. This is referred to as the *real income effect* of a price increase. In addition, if the price of DVDs goes up, consumers may find other goods more attractive and choose to buy something else instead of DVDs. This is referred to as the *substitution effect* of a price increase.

As the price of a good changes, a movement along the demand curve can be observed as consumers adjust their buying pattern in response to the price change.

Notice that the demand curve has been drawn under the ceteris paribus assumption. In other words, it was assumed that all other influences on demand were held constant in order to focus on the relationship between demand and price. There are two important implications of this procedure.

First, the price drawn on the vertical axis of a diagram such as Figure 2.1 is the *relative* price – it is the price of DVDs under the assumption that all other prices are constant.

Second, if any of the other influences on demand change, you would expect to see a shift of the whole demand curve. It is very important to distinguish between factors that induce a movement *along* a curve, and factors that induce a shift *of a* curve. This applies not only in the case of the demand curve – there are many other instances where this is important.

The two panels of Figure 2.2 show this difference. In panel (a) of the figure, the demand curve has shifted to the right because of a change in one of the factors that influences demand. In panel (b), the price of DVDs falls from P_0 to P_1, inducing a movement along the demand curve as demand expands from Q_0 to Q_1.

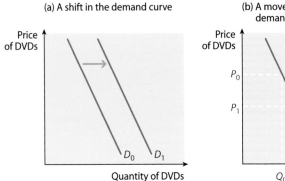

(a) A shift in the demand curve

Price of DVDs

D_0 D_1

Quantity of DVDs

(b) A movement along the demand curve

Price of DVDs

P_0

P_1

D

Q_0 Q_1 Quantity of DVDs

Figure 2.2 *A shift in the demand curve and a movement along it*

Snob effects

It is sometimes argued that for some goods a 'snob effect' may lead to the demand curve sloping upwards. The argument is that some people may value certain goods more highly simply because their price is high, especially if they know that other people will observe them consuming these goods; an example might be Rolex watches. In other words, people gain value from having other people notice that they are rich enough to afford to consume a particular good. There is thus a *conspicuous consumption* effect, which was first pointed out by Thorstein Veblen at the end of the nineteenth century.

Rolex watches may benefit from the conspicuous consumption effect

However, although there may be some individual consumers who react to price in this way, there is no evidence to suggest that there are whole markets that display an upward-sloping demand curve for this reason. In other words, most consumers would react normally to the price of such goods.

Demand and consumer incomes

The second influence on demand is consumer incomes. For a **normal good**, an increase in consumer incomes will, ceteris paribus, lead to an increase in the quantity demanded at any given price. Foreign holidays are an example of a normal good because, as people's incomes rise, they will tend to demand more foreign holidays at any given price.

Figure 2.3 illustrates this. D_0 here represents the initial demand curve for foreign holidays. An increase in consumers' incomes causes demand to be higher at any given price, and the demand curve shifts to the right – to D_1.

However, demand does not always respond in this way. For example, think about bus journeys. As incomes rise in a society, more people can afford to have a car, or to use taxis. This means that, as incomes rise, the demand for bus journeys may tend to fall. Such goods are known as **inferior goods**.

This time an increase in consumers' incomes in Figure 2.4 causes the demand curve to shift to the left, from its initial position at D_0, to D_1 where less is demanded at any given price.

The relationship between quantity demanded and income can be shown more directly on a diagram. Panel (a) of Figure 2.5 shows how this would look for a normal good. It is upward sloping, showing that the quantity demanded is higher when consumer incomes are higher. In contrast, the income demand curve for an inferior good, shown in panel (b) of the diagram, slopes downwards, indicating that the quantity demanded will be lower when consumer incomes are relatively high.

> **Key terms**
>
> **normal good:** one where the quantity demanded increases in response to an increase in consumer incomes
>
> **inferior good:** one where the quantity demanded decreases in response to an increase in consumer incomes

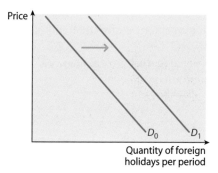

Figure 2.3 A shift in the demand curve following an increase in consumer incomes (a normal good)

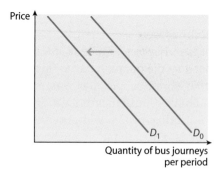

Figure 2.4 A shift in the demand curve following an increase in consumer incomes (an inferior good)

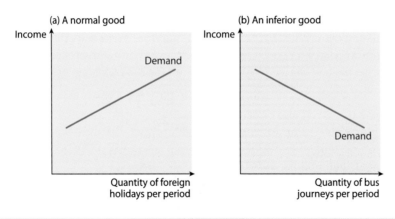

Figure 2.5
Demand and income

Exercise 2.2

Identify each of the following products as being either a normal good or an inferior good:

a   digital camera   c   potatoes   e   fine wine

b   magazine   d   bicycle   f   cheap wine

Extension point: a Giffen good

Remember that a consumer's response to a change in the price of a good is made up of a substitution effect and a real income effect (see the extension point on page 18). The substitution effect always acts in the opposite direction to the price change: in other words, an increase in the price of a good always induces a switch *away* from the good towards other goods. However, it can now be seen that the real income effect may operate in either direction, depending on whether it is a normal good or an inferior good that is being considered.

Suppose there is a good that is *very* inferior. A fall in the price of a good induces a substitution effect towards the good, but the real income effect works in the opposite direction. The fall in price is equivalent to a rise in real income, so consumers will consume less of the good. If this effect is really strong, it could overwhelm the substitution effect, and the fall in price could induce a *fall* in the quantity demanded: in other words, for such a good the demand curve could be upward sloping.

Such goods are known as *Giffen goods*, after Sir Robert Giffen, who pointed out that this could happen. However, in spite of stories about the reaction of demand to a rise in the price of potatoes during the great Irish potato famine, there have been no authenticated sightings of Giffen goods. The notion remains a theoretical curiosity.

Demand and the price of other goods

The demand for a good may respond to changes in the price of other related goods, of which there are two main types. On the one hand, two goods may be **substitutes** for each other. For example, consider two

 term

substitutes: two goods are said to be substitutes if the demand for one good is likely to rise if the price of the other good rises

---

different (but similar) breakfast cereals. If there is an increase in the price of one of the cereals, consumers may switch their consumption to the other, as the two are likely to be close substitutes for each other. Not all consumers will switch, of course – some may be deeply committed to one particular brand – but some of them are certainly likely to change over.

On the other hand, there may also be goods that are **complements** – for example, products that are consumed jointly, such as breakfast cereals and milk, or cars and petrol. Here a fall in the price of one good may lead to an increase in demand for *both* products.

 Key **term**

complements: two goods are said to be complements if an increase in the price of one good causes the demand for the other good to fall

Whether goods are substitutes or complements determines how the demand for one good responds to a change in the price of another. Figure 2.6 shows the demand curves (per period) for two goods that are substitutes – tea and coffee.

 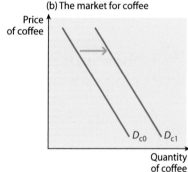

Figure 2.6
A shift in the demand curve following an increase in the price of a substitute good

If there is an increase in the price of tea from P_0 to P_1 in panel (a), more consumers will switch to coffee and the demand curve in panel (b) will shift to the right – say, from D_{c0} to D_{c1}.

For complements the situation is the reverse: in Figure 2.7 an increase in the price of tea from P_0 to P_1 in panel (a) causes the demand curve for milk to shift leftwards, from D_{m0} to D_{m1}.

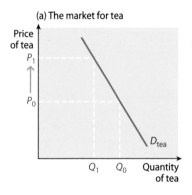 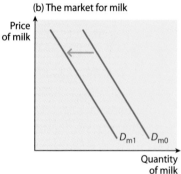

Figure 2.7
A shift in the demand curve following an increase in the price of a complementary good

Demand, consumer preferences and other influences

The discussion has shown how the demand for a good is influenced by the price of the good, the price of other goods, and by consumer incomes. It was stated earlier that almost everything else that determines demand for a good can be represented as 'consumer preferences'. In particular, this refers to whether you like or dislike a good. There may be many things that influence whether you like or dislike a product. In part it simply depends upon your own personal inclinations — some people like dark chocolate, others prefer milk chocolate. However, firms may try to influence your preferences through advertising, and sometimes they succeed. Or you might be one of those people who get so irritated by television advertising that you compile a blacklist of products that you will never buy! Even this is an influence on your demand.

In some cases your preferences may be swayed by other people's demand — again, this may be positive or negative. Fashions may influence demand, but some people like to buck (or lead) the trend.

You may also see a movement of the demand curve if there is a sudden surge in the popularity of a good — or, indeed, a sudden collapse in demand.

Exercise 2.3

Sketch some demand curves for the following situations, and think about how you would expect the demand curve to change (if at all):

a the demand for chocolate following a campaign highlighting the dangers of obesity

b the demand for oranges following an increase in the price of apples

c the demand for oranges following a decrease in the price of oranges

d the demand for DVDs following a decrease in the price of DVD players

e the demand for VCRs following a decrease in the price of DVD recorders

f the demand for private transport following an increase in consumer incomes

g the demand for public transport following an increase in consumer incomes

The above discussion has covered most of the factors that influence the demand for a good. However, in some cases it is necessary to take a time element into account. Not all of the goods bought are consumed instantly. In some cases, consumption is spread over long periods of time. Indeed, there may be instances where goods are not bought for consumption at all, but are seen by the buyer as an investment, perhaps for resale at a later date. In these circumstances, expectations about future price changes may be relevant. For example, people may buy fine wine or works of art in the expectation that prices will rise in the future. There may also be goods whose prices are expected to fall in the future. This has been common with many high-tech products; initially a newly launched product may sell at a high price, but as production levels rise, costs may fall, and prices also. People may therefore delay purchase in the expectation of future price reductions.

Summary

➤ A market is a set of arrangements that enables transactions to take place.

➤ The market demand for a good depends upon the price of the good, the price of other goods, consumers' incomes and preferences and the number of potential consumers.

➤ The demand curve shows the relationship between demand for a product and its price, ceteris paribus.

➤ The demand curve is downward sloping, as the relationship between demand and price is an inverse one.

➤ A change in price induces a movement *along* the demand curve, whereas a change in the other determinants of demand induces a shift *of* the demand curve.

➤ When the demand for a good rises as consumer incomes rise, that good is referred to as a *normal good*; when demand falls as income rises, the good is referred to as an *inferior good*.

➤ A good or service may be related to other goods by being either a *substitute* or a *complement*.

➤ For some products, demand may be related to expected future prices.

Chapter 3
The nature of supply

The previous chapter introduced you to the demand curve. The other key component of the demand and supply model is of course supply. For any market transaction, there are two parties, buyers and sellers. The question to be considered in this chapter is that of what determines the quantity that sellers will wish to supply to the market.

Learning outcomes

After studying this chapter, you should:
➤ be familiar with the notion of the supply of a good or service
➤ be aware of the relationship between the supply of a good and its price in a competitive market
➤ understand what is meant by the supply curve and the factors that influence its shape and position
➤ be able to distinguish between shifts of the supply curve and movements along it
➤ be aware of the effect of taxes and subsidies on the supply curve

Supply

In discussing demand, the focus of attention was on consumers, and on their willingness to pay for goods and services. In thinking about supply, attention switches to firms, as it is firms that take decisions about how much output to supply to the market. It is important at the outset to be clear about what is meant by a 'firm'. A **firm** exists to organise production: they bring together various factors of production, and organise the production process in order to produce output.

Key *term*

firm: an organisation that brings together factors of production in order to produce output

There are various forms that the organisation of a firm can take. A firm could be a *sole proprietor*: probably a small business such as a newsagent where the owner of the firm also runs the firm. A firm could be in the form of a *partnership* — for example, a dental practice in which profits (and debts) are shared between the partners in

the business. Larger firms may be organised as private or public *joint stock companies*, owned by shareholders. The difference between private and public joint stock companies is that the shares of a public joint stock company are traded on the stock exchange, whereas this is not the case with the private company.

In order to analyse how firms decide how much of a product to supply, it is necessary to make an assumption about what it is that firms are trying to achieve. Assume that they aim to maximise their profits, where 'profits' are defined as the difference between a firm's total revenue and its total costs.

As discussed in Chapter 2, the demand curve shows a relationship between quantity demanded and the price of a good or service. A similar relationship between the quantity supplied by firms and the price of a good can be identified in relation to the behaviour of firms in a **competitive market** — that is, a market in which individual firms cannot influence the price of the good or service that they are selling, because of competition from other firms.

In such a market it may well be supposed that firms will be prepared to supply more goods at a high price than at a lower one (ceteris paribus), as this will increase their profits. The **supply curve** illustrates how much the firms in a market will supply at any given price, as shown in Figure 3.1. As firms are expected to supply more goods at a high price than at a lower price, the supply curve will be upward sloping, reflecting this positive relationship between quantity and price.

 terms

competitive market: a market in which individual firms cannot influence the price of the good or service they are selling, because of competition from other firms

supply curve: a graph showing the quantity supplied at any given price

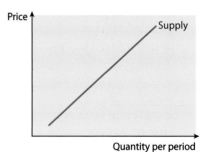

Figure 3.1 *A supply curve*

Exercise 3.1

Table 3.1 shows how the supply of oojits varies with their price. Draw the supply curve.

Price	Quantity
100	98
90	95
80	91
70	86
60	80
50	70
40	60
30	50
20	35
30	18

Table 3.1
The supply of oojits

Notice that the focus of the supply curve is on the relationship between quantity supplied and the price of a good in a given period, ceteris paribus — that is, holding other things constant. As with the demand curve, there are other factors affecting the quantity supplied. These other influences on supply will determine the position of the supply curve: if any of them changes, the supply curve can be expected to shift.

What influences supply?

We can identify five important influences on the quantity that firms will be prepared to supply to the market at any given price:

➤ production costs
➤ the technology of production
➤ taxes and subsidies
➤ the price of related goods
➤ firms' expectations about future prices

Costs and technology

If firms are aiming to maximise profits, an important influence on their supply decision will be the costs of production that they face. Chapter 1 explained that in order to produce output, firms need to use inputs of the factors of production — labour, capital, land etc. If the cost of those inputs increases, firms will in general be expected to supply less output at any given price. The effect of this is shown in Figure 3.2, where an increase in production costs induces firms to supply less output at each price. The curve shifts from its initial position at S_0 to a new position at S_1. For example, suppose the original price was £10 per unit; before the increase in costs, firms would have been prepared to supply 100 units of the product to the market. An increase in costs of £6 per unit that shifted the supply curve from S_0 to S_1 would mean that, at the same price, firms would now supply only 50 units of the good. Notice that the vertical distance between S_0 and S_1 is the amount of the change in cost per unit.

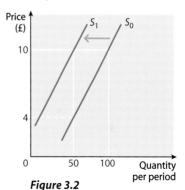

Figure 3.2
The supply curve shifts to the left if production costs increase

Improved technology means firms can produce more cost effectively

In contrast, if a new technology of production is introduced, which means that firms can produce more cost effectively, this could have the opposite effect, shifting the supply curve to the right. This is shown in Figure 3.3, where improved technology induces firms to supply more output at any given price, and the supply curve shifts from its initial position at S_0 to a new position at S_1. Thus, if firms in the initial situation were supplying 50 units with the price at £10 per unit, then a fall in costs of £6 per unit would induce firms to increase supply to 100 units (if the price remained at £10).

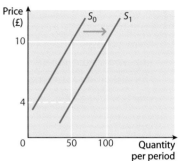

Figure 3.3
The supply curve shifts to the right if production costs fall

Taxes and subsidies

Suppose the government imposes a sales tax such as VAT on a good or service. The price paid by consumers will be higher than the revenue received by firms, as the tax has to be paid to the government. This means that firms will (ceteris paribus) be prepared to supply less output at any given market price. Again, the supply curve shifts to the left. This is shown in panel (a) of Figure 3.4, which assumes a fixed per unit tax. The supply curve shifts, as firms supply less at any given market price. On the other hand, if the government pays firms a subsidy to produce a particular good, this will reduce their costs, and induce them to supply more output at any given price. The supply curve will then shift to the right, as shown in panel (b).

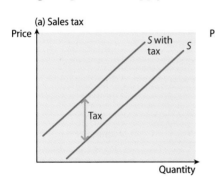

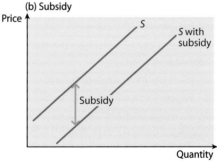

Figure 3.4
The effects of taxes and subsidies on supply

Prices of other goods

It was shown in Chapter 2 that from the consumers' perspective, two goods may be substitutes for each other, such that if the price of one good increases, consumers may be induced to switch their consumption to substitute goods. Similarly, there may be substitution on the supply side. A firm may face a situation in which there are alternative uses to which its factors of production may be put: in other words, it may be able to choose between producing a range of different products. A rise in the price of a good raises its profitability, and therefore may encourage a firm to switch production from other goods. This may happen even if there are high switching costs, provided the increase in price is sufficiently large. For example, a change in relative prices of potatoes and organic swedes might encourage a farmer to stop planting potatoes and grow organic swedes instead.

In other circumstances, a firm may produce a range of goods jointly. Perhaps one good is a by-product of the production process of another. An increase in the price of one of the goods may mean that the firm will produce more of both goods. This notion of joint supply is similar to the situation on the demand side where consumers regard two goods as complements.

Expected prices

Because production takes time, firms often take decisions about how much to supply on the basis of expected future prices. Indeed, if their product is one that can be stored, there may be times when a firm will decide to allow stocks of a product to build up in anticipation of a higher price in the future, perhaps by holding back some of its production from current sales. In some economic activities, expectations about future prices are crucial in taking supply decisions because of the length of time needed in order to increase output. For example, a firm producing palm oil, rubber or wine needs to be aware that newly planted trees or vines need several years to mature before they are able to yield their product.

Wine producers have to take supply decisions based on expected future prices

Movements along and shifts of the supply curve

As with the demand curve, it is very important to remember that there is a distinction between movements *along* the supply curve, and shifts *of* the supply curve. If there is a change in the market price, this induces a movement along the supply curve. After all, the supply curve is designed to reveal how firms will react to a change in the price of the good. For example, in Figure 3.5, if the price is initially at P_0 firms will be prepared to supply the quantity Q_0, but if the price then increases to P_1 this will induce a movement along the supply curve as firms increase supply to Q_1.

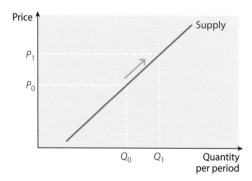

Figure 3.5
A movement along a supply curve in response to a price change

In contrast, as seen in the previous section, a change in any of the other influences on supply will induce a shift of the whole supply curve, as this affects the firms' willingness to supply at any given price.

Exercise 3.2

For each of the following, decide whether the demand curve or the supply curve will move, and in which direction:

a Consumers are convinced by arguments about the benefits of organic vegetables.

b A new process is developed that reduces the amount of inputs that firms need in order to produce bicycles.

c There is a severe frost in Brazil that affects the coffee crop.

d The government increases the rate of value added tax.

e Real incomes rise.

f The price of tea falls: what happens in the market for coffee?

g The price of sugar falls: what happens in the market for coffee?

Summary

➤ Other things being equal, firms in a competitive market can be expected to supply more output at a higher price.

➤ The supply curve traces out this positive relationship between price and quantity supplied.

➤ Changes in the costs of production, technology, taxes and subsidies or the prices of related goods may induce shifts of the supply curve, with firms being prepared to sell more (or less) output at any given price.

➤ Expectations about future prices may affect current supply decisions.

Chapter 4
Using the demand and supply model

The previous chapters introduced the notions of demand and supply, and it is now time to bring these two curves together in order to meet the key concept of market equilibrium. The model can then be further developed to see how it provides insights into how markets operate. You will encounter demand and supply in a wide variety of contexts, and begin to glimpse some of the ways in which the model can help to explain how the economic world works.

Learning outcomes

After studying this chapter, you should:
➤ understand the notion of equilibrium and its relevance in the demand and supply model
➤ be aware of what is meant by comparative static analysis
➤ understand the concept of elasticity measures and appreciate their importance and applications

Market equilibrium

The previous chapters have described the components of the demand and supply model. It only remains to bring them together, for this is how the power of the model can be appreciated. Figure 4.1 shows the demand for and supply of butter.

Suppose that the price were to be set at a relatively high price (above P^*). At such a price, firms wish to supply lots of butter to the market. However, consumers are not very keen on butter

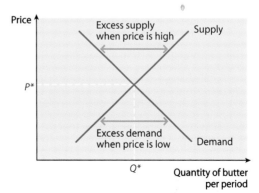

Figure 4.1
Bringing demand and supply together

at such a high price, so demand is not strong. Firms now have a problem: they find that their stocks of butter are building up. What has happened is that the price has been set at a level that exceeds the value that most consumers place on butter, so they will not buy it. There is *excess supply*. The only thing that the firms can do is to reduce the price in order to clear their stocks.

Suppose they now set their price relatively low (below P^*). Now it is the consumers who have a problem, because they would like to buy more butter at the low price than firms are prepared to supply. There is *excess demand.* Some consumers may offer to pay more than the going price in order to obtain their butter supplies, and firms realise that they can raise the price.

How will it all end? When the price settles at P^* in Figure 4.1, there is a balance in the market between the quantity that consumers wish to demand and the quantity that firms wish to supply, namely Q^*. This is the **market equilibrium**. In a free market the price can be expected to converge on this equilibrium level, through movements along both demand and supply curves.

 Key **term**

market equilibrium: a situation that occurs in a market when the price is such that the quantity that consumers wish to buy is exactly balanced by the quantity that firms wish to supply

Exercise 4.1

Identify the equilibrium market price if demand and supply are as in Figure 4.2.

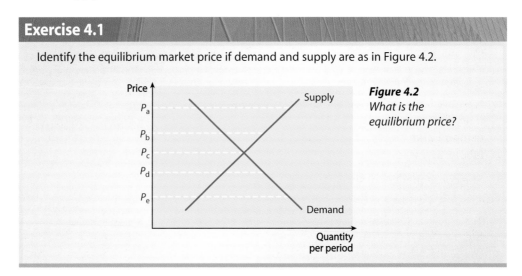

Figure 4.2
What is the equilibrium price?

Summary

➤ Bringing demand and supply together, you can identify the market equilibrium.

➤ The equilibrium price is the unique point at which the quantity demanded by consumers is just balanced by the quantity that firms wish to supply.

➤ In a free market, natural forces can be expected to encourage prices to adjust to the equilibrium level.

Examples of markets

The markets that have been discussed so far have been product markets, such as the market for DVDs, tea or butter. However, the model is much more widely applicable than this, as is shown by the examples that follow.

The labour market

Within the economy, firms demand labour and employees supply labour — so why not use demand and supply to analyse the market? This can indeed be done.

From the firms' point of view, the demand for labour is a *derived demand.* In other words, firms want labour not for its own sake, but for the output that it produces. When the 'price' of labour is low, firms will tend to demand more of it than when the 'price' of labour is high. The wage rate can be regarded as this 'price' of labour. On the employee side, it is argued that more people tend to offer themselves for work when the wage is relatively high.

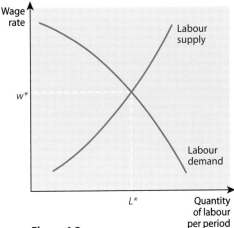

Figure 4.3
A labour market

On this basis, the demand for labour is expected to be downward sloping and the supply of labour upward sloping, as in Figure 4.3. As usual, the equilibrium in a free market will be at the intersection of demand and supply, so firms will hire L^* labour at a wage rate of w^*.

The consequences of such a market being away from equilibrium are important. Consider Figure 4.4. Suppose the wage rate is set above the equilibrium level at w_1. The high wage rate encourages more people to offer themselves for work — up to the amount of labour L_s. However, at this wage rate employers are prepared to hire only up to L_d labour. Think about what is happening here. There are people offering themselves for work who cannot find employment: in other words, there is **unemployment**. Thus, one possible cause of unemployment is a wage rate that is set above the equilibrium level.

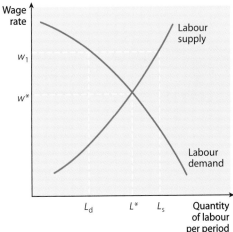

Figure 4.4
A labour market out of equilibrium

 term

unemployment: results when people seeking work at the going wage cannot find a job

The foreign exchange market

When you take your holidays in Spain, you need to buy euros. Equally, when German tourists come to visit London, they need to buy pounds. If there is buying going on, then there must be a market — remember from Chapter 1 that a market is a set of arrangements that enable transactions to be undertaken. So here is another sort of market to be considered. The exchange rate is the price at which two currencies exchange, and it can be analysed using demand and supply.

Consider the market for pounds, and focus on the exchange rate between pounds and euros, as shown in Figure 4.5. Think first about what gives rise to a demand for pounds. It is not just German tourists who need pounds to spend on holiday: anyone holding euros who wants to buy UK goods needs pounds in order to pay for them. So the demand for pounds comes from people in the euro area who want to buy UK goods or services — or assets. When the exchange rate for the pound in euros is high, potential buyers of UK goods get relatively few pounds per euro, so the demand will be relatively low, whereas if the euro per pound rate is relatively low, they get more for their money. Hence the demand curve is expected to be downward sloping.

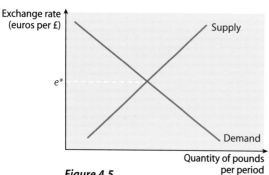

Figure 4.5
The market for pounds

Currencies are traded on the foreign exchange market

One point to notice from this is that foreign exchange is another example of a derived demand, in the sense that people want pounds not for their own sake, but for the goods or services that they can buy. One way of viewing the exchange rate is as a means by which to learn about the international competitiveness of UK exports. When the exchange rate is high, UK goods are less competitive in Europe, ceteris paribus. Notice the ceteris paribus assumption here. This is important because the exchange rate is not the only determinant of the competitiveness of UK goods: they also depend on the relative price levels in the UK and Europe.

How about the supply of pounds? Pounds are supplied by UK residents wanting euros to buy goods or services from Europe. From this point of view, when the euro/pound rate is high, UK residents get more euros for their pounds and therefore will tend to supply more pounds.

If the exchange market is in equilibrium, the exchange rate will be at e^*, where the demand for pounds is matched by the supply.

The money market

Chapter 1 highlighted the importance of money in enabling exchange to take place through the operation of markets. This implies that people have a **demand for money**. This demand for money is associated with the functions of money set out on page 13 — as a medium of exchange, store of value, unit of account and standard of deferred payment. If there is a demand for money, then perhaps there should also be a market for money?

We can think of the demand for money depending on a number of factors — in particular, upon the number of transactions that people wish to undertake — which probably depends upon income. But is there a price of money? The price of money can be viewed in terms of opportunity cost. When people choose to hold money, they incur an opportunity cost, which can be seen as the next best alternative to holding money. For example, instead of holding money, you could decide to purchase a financial asset that would provide a rate of return, represented by the rate of interest. This rate of interest can thus be interpreted as the price of holding money.

How about the supply of money? This will be discussed much later in the course, but for now, it can be assumed that the supply of money is determined by the Bank of England, and it can be assumed that this money supply will not depend upon the rate of interest. Figure 4.6 illustrates the market for money. The demand for money is shown to be downward sloping, as the higher the rate of interest, the greater the return that is sacrificed by holding money, so the smaller will be the demand for money. The supply of money does not depend upon the rate of interest (by assumption), so is shown as a vertical line. The market is in equilibrium when the rate of interest is at r^*, the level at which the demand and supply of money are equal.

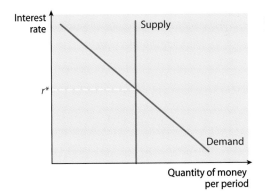

Figure 4.6
The market for money

Summary

➤ In the labour market, equilibrium is achieved through the wage rate. If the wage rate is set too high, it leads to unemployment.

➤ Demand and supply enable you to examine how the foreign exchange rate is determined.

➤ The model can also be applied to analyse the money market.

Comparative statics

In order to make good use of the demand and supply model, it is necessary to introduce another of the economist's key tools — comparative static analysis. You have seen the way in which a market moves towards equilibrium between demand and supply through price adjustments and movements along the demand and supply curves. This is called static analysis, in the sense that a ceteris paribus assumption is imposed by holding constant the factors that influence demand and supply, and focusing on the way in which the market reaches equilibrium.

In the next stage, one of these background factors is changed, and the effect of this change on the market equilibrium is then analysed. In other words, beginning with a market in equilibrium, one of the factors affecting either demand or supply is altered, and the new market equilibrium is then studied. In this way, two static equilibrium positions — before and after — will be compared. This approach is known as **comparative static analysis**.

 Key term

comparative static analysis: examines the effect on equilibrium of a change in the external conditions affecting a market

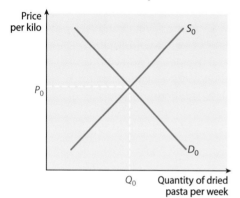

Figure 4.7
A market for dried pasta

A market for dried pasta

Begin with a simple market for dried pasta, a basic staple foodstuff obtainable in any supermarket. Figure 4.7 shows the market in equilibrium. D_0 represents the demand curve in this initial situation, and S_0 is the supply curve. The market is in equilibrium with the price at P_0, and the quantity being traded is Q_0. It is equilibrium in the sense that pasta producers are supplying just the amount of pasta that consumers wish to buy at that price. This is the 'before' position. Some experiments will now be carried out with this market by disturbing the equilibrium.

A change in consumer preferences

Suppose that a study is published highlighting the health benefits of eating pasta, backed up with an advertising campaign. The effect of this is likely to be an increase in the demand for pasta at any given price. In other words, this change in consumer preferences will shift the demand curve to the right, as shown in Figure 4.8.

The market now adjusts to a new equilibrium, with a new price P_1, and a new quantity traded at Q_1. In this case, both price and quantity have increased as a result of the change in preferences. There has been a movement along the supply curve.

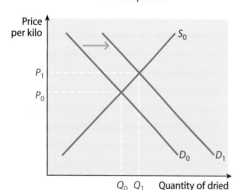

Figure 4.8
A change in consumer preferences for dried pasta

James King-Holmes/Pasta Co./SPL

Dried pasta in production

A change in the price of a substitute

A second possibility is that there is a fall in the price of fresh pasta. This is likely to be a close substitute for dried pasta, so the probable result is that some former consumers of dried pasta will switch their allegiance to the fresh variety. This time the demand curve for dried pasta moves in the opposite direction, as can be seen in Figure 4.9. Here the starting point is the original position, with market equilibrium at price P_0 and a quantity traded Q_0. After the shift in the demand curve from D_0 to D_2, the market settles again with a price of P_2 and a quantity traded of Q_2. Both price and quantity traded are now lower than in the original position.

An improvement in pasta technology

Next, suppose that a new pasta-making machine is produced, enabling dried pasta makers to produce at a lower cost than before. This advancement reduces firms' costs, and consequently they are prepared to supply more dried pasta at any given price. The starting point is the same initial position, but now it is the supply curve that shifts – to the right. This is shown in Figure 4.10.

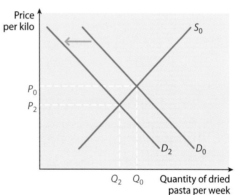

Figure 4.9
A change in the price of a substitute for dried pasta

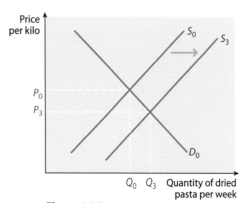

Figure 4.10
New pasta-making technology

Again, comparative static analysis can be undertaken. The new market equilibrium is at price P_3, which is lower than the original equilibrium, but the quantity traded is higher at Q_3.

An increase in labour costs

Finally, suppose that pasta producers face an increase in their labour costs. Perhaps the Pasta Workers' Union has negotiated higher wages, or the pasta producers have become subject to stricter health and safety legislation, which raises their production costs. Figure 4.11 starts as usual with equilibrium at price P_0 and quantity Q_0.

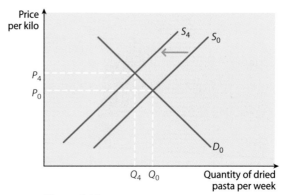

Figure 4.11
An increase in labour costs

The increase in production costs means that pasta producers are prepared to supply less dried pasta at any given price, so the supply curve shifts to the left — to S_4. This takes the market to a new equilibrium at a higher price than before (P_4), but with a lower quantity traded (Q_4).

Summary

➤ Comparative static analysis enables you to analyse the way in which markets respond to external shocks, by comparing market equilibrium before and after a shock.

➤ All you need to do is to figure out whether the shock affects demand or supply, and in which direction.

➤ The size and direction of the shifts of the demand and supply curves determine the overall effect on equilibrium price and quantity traded.

Exercise 4.2

For each of the following market situations, sketch a demand and supply diagram, and undertake a comparative static analysis to see what happens to the equilibrium price and quantity. Explain your answers.

a An increase in consumer incomes affects the demand for bus travel.

b New regulations on environmental pollution force a firm making paint to increase outlay on reducing its emission of toxic fumes.

c A firm of accountants brings in new, faster computers, which have the effect of reducing the firm's costs.

d An outbreak of bird flu causes consumers of chicken to buy burgers instead. (What is the effect on both markets?)

Exercise 4.3

In August 2001 *The Financial Times* reported that ship-owners were facing serious problems. Shipping rates (the prices that ship-owners charge for carrying freight) had fallen drastically in the second quarter of 2001.

In 2001 shipping rates fell drastically

For example, on the Europe–Asia route, rates fell by 8% eastbound and 6% westbound, causing the ship-owners' profits to be squeezed. Here are some relevant facts and issues:

a New 'superships', having been ordered a few years earlier, were coming into service with enhanced capacity for transporting freight.

b A worldwide economic slowdown was taking place; Japan was in lengthy recession and the US economy was also slowing, affecting the growth of world trade.

c Fuel prices were falling.

d The structure of the industry is fragmented, with ship-owners watching each other's orders for new ships.

e New ships take a long time to build.

f Shipping lines face high fixed costs with slender margins.

Assume that this is a competitive market. (This will allow you to draw supply and demand curves for the market.) There is some evidence for this, as shipping lines face 'slender margins' (see f). This suggests that the firms face competition from each other, and are unable to use market power to increase profit margins.

How would you expect the demand and supply curves to move in response to the first three factors mentioned (i.e. a, b and c)? Sketch a diagram for yourself.

Why should the shipping lines undertake a large-scale expansion at a time of falling or stagnant demand?

Elasticity: the sensitivity of demand and supply

Both the demand for and the supply of a good or service can be expected to depend upon its price as well as other factors. It is often interesting to know just how sensitive demand and/or supply will be to a change in either price or one of the other determinants — for example, in predicting how market equilibrium will change in response to a change in the market environment. The sensitivity of demand or supply to a change in one of its determining factors can be measured by its **elasticity**.

 terms

elasticity: a measure of the sensitivity of one variable to changes in another variable

price elasticity of demand (PED): a measure of the sensitivity of quantity demanded to a change in the price of a good or service. It is measured as:

$$\frac{\% \text{ change in quantity demanded}}{\% \text{ change in price}}$$

The price elasticity of demand

The most common elasticity measure is the **price elasticity of demand (PED)**. This measures the sensitivity of the quantity demanded of a good or service to a change in its price.

The elasticity is defined as the percentage change in quantity demanded divided by the percentage change in the price.

We define the percentage change in price as $100 \times \Delta P/P$ (where Δ means 'change in' and P stands for 'price'). Similarly, the percentage change in quantity demanded is $100 \times \Delta Q/Q$.

When the demand is highly price sensitive, the percentage change in quantity demanded following a price change will be large relative to the percentage change in price. In this case, *PED* will take on a value that is numerically greater than 1. For example, suppose that a 2% change in price leads to a 5% change in quantity demanded; the elasticity is then −5 divided by 2 = −2.5. When the elasticity is numerically greater than 1, demand is referred to as being *price elastic*.

There are two important things to notice about this. First, because the demand curve is downward sloping, the elasticity will always be negative. This is because the changes in price and quantity are always in the opposite direction. Second, you should try to calculate the elasticity only for a relatively small change in price, as it becomes unreliable for very large changes.

When demand is not very sensitive to price, the percentage change in quantity demanded will be smaller than the original percentage change in price, and the elasticity will then be numerically less than 1. For example, if a 2% change in price leads to a 1% change in quantity demanded, then the value of the elasticity will be −1 divided by 2 = −0.5. In this case, demand is referred to as being *price inelastic*.

An example

Figure 4.12 shows a demand curve for pencils. When the price of a pencil is 40p, the quantity demanded will be 20. If the price falls to 35p, the quantity demanded will rise to 30. The percentage change in quantity is $100 \times 10/20 = 50$ and the percentage change in price is $100 \times -5/40 = -12.5$. Thus, the elasticity can be calculated as $(50/-12.5) = -4$. At this price, demand is highly price elastic.

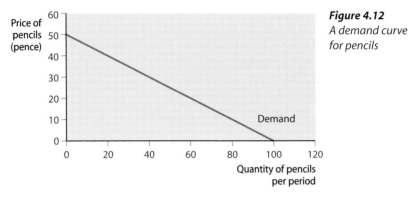

Figure 4.12
A demand curve for pencils

At a lower price, the result is quite different. Suppose that price is initially 10p, at which price the quantity demanded is 80. If the price falls to 9p, demand increases to 82. The percentage change in quantity is now $100 \times 2/80 = 2.5$, and the percentage change in price is $100 \times -1/10 = -10$, so the elasticity is calculated as $2.5/-10 = -0.25$, and demand is now price inelastic.

This phenomenon is true for any straight-line demand curve: in other words, demand is price elastic at higher prices and inelastic at lower prices. At the halfway point the elasticity is exactly −1, which is referred to as *unit elasticity*.

Why should this happen? The key is to remember that elasticity is defined in terms of the percentage changes in price and quantity. Thus, when price is relatively high, a 1p change in price is a small percentage change, and the percentage change in quantity is relatively large — because when price is relatively high, the initial quantity is relatively low. The reverse is the case when price is relatively low. Figure 4.13 shows how the elasticity of demand varies along a straight-line demand curve.

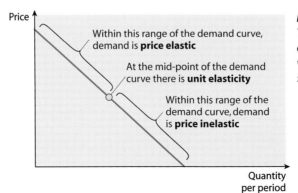

Figure 4.13
The own-price elasticity of demand varies along a straight line

The price elasticity of demand and total revenue

One reason why firms may have an interest in the price elasticity of demand is that, if they are considering changing their prices, they will be eager to know the extent to which demand will be affected. For example, they may want to know how a change in price will affect their total revenue. As it happens there is a consistent relationship between the price elasticity of demand and total revenue.

Total revenue is given by price multiplied by quantity. In Figure 4.14, if price is at P_0, quantity demanded is at Q_0 and total revenue is given by the area of the rectangle OP_0AQ_0. If price falls to P_1 the quantity demanded rises to Q_1, and you can see that total revenue has increased, as it is now given by the area OP_1BQ_1. This is larger than at price P_0, because in moving from P_0 to P_1 the area P_1P_0AC is lost, but the area Q_0CBQ_1 is gained, and the latter is the larger. As you move down the demand curve, total revenue at first increases like this, but then decreases — try sketching this for yourself to check that it is so.

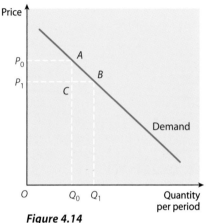

Figure 4.14
Demand and total revenue

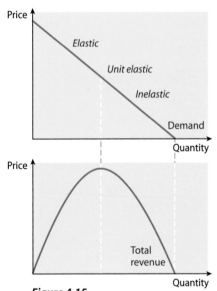

Figure 4.15
Elasticity and total revenue

For the case of a straight-line demand curve the relationship is illustrated in Figure 4.15. Remember that demand is price elastic when price is relatively high. This is the range of the demand curve in which total revenue rises as price falls. This makes sense, as in this range the quantity demanded is sensitive to a change in price and increases by more (in percentage terms) than the price falls. This implies that, as you move to the right in this segment, total revenue rises. The increase in quantity sold more than compensates for the fall in price. However, when the mid-point is reached and demand becomes unit elastic, total revenue stops rising — it is at its maximum at this point. The remaining part of the curve is inelastic: that is, the increase in quantity demanded is no longer sufficient to compensate for the decrease in price, and total revenue falls. Table 4.1 summarises the situation.

Price elasticity of demand	For a price increase, total revenue…	For a price decrease, total revenue…
Elastic	falls	rises
Unit elastic	does not change	does not change
Inelastic	rises	falls

Table 4.1
Total revenue, elasticity and a price change

Thus, if a firm is aware of the price elasticity of demand for its product, it can anticipate consumer response to its price changes, which may be a powerful strategic tool.

One very important point must be made here. If the price elasticity of demand varies along a straight-line demand curve, such a curve cannot be referred to as either elastic or inelastic. To do so is to confuse the elasticity with the *slope* of the demand curve. It is not only the steepness of the demand curve that determines the elasticity, but also the point on the curve at which the elasticity is measured.

Two extreme cases of the price elasticity of demand should also be mentioned. Demand may sometimes be totally insensitive to price, so that the same quantity will be demanded whatever price is set for it. In such a situation, demand is said to be *perfectly inelastic*. The demand curve in this case is vertical — as in D_i in Figure 4.16. In this situation, the numerical value of the price elasticity is zero, as quantity demanded does not change in response to a change in the price of the good.

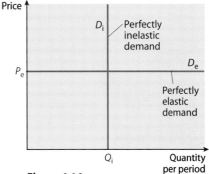

Figure 4.16
Perfectly elastic and inelastic demand

The other extreme is shown on the same figure, where D_e is a horizontal demand curve and demand is *perfectly elastic*. The numerical value of the elasticity here is infinity. Consumers demand an unlimited quantity of the good at price P_e. No firm has any incentive to lower price below this level, but if price were to rise above P_e, demand would fall to zero.

An example
A study by the Institute for Fiscal Studies for the UK found that the price elasticity of demand for wine was −1.69. This means that demand for wine is elastic. If the price of wine were to increase by 10% (ceteris paribus), there would be a fall of 16.9% in the quantity of wine demanded.

Influences on the price elasticity of demand
A number of important influences on the price elasticity of demand can now be identified. The most important is the availability of substitutes for the good or service under consideration. For example, think about the demand for cauliflower. Cauliflower and broccoli are often seen as being very similar, so if the price of cauliflower is high one week, people might quite readily switch to broccoli. The demand for cauliflower can be said to be price sensitive (elastic), as consumers can readily substitute an alternative product. On the other hand, if the price of all vegetables rises, demand will not change very much, as there are no substitutes for vegetables in the diet. Thus, goods that have close substitutes available will tend to exhibit elastic demand, whereas the demand for goods for which there are no substitutes will tend to be more inelastic.

Associated with this is the question of whether an individual regards a good or service as a necessity or as a luxury item. If a good is a necessity, then demand for it will tend to be inelastic, whereas if a good is regarded as a luxury, consumers will tend to be more price-sensitive. This is closely related to the question of substitutes, as by labelling a good as a necessity one is essentially saying that there are no substitutes for it.

Hemera Technologies

A second influence on the price elasticity of demand is the relative share of the good or service in overall expenditure. You may tend not to notice small changes in the price of an inexpensive item that is a small part of overall expenditure, such as salt or sugar. This tends to mean that demand for that good is relatively inelastic. On the other hand, an item that figures large in the household budget will be seen very differently, and consumers will tend to be much more sensitive to price when a significant proportion of their income is involved.

Finally, the time period under consideration may be important. Consumers may respond more strongly to a price change in the long run than to one in the short run. An increase in the price of petrol may have limited effects in the short run; however, in the long run, consumers may buy smaller cars or switch to diesel. Thus, the elasticity of demand tends to be more elastic in the long run than in the short run. Habit or commitment to a certain pattern of consumption may dictate the short-run pattern of consumption, but people do eventually adjust to price changes.

Demand for wine is price elastic

Summary

➤ The price elasticity of demand measures the sensitivity of the quantity of a good demanded to a change in its price.

➤ As there is an inverse relationship between quantity demanded and price, the price elasticity of demand is always negative.

➤ Where consumers are sensitive to a change in price, the percentage change in quantity demanded will exceed the percentage change in price. The elasticity of demand then takes on a value that is numerically greater than 1, and demand is said to be elastic.

➤ Where consumers are not very sensitive to a change in price, the percentage change in quantity demanded will be smaller than the percentage change in price. Elasticity of demand then takes on a value that is numerically smaller than 1, and demand is said to be inelastic.

➤ When demand is elastic, a fall (rise) in price leads to a rise (fall) in total revenue.

➤ When demand is inelastic, a fall (rise) in price leads to a fall (rise) in total revenue.

➤ The size of the price elasticity of demand is influenced by the availability of substitutes for a good, the relative share of expenditure on the good in the consumer's budget and the time that consumers have to adjust.

Exercise 4.4

Examine Table 4.2, which shows the demand for a particular red wine at different prices.

Price (£)	Quantity demanded (bottles per week)
10	20
8	40
6	60
4	80
2	100

Table 4.2
Demand for
Château Econ

a Draw the demand curve.

b Calculate the price elasticity of demand when the initial price is £8.

c Calculate the price elasticity of demand when the initial price is £6.

d Calculate the price elasticity of demand when the initial price is £4.

The income elasticity of demand

Elasticity is a measure of the sensitivity of a variable to changes in another variable. In the same way as the price elasticity of demand is determined, an elasticity measure can be calculated for any other influence on demand or supply. **Income elasticity of demand (YED)** is therefore defined as:

$$YED = \frac{\% \text{ change in quantity demanded}}{\% \text{ change in consumer income}}$$

Unlike the price elasticity of demand, the income elasticity of demand may be either positive or negative. Remember the distinction between normal and inferior goods? For normal goods the quantity demanded will increase as consumer income rises, whereas for inferior goods the quantity demanded will tend to fall as income rises. Thus, for normal goods the *YED* will be positive, whereas for inferior goods it will be negative.

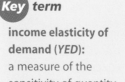

Key term

income elasticity of demand (YED):
a measure of the sensitivity of quantity demanded to a change in consumer incomes

Suppose you discover that the *YED* for wine is 0.7. How do you interpret this number? If consumer incomes were to increase by 10%, the demand for wine would increase by 10 × 0.7 = 7%. This example of a normal good may be helpful information for wine merchants, if they know that consumer incomes are rising over time.

On the other hand, if the *YED* for coach travel is –0.3, that means that a 10% increase in consumer incomes will lead to a 3% fall in the demand for coach travel — perhaps because more people are travelling by car. In this instance, coach travel would be regarded as an inferior good.

In some cases the *YED* may be very strongly positive. For example, suppose that the *YED* for digital cameras is +2. This implies that the quantity demanded of such cameras will increase by 20% for every 10% increase in incomes. An increase in income is encouraging people to devote more of their incomes to this product, which increases its share in total expenditure. Such goods are referred to as **luxury goods**.

Cross-price elasticity of demand

Another useful measure is the **cross-price elasticity of demand (*XED*)**. This is helpful in revealing the interrelationships between goods. Again, this measure may be either positive or negative, depending on the relationship between the goods. It is defined as:

$$XED = \frac{\% \text{ change in quantity demanded of good X}}{\% \text{ change in price of good Y}}$$

Key *terms*

luxury good: one for which the income elasticity of demand is positive, and greater than 1, such that as income rises, consumers spend proportionally more on the good

cross-price elasticity of demand (*XED*): a measure of the sensitivity of quantity demanded of a good or service to a change in the price of some other good or service

If the *XED* is seen to be positive, it means that an increase in the price of good Y leads to an increase in the quantity demanded of good X. For example, an increase in the price of apples may lead to an increase in the demand for pears. Here apples and pears are regarded as substitutes for each other; if one becomes relatively more expensive, consumers will switch to the other. A high value for the *XED* indicates that two goods are very close substitutes. This information may be useful in helping a firm to identify its close competitors.

On the other hand, if an increase in the price of one good leads to a fall in the quantity demanded of another good, this suggests that they are likely to be complements. The *XED* in this case will be negative. An example of such a relationship would be that between coffee and sugar, which tend to be consumed together.

Examples

A study by the Institute for Fiscal Studies using data for the UK found that the cross-price elasticity of demand for wine with respect to a change in the price of beer was −0.60, whereas the cross-price elasticity with respect to the price of spirits was +0.77. The negative cross-price elasticity with beer suggests that wine and beer are complements: a 10% increase in the price of beer would lead to a 6% fall in the quantity demanded of wine. In contrast, the cross-price elasticity of demand for wine with respect to the price of spirits is positive, suggesting that wine and spirits are substitutes. An increase in the price of spirits leads to an increase in the quantity demanded of wine.

Price elasticity of supply

As elasticity is a measure of sensitivity, its use need not be confined to influences on demand, but can also be turned to evaluating the sensitivity of quantity *supplied* to a change in its determinants — price in particular.

It was argued in Chapter 3 that the supply curve is likely to be upward sloping, so the price elasticity of supply can be expected to be positive. In other words, an increase in the market price will induce firms to supply more output to the market. The **price elasticity of supply (PES)** is defined as:

$$PES = \frac{\% \text{ change in the quantity supplied}}{\% \text{ change in price}}$$

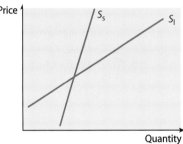

> **Key term**
>
> **price elasticity of supply (PES):** a measure of the sensitivity of quantity supplied of a good or service to a change in the price of that good or service

So, if the price elasticity of supply is 0.8, an increase in price of 10% will encourage firms to supply 8% more. As with the price elasticity of demand, if the elasticity is greater than 1, supply is referred to as being elastic, whereas if the value is between 0 and 1, supply is considered inelastic. *Unit elasticity* occurs when the price elasticity of supply is exactly 1, so that a 10% increase in price induces a 10% increase in quantity supplied.

The value of the elasticity will depend on how willing and able firms are to increase their supply. For example, if firms are operating close to the capacity of their existing plant and machinery, they may be unable to respond to an increase in price, at least in the short run. So here again, supply can be expected to be more elastic in the long run than in the short run. Figure 4.17 illustrates this. In the short run, firms may be able to respond to an increase in price only in a limited way, and so supply may be relatively inelastic, as shown by S_s in the figure. However, firms can become more flexible in the long run by installing new machinery or building new factories, so supply can then become more elastic, moving to S_l.

There are two limiting cases of supply elasticity. For some reason, supply may be fixed such that, no matter how much price increases, firms will not be able to supply any more. For example, it could be that a certain amount of fish is available in a market, and however high the price goes, no more can be obtained. Equally, if the fishermen know that the fish they do not sell today cannot be stored for another day, they have an incentive to sell however low the price goes. In these cases, supply is perfectly inelastic. At the other extreme is perfectly elastic supply, where firms would be prepared to supply any amount of the good at the going price.

These two possibilities are shown in Figure 4.18. Here S_i represents a perfectly inelastic supply curve: firms will supply Q_i whatever the price, perhaps because that is the amount available for sale. Supply here is vertical. At the opposite extreme, if supply is perfectly elastic then firms are prepared to supply any amount at the price P_e, and the supply curve is given by the horizontal line S_e.

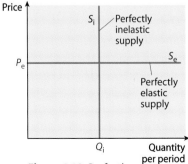

Figure 4.17
Short- and long-run supply

Figure 4.18 Perfectly elastic and inelastic supply

Exercise 4.5

Imagine the following scenario. You are considering a pricing strategy for a bus company. The economy is heading into recession, and the company is running at a loss. Your local rail service provider has announced an increase in rail fares. How (if at all) do you use the following information concerning the elasticity of bus travel with respect to various variables to inform your decision on price? Do you raise or lower price?

➤ price elasticity of demand   −1.58

➤ income elasticity of demand   −2.43

➤ cross-price elasticity of demand with respect to rail fares   +2.21

➤ your price elasticity of supply   +1.15

Summary

➤ The income elasticity of demand (*YED*) measures the sensitivity of quantity demanded to a change in consumer incomes. It serves to distinguish between normal, luxury and inferior goods.

➤ The cross-price elasticity of demand (*XED*) measures the sensitivity of the quantity demanded of one good or service to a change in the price of some other good or service. It can serve to distinguish between substitutes and complements.

➤ The price elasticity of supply (*PES*) measures the sensitivity of the quantity supplied to a change in the price of a good or service. The price elasticity of supply can be expected to be greater in the long run than in the short run, as firms have more flexibility to adjust their production decisions in the long run.

Chapter 5
Prices, resource allocation and market failure

Now that you are familiar with the use of the demand and supply model, it is time to take a wider view of the process of resource allocation within society. An important question is whether markets can be relied upon to guide this process, or whether there are times when markets will fail. This chapter begins to address this by examining how prices can act as market signals to guide resource allocation, and by identifying circumstances in which this process may not work effectively. In this discussion, some new tools will be needed in order to identify what constitutes an efficient allocation of resources.

Learning outcomes

After studying this chapter, you should:
- ➤ have an overview of how the price mechanism works to allocate resources
- ➤ understand the meaning and significance of consumer surplus
- ➤ be able to see how prices provide incentives to producers
- ➤ understand the meaning and significance of producer surplus
- ➤ be aware of the effects of the entry and exit of firms into and out of a market
- ➤ understand the concepts of productive and allocative efficiency
- ➤ be familiar with the way in which resources are allocated in a free market economy
- ➤ appreciate the situations in which markets may fail to allocate resources effectively

Prices and resource allocation

The coordination problem

As Chapter 1 indicated, all societies face the fundamental economic problem of scarcity. Because there are unlimited wants but finite resources, it is necessary to take decisions on which goods and services should be produced, how they should be produced and for whom they should be produced. For an economy the size of the UK, there is thus an immense coordination problem. Another way of looking at this is to ask how consumers can express their preferences between alternative goods so that producers can produce the best mix of goods and services.

Some alternative possibilities for handling this problem will now be considered. In a **free market economy**, market forces are allowed to allocate resources. At the other extreme, in a centrally planned economy the state plans and directs resources into a range of uses. In between there is the mixed economy. In order to evaluate these alternatives, it is necessary to explore how each of them operates.

In a free market economy, prices play the key role; this is sometimes referred to as the laissez-faire approach to resource allocation.

Prices and preferences

How can consumers signal their preferences to producers? Demand and supply analysis provides the clue. Figure 5.1 shows the demand and supply for laptop computers. These have become popular goods in recent years. That is to say, over time there has been a rightward shift in the demand curve – in the figure, from D_0 to D_1. This simply means that consumers are placing a higher value on these goods; they are prepared to demand more at any given price. The result, as you know from comparative static analysis, is that the market will move to a new equilibrium, with price rising from P_0 to P_1 and quantity traded from Q_0 to Q_1: there is a movement along the supply curve.

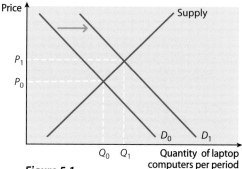

Figure 5.1
The market for laptop computers

The shift in the demand curve is an expression of consumers' preferences; it embodies the fact that they value laptop computers more highly now than before. The price that consumers are willing to pay represents their valuation of laptop computers.

Consumer surplus

Think a little more carefully about what the demand curve represents. Figure 5.2 again shows the demand curve for laptop computers. Suppose that the price is set at P^* and quantity demanded is thus Q^*. P^* can be seen as the value that the last customer places on a laptop. In other words, if the price were even slightly above P^*, there would be one consumer who would choose not to buy: this individual will be referred to as the *marginal consumer*.

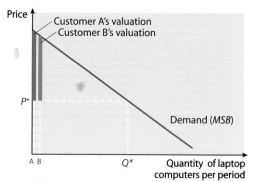

Figure 5.2
Price as marginal benefit

To that marginal consumer, P^* represents the marginal benefit derived from consuming this good — it is the price that just reflects the consumer's benefit from a laptop, as it is the price that just induces her to buy. Thinking of the society as a whole (which is made up of all the consumers within it), P^* can be regarded as the **marginal social benefit (MSB)** derived from consuming this good. The same argument could be made about any point along the demand curve, so the demand curve can be interpreted as the marginal benefit to be derived from consuming laptop computers.

Consumer demand for laptops has risen over the last few years

In most markets, all consumers face the same prices for goods and services. This leads to an important concept in economic analysis. P^* may represent the value of laptops to the *marginal* consumer, but what about all the other consumers who are also buying laptops at P^*? They would all be willing to pay a higher price for a laptop. Indeed, consumer A in Figure 5.2 would pay a very high price indeed, and thus values a laptop much more highly than P^*. When consumer A pays P^* for a laptop, he gets a great deal, as he values the good so much more highly — as represented by the vertical green line on Figure 5.2. Consumer B also gains a surplus above her willingness to pay (the blue line).

If all these surplus values are added up, they sum to the total surplus that society gains from consuming laptops. This is known as the **consumer surplus**, represented by the shaded triangle in Figure 5.3. It can be interpreted as the welfare that society gains from consuming the good, over and above the price that has to be paid for it.

> **Key terms**
>
> **marginal social benefit (MSB):** the additional benefit that society gains from consuming an extra unit of a good
>
> **consumer surplus:** the value that consumers gain from consuming a good or service over and above the price paid

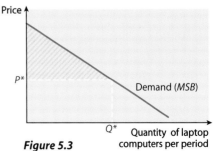

Figure 5.3
Consumer surplus

Prices as signals and incentives

From the producers' perspective, the question is how they receive signals from consumers about their changing preferences. Price is the key. Figure 5.1 shows how an increase in demand for laptop computers leads to an increase in the equilibrium market price. The shift in the demand curve leads to an increase in the equilibrium price, which encourages producers to supply more computers – there is a movement *along* the supply curve. This is really saying that producers find it profitable to expand their output of laptop computers at that higher price. The price level is thus a signal to producers about consumer preferences.

Notice that the price signal works equally well when there is a *decrease* in the demand for a good or service. Figure 5.4, for example, shows the market for video recordings. With the advent of DVDs, there has been a large fall in the demand for video recordings, so the demand for them has shifted to the left – consumers are demanding fewer videos at any price. Thus, the demand curve shifts from D_0 to D_1. Producers of video recordings are beginning to find that they cannot sell as many videos at the original price as before, so they have to reduce their price to avoid an increase in their unsold stocks. They have less incentive to produce videos, and will supply less. There is a movement *along* the supply curve to a lower equilibrium price at P_1, and a lower quantity traded at Q_1. You may like to think of this as a movement along the firm's production possibility curve for DVDs and videos.

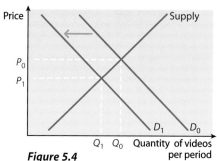

Figure 5.4
The market for video recordings

Thus, you can see how existing producers in a market receive signals from consumers in the form of changes in the equilibrium price, and respond to these signals by adjusting their output levels.

Producer surplus

Parallel to the notion of consumer surplus is the concept of **producer surplus**. Think about the nature of the supply curve: it reveals how much output firms are prepared to supply at any given price in a competitive market. Figure 5.5 depicts a supply curve. Assume the price is at P^*, and that all units are sold at that price. P^* represents the value to firms of the marginal unit sold. In other words, if the price had been set slightly below P^*, the last unit would not have been supplied, as firms would not have found this profitable.

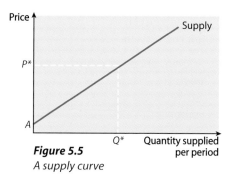

Figure 5.5
A supply curve

Key term

producer surplus: the difference between the price received by firms for a good or service and the price at which they would have been prepared to supply that good or service

Notice that the threshold at which a firm will decide it is not profitable to supply is the point at which the price received by the firm reaches the cost to the firm of producing the last unit of the good. Thus, in a competitive market the supply curve reflects **marginal cost**.

The supply curve shows that, in the range of prices between point *A* and *P**, firms would have been willing to supply positive amounts of this good or service. So at *P**, they would gain a surplus value on all units of the good supplied below *Q**. The total area is shown in Figure 5.6 – it is the area above the supply curve and below *P**, shown as the shaded triangle.

One way of defining this producer surplus is as the surplus earned by firms over and above the minimum that would have kept them in the market. It is the *raison d'être* of firms.

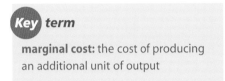

Key term

marginal cost: the cost of producing an additional unit of output

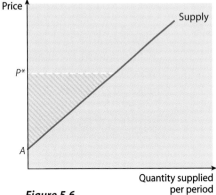

Figure 5.6
Producer surplus

Entry and exit of firms

The discussion so far has focused on the reactions of existing firms in a market to changes in consumer preferences. However, this is only part of the picture. Think back to Figure 5.1, where there was an increase in demand for laptop computers following a change in consumer preferences. The equilibrium price rose, and existing firms expanded the quantity supplied in response. Those firms are now earning a higher producer surplus than before. Other firms not currently in the market will be attracted by these surpluses, perceiving this to be a profitable market in which to operate.

If there are no barriers to entry, more firms will join the market. This in turn will tend to shift the supply curve to the right, as there will then be more firms prepared to supply. As a result, the equilibrium market price will tend to drift down again, until the market reaches a position in which there is no further incentive for new firms to enter the market. This will occur when the rate of return for firms in the laptop market is no better than in other markets.

Figure 5.7 illustrates this situation. The original increase in demand leads, as before, to a new equilibrium with a higher price P_1. As new firms join the market in quest of producer surplus, the supply curve shifts to the right to S_2, pushing the price back down to P_0, but with the quantity traded now up at Q_2.

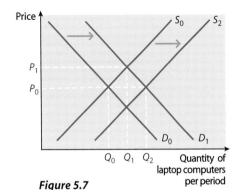

Figure 5.7
The market for laptop computers revisited

If the original movement in demand is in the opposite direction, as it was for video recordings in Figure 5.4, a similar long-run adjustment takes place. As the market price falls, some firms in the market may decide that they no longer wish to remain in production, and will exit from the market altogether. This will shift the supply curve to the left in Figure 5.8 (to S_2) until only firms that continue to find it profitable will remain in the market. In the final position price is back to P_0, and quantity traded has fallen to Q_2.

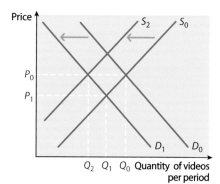

Figure 5.8
The market for video recordings

Exercise 5.1

a Sketch a demand and supply diagram and mark on it the areas that represent consumer and producer surplus.

b Using a demand and supply diagram, explain the process that provides incentives for firms to adjust to a decrease in the demand for fountain pens in a competitive market.

c Think about how you could use demand and supply analysis to explain recent movements in the world price of oil.

Summary

➤ If market forces are to allocate resources effectively, consumers need to be able to express their preferences for goods and services in such a way that producers can respond.

➤ Consumers express their preferences through prices, as prices will adjust to equilibrium levels following a change in consumer demand.

➤ Consumer surplus represents the benefit that consumers gain from consuming a product over and above the price they pay for that product.

➤ Producer surplus represents the benefit gained by firms over and above the price at which they would have been prepared to supply a product.

➤ Producers have an incentive to respond to changes in prices. In the short run this occurs through output adjustments of existing firms (movements along the supply curve), but in the long run firms will enter the market (or exit from it) until there are no further incentives for entry or exit.

Aspects of efficiency

In tackling the fundamental economic problem of scarcity, a society needs to find a way of using its limited resources as effectively as possible. In normal parlance it might be natural to refer to this as a quest for *efficiency*. From an economist's point of view there are two key aspects of efficiency, both of which are important in evaluating whether markets in an economy are working effectively.

Chapter 1 introduced one of these aspects in relation to the production possibility curve (*PPC*). Figure 5.9 shows a country's production possibility curve. One of the choices to be made in allocating resources in this country is between producing agricultural or manufactured goods.

In Chapter 1 it was seen that at a production point such as *A* the economy would not be using its resources fully, since by moving to a point *on* the *PPC* it would be possible to produce more of both types of good. For example, if production took place at point *B*, then more of both agricultural and manufactured goods could be produced, so that society would be better off than at *A*.

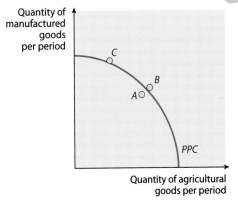

Figure 5.9
Productive efficiency

A similar claim could be made for any point along the *PPC*: it is more efficient to be at a point *on* the frontier than at some points *within* it. However, if you compare point *B* with point *C*, you will notice that the economy produces more manufactured goods at *C* than at *B* — but only at the expense of producing fewer agricultural goods.

This draws attention to the trade-off between the production of the two sorts of goods. It is difficult to judge whether society is better off at *B* or at *C* without knowing more about the preferences of consumers.

This discussion highlights the two aspects of efficiency. On the one hand, there is the question of whether society is operating on the *PPC*, and thus using its resources effectively. On the other hand, there is the question of whether society is producing the balance of goods that consumers wish to consume. These two aspects of efficiency are known as **productive efficiency** and **allocative efficiency**, and are discussed in more detail below.

In terms of Figure 5.9, both *B* and *C* are on the *PPC*, so both are productively efficient points, but it is not possible to judge which of the two is better without knowing consumers' preferences.

An efficient point for a society would be one in which no redistribution of resources could make any individual better off without making some other individual worse off. This is known as the *Pareto criterion*, after the nineteenth-century economist Vilfredo Pareto, who first introduced the concept.

Notice, however, that *any* point along the *PPC* is a **Pareto optimum**: with a different distribution of income among individuals in a society, a different overall equilibrium will be reached.

Key terms

productive efficiency: attained when a firm operates at minimum average total cost, choosing an appropriate combination of inputs (cost efficiency) and producing the maximum output possible from those inputs (technical efficiency)

allocative efficiency: achieved when society is producing an appropriate bundle of goods relative to consumer preferences

Pareto optimum: an allocation of resources is said to be a Pareto optimum if no reallocation of resources can make an individual better off without making some other individual worse off

Efficiency in a market

Aspects of efficiency can be explored further by considering an individual market. First, however, it is necessary to identify the conditions under which productive and allocative efficiency can be attained.

Productive efficiency

The production process entails combining a range of inputs of factors of production in order to produce output. Firms may find that there are benefits from large-scale production, so that efficiency may improve as firms expand production.

One way of measuring productive efficiency is in terms of the **average total cost** of production. This is simply the total cost of production divided by the quantity of output produced. Productive efficiency can then be defined in terms of the minimum average cost at which output can be produced, noting that average cost is likely to vary at different scales of output. **Economies of scale** occur when an increase in the scale of production leads to production at lower long-run average cost.

There are two aspects to productive efficiency. One entails making the best possible use of the inputs of factors of production: in other words, it is about producing as much output as possible from a given set of inputs. This is sometimes known as **technical efficiency**. However, there is also the question of whether the *best* set of inputs has been chosen. For example, there may be techniques of production that use mainly capital and not much labour, and alternative techniques that are more labour intensive. The firm's choice between these techniques will depend crucially on the relative prices of capital and labour. This is sometimes known as **cost efficiency**.

Key terms

average total cost: total cost divided by the quantity produced

economies of scale: occur for a firm when an increase in the scale of production leads to production at lower long-run average cost

technical efficiency: attaining the maximum possible output from a given set of inputs

cost efficiency: the appropriate combination of inputs of factors of production, given the relative prices of those factors

To attain productive efficiency, both technical efficiency and cost efficiency need to be achieved. In other words, productive efficiency is attained when a firm chooses the appropriate combination of inputs (cost efficiency) and produces the maximum output possible from those inputs (technical efficiency).

It is worth noting that the choice of technique of production may depend crucially upon the level of output that the firm wishes to produce. The balance of factors of production may well change according to the scale of activity. If the firm is producing very small amounts of output, it may well choose a different combination of capital and labour than if it were planning mass production on a large scale.

Thus, the firm's decision process is a three-stage procedure. First, the firm needs to decide how much output it wants to produce. Second, it has to choose an appropriate combination of factors of production, given that intended scale of production.

Third, it needs to produce as much output as possible, given those inputs. Once the intended scale of output has been decided, the firm has to minimise its costs of production. These decisions are part of the response to the question of *how* output should be produced. Remember also the concept of *marginal cost*, which refers to the cost faced by a firm in changing the output level by a small amount. This becomes an important part of the discussion.

Allocative efficiency

Allocative efficiency is about whether an economy allocates its resources in such a way as to produce a balance of goods and services that matches consumer preferences. In a complex modern economy, it is clearly difficult to identify such an ideal result. How can an appropriate balance of goods and services be identified?

Take the market for an individual product, such as the market for laptop computers that was considered earlier in the chapter. It was then argued that, in the long run, the market could be expected to arrive at an equilibrium price and quantity at which there was no incentive for firms either to enter the market or to exit from it. Figure 5.10 will remind you of the market situation.

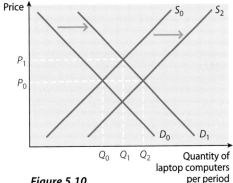

Figure 5.10
The market for laptop computers revisited again

The sequence of events in the diagram shows that, from an initial equilibrium with price at P_0 and quantity traded at Q_0, there was an increase in demand, with the demand curve shifting to D_1. In response, existing firms expanded their supply, moving up the supply curve. However, the lure of the producer surplus (abnormal profits) that was being made by these firms then attracted more firms into the market, such that the supply curve shifted to S_2, a process that brought the price back down to the original level of P_0.

Now think about that price from the point of view of a firm. P_0 is at a level where there is no further incentive to attract new firms, but no firm wishes to leave the market. In other words, no surplus is being made on that marginal unit, and the marginal firm is just breaking even on it. The price in this context would seem to be just covering the marginal cost of production.

However, it was also argued that from the consumers' point of view any point along the demand curve could be regarded as the marginal benefit received from consuming a good or service.

Where is all this leading? Putting together the arguments, it would seem that market forces can carry a market to a position in which, from the firms' point of view, the price is equal to marginal cost, and from the consumers' point of view, the price is equal to marginal benefit.

This is an important result. Suppose that the marginal benefit from consuming a good were higher than the marginal cost to society of producing it. It could then be argued that society would be better off producing more of the good because, by increasing production, more could be added to benefits than to costs. Equally, if the marginal cost were above the marginal benefit from consuming a good, society would be producing too much of the good and would benefit from producing less. The best possible position is thus where marginal benefit is equal to marginal cost — in other words, where *price is set equal to marginal cost.*

If all markets in an economy operated in this way, resources would be used so effectively that no reallocation of resources could generate an overall improvement. Allocative efficiency would be attained. The key question is whether the market mechanism will work sufficiently well to ensure that this happens — or whether it will fail. In other words, are there conditions that could arise in a market, in which price would not be set at marginal cost?

Exercise 5.2

Consider Figure 5.11, which shows a production possibility curve (*PPC*) for an economy that produces consumer goods and investment goods.

Identify each of the following (*Hint*: in some cases more than one answer is possible):

a a point of productive inefficiency

b a point that is Pareto-superior to *B*

c a point of productive efficiency

d a point of allocative efficiency

e an unattainable point (*Hint*: think about what would need to happen for society to reach such a point)

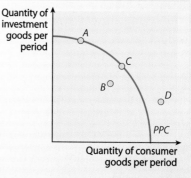

Figure 5.11 *A production possibility curve*

Summary

➤ A society needs to find a way of using its limited resources as efficiently as possible.

➤ Productive efficiency occurs when firms have chosen appropriate combinations of factors of production and produce the maximum output possible from those inputs.

➤ Allocative efficiency occurs when firms produce an appropriate bundle of goods and services, given consumer preferences.

➤ An allocation of resources is said to be a Pareto optimum if no reallocation of resources can make an individual better off without making some other individual worse off.

➤ An individual market exhibits aspects of allocative efficiency when the marginal benefit received by society from consuming a good or service matches the marginal cost of producing it — that is, when price is equal to marginal cost.

The working of a market economy

The previous section showed that the price mechanism allows a society to allocate its resources effectively if firms respond to changes in prices. Consumers express changes in their preferences by their decisions to buy (or not to buy) at the going price, which leads to a change in the equilibrium price. Firms thus respond to changes in consumer demand, given the incentive of profitability, which is related to price. In the short run, existing firms adjust their output levels along the supply curve. In the long run, firms enter into markets (or exit from them) in response to the relative profitability of the various economic activities that take place in the economy. But how does this work out in practice in a 'real-life' economy?

One way of viewing this system is through the notion of opportunity cost, introduced in Chapter 1. For example, in choosing to be active in the market for video recordings, a firm faces an opportunity cost. If it uses its resources to produce video recordings, it is *not* using those resources to produce DVDs. There may come a point at which the cost of producing video recordings becomes too high, if the profitability of DVDs is so much higher than that for video recordings, because of changes in the pattern of consumer demand. When the firm finds that it is not covering its opportunity costs, it will transfer production from the video market to the DVD market.

This sort of system of resource allocation is often referred to as **capitalism**. The key characteristic of capitalism is that individuals own the means of production, and can pursue whatever activities they choose — subject, of course, to the legal framework within which they operate.

The government's role in a free capitalist economy is relatively limited, but nonetheless important. A basic framework of *property rights* is essential, together with a basic legal framework. However, the state does not intervene in the production process directly. Secure property rights are significant, as this assures the incentives for the owners of capital.

Within such a system, consumers try to maximise the satisfaction they gain from consuming a range of products, and firms seek to maximise their profits by responding to consumer demand through the medium of price signals.

As has been shown, this is a potentially effective way of allocating resources. In the eighteenth century Adam Smith discussed this mechanism, arguing that when consumers and firms respond to incentives in this way resources are allocated effectively through the operation of an **invisible hand**, which guides firms to produce the goods and services that consumers wish to consume. Although individuals pursue their self-interest,

capitalism: a system of production in which there is private ownership of productive resources, and individuals are free to pursue their objectives with minimal interference from government

invisible hand: term used by Adam Smith to describe the way in which resources are allocated in a market economy

the market mechanism ensures that their actions will bring about a good result for society overall. A solution to the coordination problem is thus found through the free operation of markets. Such market adjustments provide a solution to Samuelson's three fundamental economic questions of what? how? and for whom?

However, Adam Smith also sounded a word of warning. He felt that there were too many factors that interfered with the free market system, such as over-protectionism and restrictions on trade. At the same time, he was not utterly convinced that a free market economy would be wholly effective, noting also that firms might at times collude to prevent the free operation of the market mechanism:

> People of the same trade seldom meet together, even for merriment and diversion, but the conversation ends in a conspiracy against the public, or in some contrivance to raise prices...
>
> Adam Smith, *The Wealth of Nations*, Vol. I

So there may be situations in which consumer interests need to be protected, if there is some sort of **market failure** that prevents the best outcome from being achieved.

Causes of market failure

The following chapters explore a number of ways in which markets may fail to bring the best result for society as a whole. In each case, the failure will arise because a market settles in a position in which marginal social cost diverges from marginal social benefit. The remainder of this chapter introduces the most important reasons for market failure.

> **Key term**
>
> **market failure:**
> a situation in which the free market mechanism does not lead to an optimal allocation of resources — for example, where there is a divergence between marginal social benefit and marginal social cost

Imperfect competition

The discussion of market adjustment outlined above argued that the entry and exit of firms ensures that a market will evolve towards a situation in which price is equal to marginal cost. However, this rested on the assumption that markets are competitive. Firms were fairly passive actors in these markets, responding perhaps rather tamely to changes in consumer preferences. The real world is not necessarily like that, and in many markets, firms have more power over their actions than has so far been suggested.

In the extreme, there are markets in which production is dominated by a single firm. In 1998 Microsoft was taken to court in the USA, accused of abusing its dominant position. At the time, Microsoft was said to control 95% of the market for operating systems for PC computers — and not just in the USA: this was 95% of the *world* market. When a firm achieves such dominance, there is no guarantee that it will not try to exploit its position at the expense of consumers.

The very fact that there was a court case against Microsoft bears witness to the need to protect consumers against dominant firms. In the UK, the Office of Fair Trading (OFT) and the Competition Commission have a brief to monitor the way in which markets operate and to guard against anti-competitive acts by firms.

This is one example of how imperfect competition can lead to a distortion in the allocation of resources. Firms with a dominant position in a market may be able to drive prices to a level that is above marginal cost; consumers then lose out in terms of allocative efficiency.

Externalities

If market forces are to guide the allocation of resources, it is crucial that the costs that firms face and the prices to which they respond fully reflect the actual costs and benefits associated with the production and consumption of goods. However, there are a number of situations and markets in which this does not happen because of **externalities**. These cause a divergence between marginal social cost and marginal social benefit in a market equilibrium situation. In the presence of such externalities, a price will emerge that is not equal to the 'true' marginal cost.

externality: a cost or a benefit that is external to a market transaction, and is thus not reflected in market prices

There are many examples of such externalities. An obvious one is pollution. A firm that causes pollution in the course of its production process imposes costs on others, but does not have to pay these costs. As a result, these costs are not reflected in market prices. This causes a distortion in the allocation of resources.

Pollution is a cost to society that may not be reflected in a good's market price

Not all externalities are negative. There may be situations in which a firm takes an action that benefits others. For example, if a firm chose to upgrade the road that ran past its factory, this would benefit other users of the road, even though they did not have to contribute to the cost of the upgraded road.

Not all externalities are on the supply side of the market. There may also be externalities in consumption, which may be positive or negative. If your neighbours mount an excellent firework display on 5 November, you can benefit without having to pay.

Externalities are discussed in Chapter 6.

Information failure

If markets are to perform a role in allocating resources, it is extremely important that all relevant economic agents (buyers and sellers) have good information about market conditions; otherwise they may not be able to take rational decisions.

It is important that consumers can clearly perceive the benefits to be gained by their consuming particular goods or services, in order to determine their own willingness to pay. Such benefits may not always be clear. For example, people may not fully perceive the benefits to be gained from education — or they may fail to appreciate the harmfulness of smoking tobacco.

In other market situations, economic agents on one side of the market may have different information from those on the other side: for example, sellers may have information about the goods that they are providing that buyers cannot discern. Chapter 7 explains that such information failure can also lead to a suboptimal allocation of resources.

Public goods

There is a category of goods known as public goods, which because of their characteristics cannot be provided by a purely free market. Street lighting is one example: there is no obvious way in which a private firm could charge all the users of street lighting for the benefits that they receive from it. Such goods are also discussed in Chapter 7.

Income distribution

Chapter 8 discusses equity. It is commonly accepted that safeguards need to be in place in any economy to ensure that the distribution of income does not become so skewed that poverty escalates. If there is substantial poverty in a society, the allocation of resources is unlikely to be optimal. Chapter 8 examines the extent to which inequality in the distribution of income can be considered a form of market failure that requires some intervention by government. In addition, Chapter 8 also examines some ways in which government intervention may have unintended effects — in other words, situations in which there may be *government failure*.

Summary

➤ Free markets do not always lead to the best possible allocation of resources: there may be market failure.

➤ Markets may fail when there is imperfect competition, so that firms are able to utilise market power to disadvantage consumers.

➤ When there are costs or benefits that are external to the price mechanism, the economy will not reach allocative efficiency.

➤ Markets can operate effectively only when participants in the market have full information about market conditions.

➤ Public goods have characteristics that prevent markets from supplying the appropriate quantity.

➤ Most societies are concerned to some extent with notions of equity.

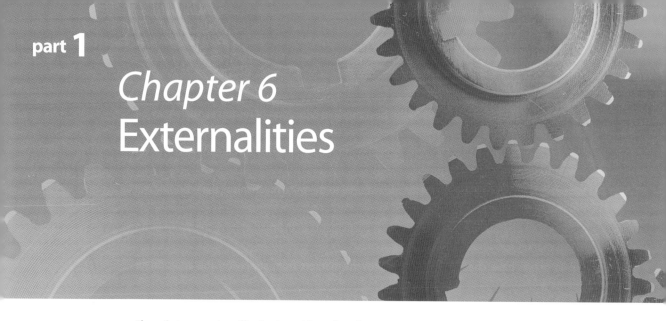

Chapter 6
Externalities

If markets are to be effective in guiding the allocation of resources in society, a precondition is that market prices are able to reflect the full costs and benefits associated with market transactions. However, there are many situations in which this is not so, and there are costs or benefits that are external to the workings of the market mechanism. This chapter examines the circumstances in which this may happen, and provides a justification for government intervention to improve the workings of the market.

Learning outcomes

After studying this chapter, you should:

➤ recognise situations in which the free market mechanism may fail to take account of costs or benefits that are associated with market transactions
➤ be familiar with situations in which there may be a divergence between private and social costs or benefits, such that price is not set equal to marginal cost
➤ be able to use diagrams to analyse positive and negative externalities in either production or consumption
➤ appreciate reasons why government may need to intervene in markets in which externalities are present
➤ be familiar with a wide range of examples of externalities
➤ recognise ways in which external costs or benefits may be valued
➤ be familiar with possible solutions to the problem of externalities

Key term

externality: a cost or a benefit that is external to a market transaction, and is thus not reflected in market prices

What is an externality?

Externality is one of those ugly words invented by economists, which says exactly what it means. It simply describes a cost or a benefit that is external to the market mechanism.

An externality will lead to a form of market failure because, if the cost or benefit is not reflected in market prices, it cannot be taken into consideration by all parties to a transaction. In other

words, there may be costs or benefits resulting from a transaction that are borne (or enjoyed) by some third party not directly involved in that transaction. This in turn implies that decisions will not be aligned with the best interests of society.

For example, if there is an element of costs that is not borne by producers, it is likely that 'too much' of the good will be produced. Where there are benefits that are not included, it is likely that too little will be produced. Later in the chapter, it will be shown that this is exactly what does happen. Externalities can affect either demand or supply in a market: that is to say, they may arise either in **consumption** or in **production**.

In approaching this topic, begin by tackling Exercise 6.1, which offers an example of each type of externality.

> ### Key terms
>
> **consumption externality:** an externality that affects the consumption side of a market, which may be either positive or negative
>
> **production externality:** an externality that affects the production side of a market, which may be either positive or negative

Exercise 6.1

Each of the following situations describes a type of externality. Do they affect production or consumption?

a   A factory situated in the centre of a town, and close to a residential district, emits toxic fumes through a chimney during its production process. As a result, residents living nearby have to wash their clothes more frequently, and incur higher medical bills as a result of breathing in the fumes.

b   Residents living along a main road festoon their houses with lavish Christmas lights and decorations during the month of December, helping passers-by to capture the festive spirit.

Toxic fumes

Example (a) is a negative production externality. The factory emits toxic fumes that impose costs on the residents (third parties) living nearby, who incur high washing and medical bills. The households face costs as a result of the production activities of the firm, so the firm does not face the full costs of its activity.

Thus, the **private costs** faced by the producer are lower than the social costs: that is, the costs faced by society as a whole. The producer will take decisions based only on its private costs, ignoring the **external costs** it imposes on society.

> ### Key terms
>
> **private cost:** a cost incurred by an individual (firm or consumer) as part of its production or other economic activities
>
> **external cost:** a cost that is associated with an individual's (a firm or household's) production or other economic activities, which is borne by a third party

Figure 6.1 illustrates this situation under the assumption that firms operate in a competitive market (i.e. there is not a monopoly). Here, D (MSB) represents the demand curve, which was characterised in Chapter 5 as representing the marginal social benefit derived from consuming a good. In other words, the demand curve represents consumers' willingness to pay for the good, and thus reflects their marginal valuation of the product.

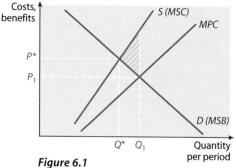

Figure 6.1
A negative production externality

Producers face marginal private costs given by the line MPC, but in fact impose higher costs than this on society. Thus S represents the supply curve that includes these additional costs imposed on society. This may be regarded as being the marginal social cost (MSC) of the firms' production.

If the market is unregulated by the government, firms will choose how much to supply on the basis of the marginal (private) cost they face, shown by MPC in Figure 6.1. The market equilibrium will thus be at quantity traded Q_1, where firms just break even on the marginal unit sold; price will be set at P_1.

This is not a good outcome for society, as it is clear that there is a divergence between the price in the market and the 'true' marginal cost – in other words, a divergence between marginal social benefit and marginal social cost. It is this divergence that is at the heart of the market failure. The last unit of this good sold imposes higher costs on society than the marginal benefit derived from consuming it. Too much is being produced.

In fact, the optimum position is at Q^*, where marginal social benefit is equal to marginal social cost. This will be reached if the price is set equal to (social) marginal cost at P^*. Less of the good will be consumed, but also less pollution will be created, and society will be better off than at Q_1.

The extent of the welfare loss that society suffers can be identified: it is shown by the shaded triangle in Figure 6.1. Each unit of output that is produced above Q^* imposes a cost equal to the vertical distance between MSC and MPC. The shaded area thus represents the difference between marginal social cost and marginal benefit over the range of output between the optimum output and the free market level of output.

Christmas lights

Example (b) in Exercise 6.1 is an example of a positive consumption externality. Residents of this street decorate their homes in order to share the Christmas spirit with passers-by. The benefit they gain from the decorations spills over and adds to the enjoyment of others. In other words, the social benefits from the residents' decision to provide Christmas decorations go beyond the private enjoyment that they receive.

chapter

Christmas lights have a positive consumption externality

Figure 6.2 illustrates this situation. *MPB* represents the marginal private benefits gained by residents from the Christmas lights; but *MSB* represents the full marginal social benefit that the community gains, which is higher than the *MPB*. Residents will provide decorations up to the point Q_2, where their marginal private benefit is just balanced by the marginal cost of the lights. However, if the full social benefits received are taken into account, Q^* would be the optimum point: the residents do not provide enough décor for the community to reach the optimum. The shaded triangle in Figure 6.2 shows the welfare loss, that is, the amount of social benefit forgone if the outcome is at Q_2 instead of Q^*.

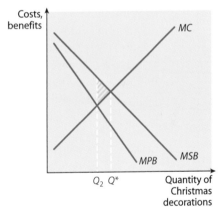

Figure 6.2
A positive consumption externality

Positive and normative revisited

Example (b) is a reminder of the distinction between positive and normative analysis, which was introduced in Chapter 1. Economists would agree that Figure 6.2 shows the effects of a beneficial consumption externality. However, probably not everyone would agree that the lavish Christmas decorations are providing such benefits. This is where a *normative judgement* comes into play. It could equally be argued that the lavish Christmas decorations are unsightly and inappropriate, or that they constitute a distraction for drivers and are therefore likely to cause accidents. After all, not everyone enjoys the garish.

Exercise 6.1 (continued)

Discussion has centred around two examples of externalities: a production externality that had negative effects, and a consumption externality that was beneficial to society. In fact, there are two other possibilities.

c   A factory that produces chemicals, which is located on the banks of a river, installs a new water purification plant that improves the quality of water discharged into the river. A trout farm located downstream finds that its productivity increases, and that it has to spend less on filtering the water.

d   Liz, a 'metal' enthusiast, enjoys playing her music at high volume late at night, in spite of the fact that she lives in a flat with inadequate sound insulation. The neighbours prefer rock, but cannot escape the metal.

Water purification

Example (c) is a production externality that has *positive* effects. The action taken by the chemical firm to purify its waste water has beneficial effects on the trout farm, which finds that its costs have been reduced without it having taken any action whatsoever. Indeed, it finds that it has to spend less on filtering the water.

Figure 6.3 shows the position facing the chemicals firm. It faces relatively high marginal private costs given by *MPC*. However, its actions have reduced the costs faced by the trout farm, so the 'social' cost of the firm's production activities is lower than its private cost. Thus, in this case marginal social cost, shown by *MSC* in the figure, is lower than marginal private cost. The firm will produce up to the point where *MPC* equals marginal social benefit: that is, at Q_3.

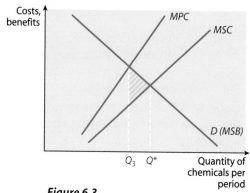

Figure 6.3
A positive production externality

In this market position, notice that the marginal benefit that society receives from consuming the product is higher than the marginal social cost of producing it, so too little of the product is being consumed for society's good. Society would be better off at Q^*, where marginal social benefit is equal to marginal social cost.

Again, the shaded triangle in Figure 6.3 represents the extent of the inefficiency: it is given by the excess of marginal social benefit over marginal social cost over the range of output between the market outcome and society's optimum position.

Rock and metal

Example (d) is a *negative* consumption externality. Liz, the metal fan, gains benefit from listening to her music at high volume, but the neighbours also hear her music and suffer as a result. Indeed, it may be that when they try to listen to rock, the metal interferes with their enjoyment. Their benefit is reduced by having to hear the metal.

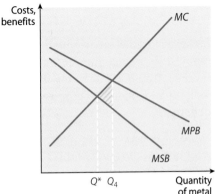

Figure 6.4 *A negative consumption externality*

Figure 6.4 illustrates this. The situation can be interpreted in terms of the benefits that accrue as a result of Liz's consumption of loud metal music. Liz gains benefit as shown by the line *MPB*, which represents marginal private benefit. However, the social benefit is lower than this if the vexation suffered by the neighbours is taken into account, so *MSB* in Figure 6.4 represents the marginal social benefits from Liz's metal.

Liz will listen to metal up to the point where her marginal private benefit is just equal to the marginal cost of playing it, at Q_4. However, the optimal position that takes the neighbours into consideration is where marginal social benefit is equal to marginal cost — at Q^*. Thus, Liz plays too much metal for the good of society.

Summary

➤ Markets can operate effectively only if all relevant costs and benefits are taken into account in decision making.

➤ Some costs and benefits are external to the market mechanism, and are thus neglected, causing a distortion in resource allocation.

➤ Such external costs and benefits are known as 'externalities'.

➤ Externalities may occur in either production or consumption, thereby affecting either demand or supply.

➤ Externalities may be either positive or negative, but either way resources will not be optimally allocated if they are present.

Exercise 6.2

Discuss examples of some externalities that you meet in everyday situations, and classify them as affecting either production or consumption.

Externalities occur in a wide variety of market situations, and constitute an important source of market failure. This means that externalities may hinder the achievement of good resource allocation from society's perspective. The final section of this chapter explores some ways in which attempts have been made to measure the social costs imposed by externalities. First, however, a number of other externalities that appear in various parts of the economy will be examined.

Externalities and the environment

Concern for the environment has been growing in recent years, with 'green' lobbyist groups demanding attention, sometimes through demonstrations and protests. There are so many different facets to this question that it is sometimes difficult to isolate the core issues. Externalities lie at the heart of much of the debate.

Some of the issues are international in nature, such as the debate over global warming. At the heart of this concern is the way in which emissions of greenhouse gases are said to be warming up the planet. Sea levels are rising and major climate change seems imminent.

One reason why this question is especially difficult to tackle is that actions taken by one country can have effects on other countries. Scientists argue that the problem is caused mainly by pollution created by transport and industry, especially in the richer countries of the world. However, poorer countries suffer the consequences as well, especially countries such as Bangladesh, where much of the land is low lying and prone to severe flooding — indeed, two-thirds of the country was under water during the floods of 2004.

In principle, this is very similar to example (a) in Exercise 6.1: it is an example of a negative production externality, in which the nations causing most of the damage face only part of the costs caused by their lifestyles and production processes. The inevitable result in an unregulated market is that too much pollution is produced.

When externalities cross international borders in this way, the problem can be tackled only through international cooperation. For example, at the Kyoto World Climate Summit held in Japan in 1997, almost every developed nation agreed to cut greenhouse gas emissions by 6% by 2010. (The USA, the largest emitter of carbon dioxide, withdrew from the agreement in early 2001, fearing the consequences of such a restriction on the US economy.)

Global warming is not the only example of international externality effects. Scandinavian countries have suffered from acid rain caused by pollution in other European countries, including the UK. Forest fires left to burn in Indonesia have caused air pollution in neighbouring Singapore.

Another environmental issue concerns rivers. Some of the big rivers of the world, such as the Nile in Africa, pass through several countries on their way to the sea. For Egypt, through which the river runs at the end of its journey, the Nile is crucial for the livelihood of the economy. If countries further upstream were to increase their usage of the river, perhaps through new irrigation projects, this could have disastrous effects on Egypt. Again, the actions of one set of economic agents would be having damaging effects on others, and these effects would not be reflected in market prices, in the sense that the upstream countries would not have to face the full cost of their actions.

Part of the problem here can be traced back to the difficulty of enforcing property rights. If the countries imposing the costs could be forced to make appropriate payment for their actions, this would help to bring the costs back within the market mechanism. Such a process is known in economics as 'internalising the externality', and will be examined later in this chapter.

Concern has also been expressed about the loss of *biodiversity*, a word that is shorthand for 'biological diversity'. The issue here is that when a section of rain-forest is cleared to plant soya, or for timber, it is possible that species of plants, insects or even animals whose existence is not even known at present may be wiped out. Many modern medicines are based on chemicals that occur naturally in the wild. By eradicating species before they have been discovered, possible scientific advances will be forgone. Notice that when it comes to measuring the value of what is being destroyed, biodiversity offers particular challenges — namely, the problem of putting a value on something that might not even be there!

Externalities and transport

With the introduction of the congestion charge in parts of central London, the London authorities have been attempting to tackle congestion. When traffic on the roads reaches a certain volume, congestion imposes heavy costs on road users. This is another example of an externality.

Figure 6.5 illustrates the situation. Suppose that D (MSB) represents the demand curve for car journeys along a particular stretch of road. When deciding whether or not to undertake a journey, drivers will balance the marginal benefit gained from making the journey against the marginal cost that they face. This is given by MPC — the marginal private cost of undertaking journeys. When the road is congested, a motorist who decides to undertake the journey adds to the congestion, and slows the traffic. The MPC curve incorporates the cost to the motorist of joining a congested road, and the chosen number of journeys will be at Q_1.

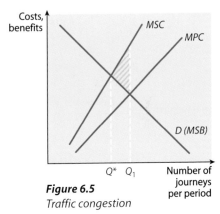

Figure 6.5
Traffic congestion

However, in adding to the congestion the motorist not only suffers the costs of congestion, but also imposes some marginal increase in costs on all other users of the road, as everyone suffers from the slower journeys resulting from the extra congestion. Thus, the marginal social costs (MSC) of undertaking journeys are higher than the cost faced by any individual motorist. MSC is therefore higher than MPC. Society would be better off with lower congestion: that is, with the number of journeys undertaken being limited to Q^*, where marginal social benefit equals marginal social cost. By imposing a charge on motorists entering central London, the authorities are trying to ensure that drivers face at least part of the social costs that they impose on others by using congested roads.

Externalities and health

Healthcare is a sector in which there is often public provision, or at least some state intervention in support of the health services. In the UK, the National Health Service is the prime provider of healthcare, but private healthcare is also available, and the use of private health insurance schemes is on the increase. Again, externalities can help to explain why there should be a need for government to intervene.

Consider the case of vaccination against a disease such as measles. Suppose an individual is considering whether or not to be vaccinated. Being vaccinated reduces the probability of that individual contracting the disease, so there are palpable potential benefits. However, these benefits must be balanced against the costs. There may be a direct charge for the vaccine; some individuals may have a phobia against needles; or they may be concerned about possible side-effects. Individuals will opt to be vaccinated only if the marginal expected benefit to them is at least as large as the marginal cost.

There are palpable potential benefits from a vaccination programme

From society's point of view, however, there are potential benefits that individuals will not take into account. After all, if they do contract measles, there is a chance of their passing it on to others. Indeed, if lots of people decide not to be vaccinated, there is the possibility of a widespread epidemic, which would be costly and damaging to many.

Figure 6.6 illustrates this point. The previous paragraph argues that the social benefits to society of having people vaccinated against measles exceed the private benefits that will be perceived by individuals, so that marginal social benefits exceed marginal private benefits. Private individuals will choose to balance marginal private benefit against marginal private cost at Q_1, whereas society would prefer more people to be vaccinated at Q^*. This parallels the discussion of a positive consumption externality. Chapter 7 returns to consider another aspect of healthcare provision.

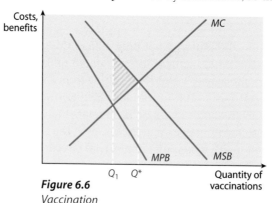

Figure 6.6
Vaccination

Externalities and education

As you are reading this textbook, it is reasonably safe to assume that you are following a course in AS economics. You have decided to demand education. This is yet another area in which externalities may be important.

When you decided to take A-levels (including economics), there were probably a number of factors that influenced your decision. Perhaps you intend to demand even more education in the future, by proceeding to study at university. Part of your decision process probably takes into account the fact that education improves your future earnings potential. Your expected lifetime earnings depend in part upon the level of educational qualifications that you attain. Research has shown that, on average, graduates earn more during their lifetimes than non-graduates. This is partly because there is a productivity effect: by becoming educated, you cultivate a range of skills that in later life will make you more productive, and this helps to explain why you can expect higher lifetime earnings than someone who chooses not to demand education. There is also a signalling effect, as having a degree signals to potential employers that you have the ability to cope with university study and have gained a range of skills.

What does society get out of this? Evidence suggests that, not only does education improve productivity, but a *group* of educated workers cooperating with each other become even more productive. This is an externality effect, as it depends upon interaction between educated workers – but each individual perceives only the individual benefit, and not the benefits of cooperation.

In other words, when you decide to undertake education, you do so on the basis of the expected private benefits that you hope to gain from education. However, you do not take into account the additional benefits through cooperation that society will reap. So here is another example of a positive consumption externality. As with healthcare, some other aspects of education will be discussed in Chapter 7.

Externalities and tourism

As international transport has become easier and cheaper, more people are wanting to travel to new and different destinations. For less developed countries, this offers an opportunity to earn much-needed foreign exchange.

There has been some criticism of this. The building of luxury hotels in the midst of the poverty that characterises many less developed countries is said to have damaging effects on the local population by emphasising differences in living standards.

However, constructing the infrastructure that tourists need may have beneficial effects on the domestic economy. Improved roads and communication systems can benefit local businesses. This effect can be interpreted as an externality, in the sense that the local firms will face lower costs as a result of the facilities provided for the tourist sector.

Extension material: social cost–benefit analysis

The importance of externalities in regard to environmental issues means that it is especially important to be aware of externalities when taking decisions that are likely to affect the environment. One area in which this has been especially contentious in recent years is road-building programmes. If decisions to build new roads, or to expand existing ones such as the M25, are taken only by reference to commercial considerations, there could be serious implications for resource allocation.

In taking such decisions, it is desirable to weigh up the costs and benefits of a scheme. If it turns out that the benefits exceed the costs, it might be thought appropriate to go ahead. However, in valuing the costs and the benefits, it is clearly important to include some estimate for the externalities involved in order that the decision can be based on all relevant factors. In other words, it is important to take a 'long and wide view' and not to focus too narrowly on purely financial costs and benefits.

A further complication is that with many such schemes the costs and benefits will be spread out over a long period of time, and it is important to come to a reasonable balance between the interests of present and future generations.

Social cost–benefit analysis is a procedure for bringing together the information needed to make appropriate decisions on such large-scale schemes. This entails a sequence of key steps.

1 Identify relevant costs and benefits

The first step is to identify all relevant costs and benefits. This needs to cover all of the direct costs of the project. These can probably be identified relatively easily, and include the production costs, labour costs and so on. The indirect costs also need to be identified, and this is where externality effects need to be considered. For example, in a road-building scheme, it is important to think in terms not only of the costs of construction, but also of the opportunity cost — how else could the land being used for the road have been used? How will the increase in traffic affect the quality of life enjoyed by local residents? For example, they may suffer from noise from the traffic using the road, or from the traffic fumes. Similarly, direct and indirect benefits need to be identified.

2 Valuation

If the costs and benefits are to be compared, they all need to be given a monetary valuation. It is likely that some of them will be items that have a market price attached to them. For these, valuation is not a problem. However, for externalities, or for other indirect costs and benefits without a market valuation, it is necessary to establish a **shadow price** — an estimate of the monetary value of each item.

 Key terms

social cost–benefit analysis: a process of evaluating the worth of a project by comparing its costs and benefits, including both direct and social costs and benefits — including externality effects

shadow price: an estimate of the monetary value of an item that does not carry a market price

3 Discounting the future

It is also important to recognise that costs and benefits that will flow from the project at some point in the future need to be expressed in terms of their value in the present. From today's perspective, a benefit that is immediate is more valuable than one that will only become relevant in 20 years' time. In order to incorporate this notion into the calculations, we need to **discount** the future at an appropriate rate, and calculate the **net present value** of the future stream of costs and benefits associated with the project under consideration.

 terms

discount: a process whereby the future valuation of a cost or benefit is reduced (discounted) in order to provide an estimate of its present value

net present value: the estimated value in the current time period of the discounted future net benefit of a project

Summary

➤ Externalities arise in many aspects of economic life.

➤ Environmental issues are especially prone to externality effects, as market prices do not always incorporate environmental issues, especially where property rights are not assigned.

➤ Congestion on the roads can also be seen as a form of externality.

➤ Externalities also arise in the areas of healthcare provision and education, where individuals do not always perceive the full social benefits that arise.

➤ A number of approaches have been proposed to measure externalities. Measurement may enable a social cost–benefit analysis to be made of projects involving a substantial externality element.

Exercise 6.3

Suppose there is a proposal to construct a new industrial estate close to where you live. Identify the costs and benefits of the scheme, including direct costs and benefits and not forgetting externalities.

Dealing with externalities

Externalities arise in situations where there are items of cost or benefit associated with transactions, and these are not reflected in market prices. In these circumstances a free market will not lead to an optimum allocation of resources. One approach to dealing with such market situations is to bring those externalities into the market mechanism — a process known as **internalising an externality**. The London congestion charge may be seen as an attempt to internalise

 term

internalising an externality: an attempt to deal with an externality by bringing an external cost or benefit into the price system

the externality effects of traffic congestion. In the case of pollution this principle would entail forcing the polluting firms to face the full social cost of their production activities. This is sometimes known as the *polluter pays* principle.

Pollution

Figure 6.7 illustrates a negative production externality: pollution. Suppose that firms in the market for chemicals use a production process that emits toxic fumes, thereby imposing costs on society that the firms themselves do not face. In other words, the marginal private costs faced by these firms are less than the marginal social costs that are inflicted on society. As explained earlier in the chapter, firms in this market will choose to produce up to point Q_1 and charge a price of P_1 to consumers. At this point, marginal social benefit is below the marginal cost of producing the chemicals, so it can be claimed that 'too much' of the product is being produced – that society would be better off if production were at Q^*, with a price charged at P^*.

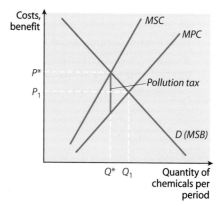

Figure 6.7 Pollution

Note that this optimum position is not characterised by *zero* pollution. In other words, from society's point of view it pays to abate pollution only *up to* the level where the marginal benefit of reducing pollution is matched by the marginal cost of doing so. Reducing pollution to zero would be too costly.

How can society reach the optimum output of chemicals at Q^*? In line with the principle that the polluter should pay, one approach would be to impose a tax on firms such that polluters face the full cost of their actions. In Figure 6.7, if firms were required to pay a tax equivalent to the vertical distance between marginal private cost (*MPC*) and marginal social cost (*MSC*), they would choose to produce at Q^*, paying a tax equal to the green line on the figure.

An alternative way of looking at this question is via a diagram showing the marginal benefit and marginal cost of emissions reduction. In Figure 6.8, *MB* represents the marginal social benefits from reducing emissions of some pollutant and *MC* is the marginal costs of reducing emissions. The optimum amount of reduction is found where marginal benefit equals marginal cost, at e^*. Up to this point, the marginal benefit to society of reducing emissions exceeds the marginal cost of the reduction, so it is in the interest of society to reduce pollution. However, beyond that point the marginal cost of reducing the amount of

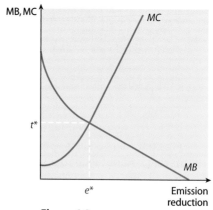

Figure 6.8
Reducing the emission of toxic fumes

pollution exceeds the benefits that accrue, so society will be worse off. Setting a tax equal to t^* in Figure 6.8 will induce firms to undertake the appropriate amount of emission reduction.

This is not the only way of reaching the objective, however. Figure 6.8 suggests that there is another possibility — namely, to impose environmental standards, and to prohibit emissions beyond e^*. This amounts to controlling quantity rather than price; and, if the government has full information about marginal costs and marginal benefits, the two policies will produce the equivalent result.

Either of the approaches outlined above will be effective — *if* the authorities have full information about the marginal costs and benefits. But how likely is this? There are many problems with this proviso. The measurement of both marginal benefits and marginal costs is fraught with difficulties.

The marginal social benefits of reducing pollution cannot be measured with great precision, for many reasons. It may be argued that there are significant gains to be made in terms of improved health and lower death rates if pollution can be reduced, but quantifying this is not straightforward. Even if it were possible to evaluate the saving in resources that would need to be devoted to future medical care resulting from the pollution, there are other considerations: quantification of the direct improvements to quality of life; whether or not to take international effects into account when formulating domestic policy; and the appropriate discount rate for evaluating benefits that will be received in the future. Moreover, the environmentalist and the industrialist may well arrive at different evaluations of the benefits of pollution control, reflecting their different viewpoints.

The measurement of costs may also be problematic. For example, it is likely that there will be differences in efficiency between firms. Those using modern technology may face lower costs than those using relatively old capital equipment. Do the authorities try to set a tax that is specific to each firm to take such differences into account? If they do not, but instead set a flat-rate tax, then the incentives may be inappropriate. This would mean that a firm using modern technology would face the same tax as one using old capital. The firm using new capital would then tend to produce too little output relative to those using older, less efficient capital.

Pollution permits

Another approach is to use a *pollution permit system*, under which the government issues or sells permits to firms, allowing them to pollute up to a certain limit. These permits are then tradable, so that firms that are relatively 'clean' in their production methods and do not need to use their full allocation of permits can sell their polluting rights to other firms, whose production methods produce greater levels of pollution.

One important advantage of such a scheme lies in the incentives for firms. Firms that pollute because of their relatively inefficient production methods will find they are at a disadvantage because they face higher costs. Rather than continuing to purchase permits, they will find that they have an incentive to produce less pollution — which, of course, is what the policy is intended to achieve. In this way, the permit

A system of pollution permits could be effective in regulating pollution

system uses the market to address the externality problem – in contrast to direct regulation of environmental standards, which tries to solve pollution by overriding the market.

A second advantage is that the overall level of pollution can be controlled by this system, as the authorities control the total amount of permits that are issued. After all, the objective of the policy is to control the overall level of pollution, and a mixture of 'clean' and 'dirty' firms may produce the same amount of total emissions as uniformly 'slightly unclean' firms.

However, the permit system may not be without its problems. In particular, there is the question of enforcement. For the system to be effective, sanctions must be in place for firms that pollute beyond the permitted level, and there must be an operational and cost-effective method for the authorities to check the level of emissions.

Furthermore, it may not be a straightforward exercise for the authorities to decide upon the appropriate number of permits to issue in order to produce the desired reduction in emission levels. Some alternative regulatory systems share this problem, as it is not easy to measure the extent to which marginal private and social costs diverge.

One possible criticism that is unique to a permit form of regulation is that the very different levels of pollution produced by different firms may seem inequitable – as if those firms that can afford to buy permits can pollute as much as they like. On the other hand, it might be argued that those most likely to suffer from this are the polluting firms, whose public image is likely to be tarnished if they acquire a reputation as heavy polluters. This possibility might strengthen the incentives of such firms to clean up their production. Taking the strengths and weaknesses of this approach together, it seems that on balance such a system could be effective in regulating pollution.

Global warming

Global warming is widely seen to require urgent and concerted action at a worldwide level. The Kyoto summit of 1997 laid the foundations for action, with many of the developed nations agreeing to take action to reduce emissions of carbon dioxide and other 'greenhouse' gases that are seen to be causing climate change. Although the USA withdrew from the agreement in early 2001, apparently concerned that the US economy might be harmed, in November of that year 178 other countries did reach agreement on how to enforce the Kyoto Accord. The absence of US cooperation is potentially significant, however, as the USA is the world's largest emitter of carbon dioxide, responsible for about a quarter of the world's greenhouse gas emissions.

At the heart of the Kyoto Accord is the decision of countries to reduce their greenhouse gas emissions by an agreed percentage by 2010. The method chosen to achieve these targets was based on a tradable pollution permit system. This was seen to be especially demanding for countries such as Japan, whose industry is already relatively energy-efficient. Japan was thus concerned that there should be sufficient permits available for purchase. More explicitly, it was concerned that sloppy compliance by Russia would limit the amount of permits on offer. The issues of monitoring and compliance are thus seen as critical.

A further summit meeting was held in Bali in December 2007 in an attempt to reach agreement on how to proceed when the first phase of the Kyoto protocol expires at the end of 2012. Some progress was made, but countries such as the USA, Canada and Japan remained sceptical, and China was reluctant to negotiate beyond Kyoto. This was significant, as China is soon expected to overtake the USA as the world's largest emitter of greenhouse gases.

The NIMBY syndrome

One problem that arises in trying to deal with externalities is that you cannot please all of the people all of the time. For example, it may well be that it is in society's overall interests to relocate unsightly facilities — it may even be that everyone would agree about this; but such facilities have to be located somewhere, and someone is almost bound to object because they are the ones to suffer. This is the **NIMBY (not in my back yard)** syndrome.

 Key *term*

NIMBY (not in my back yard): a syndrome under which people are happy to support the construction of an unsightly or unsocial facility, so long as it is not in their back yard

For example, many people would agree that it is desirable for the long-run sustainability of the economy that cleaner forms of energy are developed. One possibility is to build wind farms. People may well be happy for these to be constructed — *as long as* they do not happen to be living near them. This may not be the best example, however, as the effectiveness of wind farms is by no means proven, and there is a strong movement against their use on these grounds.

Exercise 6.4

You discover that your local authority has chosen to locate a new landfill site for waste disposal close to your home. What costs and benefits for society would result? Would these differ from your private costs and benefits? Would you object?

Property rights

The existence of a system of secure property rights is essential as an underpinning for the economy. The legal system exists in part to enforce property rights, and to provide the set of rules under which markets operate. When property rights fail, there is a failure of markets.

One of the reasons underlying the existence of some externalities is that there is a failing in the system of property rights. For example, think about the situation in which a factory is emitting toxic fumes into a residential district. One way of viewing this is that the firm is interfering with local residents' clean air. If those residents could be given property rights over clean air, they could require the firm to compensate them for the costs it was inflicting. However, the problem is that, with such a wide range of people being affected to varying degrees (according to prevailing winds and how close they live to the factory), it is impossible in practical terms to use the assignment of property rights to internalise the pollution externality. This is because the problem of coordination requires high transaction costs in order for property rights to be individually enforced. Therefore, the government effectively takes over the property rights on behalf of the residents, and acts as a collective enforcer.

Nobel prize winner Ronald Coase argued that externality effects could be internalised in conditions where property rights could be enforced, and where the transaction costs of doing so were not too large.

Summary

➤ In seeking to counter the harmful effects of externalities, governments look for ways of internalising the externality, by bringing external costs and benefits within the market mechanism.

➤ For example, the 'polluter pays' principle argues that the best way of dealing with a pollution externality is to force the polluter to face the full costs of its actions.

➤ Attempts have been made to tackle pollution through taxation, the regulation of environmental standards and the use of pollution permits.

➤ In some cases the allocation of property rights can be effective in curbing the effects of externalities — so long as the transaction costs of implementing it are not too high.

Chapter 7
Other forms of market failure

Externalities are not the only form of market failure. There are also situations where the characteristics of a good or service can affect the effective operation of a market. This chapter explores goods with unusual economic characteristics and markets that may fail as a result of problems with information.

Learning outcomes

After studying this chapter, you should:
➤ understand the nature of public goods and problems that arise in their provision
➤ be able to identify examples of public goods
➤ be aware of the characteristics of merit and demerit goods
➤ be able to give examples of possible merit and demerit goods
➤ appreciate the significance of asymmetric information as a source of market failure

Public goods

Private goods

Most of the goods that individuals consume are **private goods**. You buy a can of Diet Coke, you drink it, and it's gone. You may choose to share it with a friend, but you do not have to: by drinking it you can prevent anyone else from doing so. Furthermore, once it is gone, it's gone: nobody else can subsequently consume that Coke.

The two features that characterise a private good are:
➤ other people can be excluded from consuming it
➤ once consumed by one person, it cannot be consumed by another

The first feature can be described as *excludability*, whereas the second feature might be described by saying that consumption of a private good is *rivalrous*: the act of consumption uses up the good.

 Key *term*

private good: a good that, once consumed by one person, cannot be consumed by somebody else; such a good has excludability and is rivalrous

Public goods

Not all goods and services have these two characteristics. There are goods that, once provided, are available to all. In other words, people cannot be excluded from consuming such goods. There are other goods that do not diminish through consumption, so they are non-rivalrous in consumption. Goods that have the characteristics of *non-excludability* and *non-rivalry* are known as **public goods**.

Examples of public goods that are often cited include street lighting, a lighthouse and a nuclear deterrent. For example, once street lighting has been provided in a particular street, anyone who walks along that street at night benefits from the lighting — no one can be excluded from consuming it. So street lighting is non-exclusive. In addition, the fact that one person has walked along the street does not mean that there is less street lighting left for later walkers. So street lighting is also non-rivalrous.

The key feature of such a market is that, once the good has been provided, there is no incentive for anyone to pay for it — so the market will fail, as no firm will have an incentive to supply the good in the first place. This is often referred to as the **free-rider problem**, as individual consumers can free-ride and avoid having to pay for the good if it is provided.

 terms

public good: a good that is non-exclusive and non-rivalrous — consumers cannot be excluded from consuming the good, and consumption by one person does not affect the amount of the good available for others to consume

free-rider problem: when an individual cannot be excluded from consuming a good, and thus has no incentive to pay for its provision

Extension material

A key question is how well the market for a public good is likely to operate. In particular, will a free market reach a position where there is allocative efficiency, with price equal to marginal social cost?

Think about the supply and demand curves for a public good such as street lighting. To simplify matters, suppose there are just two potential demanders of the good, *a* and *b*. Consider Figure 7.1. If it is assumed that the supply is provided in a competitive market, *S* represents the supply curve, reflecting the marginal cost of providing street lighting. The curves d_a and d_b represent the demand curves of the two potential demanders. For a given quantity Q_1, *a* would be prepared to pay P_a and *b* would pay P_b.

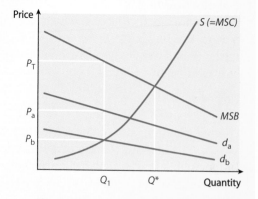

Figure 7.1
Demand and supply of a public good

If these prices are taken to be the value that each individual places on this amount of the good, then $P_a + P_b = P_T$ represents the social benefit derived from consuming Q_1 units of street lighting. Similarly, for any given quantity of street lighting, the marginal social benefit derived from consumption can be calculated as the vertical sum of the two demand curves. This is shown by the curve MSB. So the optimal provision of street lighting is given by Q^*, at which point the marginal social benefit is equated with the marginal cost of supplying the good.

However, if person a were to agree to pay P_a for the good, person b could then consume Q_1 of the good free of charge, but would not be prepared to pay in order for the supply to be expanded beyond this point — as person b's willingness to pay is below the marginal cost of provision beyond this point. So the social optimum at Q^* cannot be reached. Indeed, when there are many potential consumers, the likely outcome is that *none* of this good will be produced: why should any individual agree to pay if he or she can free-ride on others?

The free-rider problem helps to explain why these sorts of goods have typically been provided through state intervention. This begs the question of how the state can identify the optimal quantity of the good to be provided — in other words, how the government determines Q^*. The extent to which individuals value a particular good cannot be directly observed. However, by including statements about the provision of public goods in their election manifestos, politicians can collect views about public goods provision via the medium of the ballot box. This is an indirect method, but it provides some mandate for the government to take decisions.

Note that public goods are called 'public goods' not because they are publicly provided, but because of their characteristics.

The free-rider problem makes it difficult to charge for a public good, so the private sector will be reluctant to supply such goods. In fact, pure public goods are relatively rare, but there are many goods that have some but not all of the required characteristics. On the face of it, the lighthouse service seems to be a good example of a public good. Once the lighthouse has been constructed and is sending out its signal, all boats and ships that pass within the range of its light can benefit from the service: that is, it is non-excludable. Moreover, the fact that one ship has seen the lighthouse signal does not reduce the amount of light available to the next ship, so it is also non-rivalrous.

However, this does not mean that ships cannot be charged for their use of lighthouse services. In 2002 an article in the *Guardian* reported that ships were complaining about the high charges to which they were subjected for lighthouse services. Ships of a certain size must pay 'light dues' every time they enter or leave UK ports, and the fees collected are used to fund lighthouses, buoys and beacons around the coast. In principle, it could be argued that this renders lighthouses excludable, as ships can be prevented from sailing if they have not paid their dues, and so could not consume the lighthouse services. At the heart of the complaints from the shipping companies was the fact that leisure craft below a certain

threshold did not have to pay the charges, and they made more use of the light-houses than the larger vessels. This is one example of the way in which it becomes necessary to design a charging system to try to overcome the free-rider problem associated with the provision of public goods.

In fact, there are many goods that are either non-rivalrous or non-excludable, but not both. One example of this is a football match. If I go to watch a premiership football match, my 'consumption' of the match does not prevent the person sitting next to me from also consuming it, so it is non-rivalrous. However, if I go along without my season ticket (or do not have a ticket), I can clearly be excluded from consuming the match, so it is *not* non-exclusive.

A stretch of road may be considered non-exclusive, as road users are free to drive along it. However, it is not non-rivalrous, in the sense that as congestion builds up consumption is affected. This example is also imperfect as a public good because, by installing toll barriers, users can be excluded from consuming it.

Where goods have some features of a public good, the free market may fail to produce an ideal outcome for society. Exercise 7.1 provides some examples of goods: to what extent may each of these be considered to be non-rivalrous or non-excludable?

Exercise 7.1

For each of the following goods, think about whether they have elements of non-rivalry, non-excludability, both or neither:

a   a national park
b   a playground
c   a theatre performance
d   an apple
e   a television programme

f   a firework display
g   police protection
h   a lecture
i   a DVD recording of a film
j   the national defence

Tackling the public goods problem

For some public goods, the failure of the free market to ensure provision may be regarded as a serious problem — for example, in such cases as street lighting or law and order. Some government intervention may thus be needed to make sure that a sufficient quantity of the good or service is provided. Notice that this does not necessarily mean that the government has to provide the good itself. It may be that the government will raise funds through taxation in order to ensure that street lighting is provided, but could still make use of private firms to supply the good through some sort of subcontracting arrangement. In the UK, it may be that the government delegates the responsibility for provision of public goods to local authorities, which in turn may subcontract to private firms.

In some other cases, it may be that changes in technology may alter the economic characteristics of a good. For example, in the case of television programmes, originally provision was entirely through the BBC, funded by the licence fee.

Subsequently, ITV set up in competition, using advertising as a way of funding its supply. More recently, the advent of satellite and digital broadcasting has reduced the degree to which television programmes are non-excludable, allowing private firms to charge for transmissions.

Summary

➤ A private good is one that, once consumed by one person, cannot be consumed by anyone else — it has characteristics of excludability and rivalry.
➤ A public good is non-exclusive and non-rivalrous.
➤ Because of these characteristics, public goods tend to be underprovided by a free market.
➤ One reason for this is the free-rider problem, whereby an individual cannot be excluded from consuming a public good, and thus has no incentive to pay for it.
➤ Public goods, or goods with some of the characteristics of public goods, must be provided with the assistance of the government or its agents.

Merit goods

There are some goods that the government believes everyone should consume, whether or not they wish to, and whether or not they have the means to do so. The key argument is that individuals do not fully perceive the benefits that they will gain from consuming such goods. These are known as **merit goods**.

Clearly, there is a strong political element involved in identifying the goods that should be regarded as merit goods: indeed, there is a subjective or normative judgement involved, since declaring a good to be a merit good requires the decision-maker to make a paternalistic choice on behalf of the population.

Key term

merit good: a good that brings unanticipated benefits to its consumers, such that society believes that it should be consumed by individuals regardless of whether they have the means or the willingness to do so

One way of viewing merit goods is that they reflect a divergence between the value that individual members of society place on goods and the decision-maker's views about their value to society as a whole. There is clearly a danger here that the decision-makers will force their views on the rest of society, and again, the ballot box may be the ultimate way of preventing this.

Another aspect of the merit good phenomenon is that the government may be in a better position than individuals to take a long-term view of what is good for society. In particular, governments may need to take decisions on behalf of future generations as well as the present. Resources need to be used wisely in the present in order to protect the interests of tomorrow's citizens. Again, this may require decision-makers to make normative judgements about the appropriate weighting to be given to the present as opposed to the future.

At the heart of the notion of a merit good, therefore, is the decision-maker's perception that there is a divergence between the marginal benefit that individuals perceive to arise from consuming a good, and the social benefit that actually

accrues from its consumption. This is reminiscent of the arguments in Chapter 6 about consumption externalities, where a positive consumption externality arises when the marginal social benefit from consuming a good is greater than the marginal private benefit.

Figure 7.2 shows how this situation can be analysed. The example used here is education. In the UK everyone is required to attend school, at least up to age 16. Part of this requirement may be attributed to a merit good argument. It can be argued that education provides benefits to society in excess of those that are perceived by individuals. In other words, society believes that individuals will derive a benefit from education that they will not realise until after they have acquired that education. Thus, the government decrees that everyone must consume education up to the age of 16, whether they want to or not and whether they have the means to do so or not. This is a merit good argument. In Figure 7.2 marginal social benefit (*MSB*) is shown as being higher than marginal private benefit (*MPB*). Thus, society would like to provide Q^* education, where $MSB = MC$ (marginal social cost), but individuals would choose to consume only Q_1 education, where $MPB = MC$, because they do not expect the future benefits to be as high as the government does.

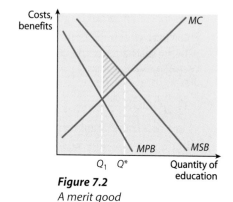

Figure 7.2
A merit good

In this case there may be other issues affecting the market for education. Chapter 6 argued that there would also be positive externality effects if educated workers were better able to cooperate with each other. There may be a further argument that individuals may fail to demand sufficient education because of information failure: in other words, they may not perceive the full benefits that will arise from education. The situation may be aggravated if parents have the responsibility of financing their children's education, because they are taking decisions *on behalf of* their children. In the case of tertiary education, there is no guarantee that parents will agree with their children about the benefits of a university education — it could go either way.

Another important issue that arises in the context of education concerns equity in access to higher education. Research has shown that graduates tend to enjoy higher lifetime earnings than non-graduates. However, if some groups have better access to credit markets than others, then those groups may be more able to take advantage of a university education. Specifically, it has been argued that people from low-income households may be discouraged from taking up university places because of failure in credit markets. In other words, the difficulty of raising funds in the present to pay for a university education may prevent people from gaining the longer-term benefits of having received a university education — hence the launching of student loan schemes, which should help to address this particular form of market failure.

In some societies it has been suggested that the merits of education are better perceived by some groups in society than others. Thus in some less developed countries, individuals in relatively well-off households demand high levels of education, as they realise the long-run benefits that they can receive in terms of higher earnings – and, perhaps, political influence. In contrast, low-income households in remote rural areas may not see the value of education. As a result, drop-out from secondary – and even primary – education tends to be high. This is clearly a merit good argument that may need to be addressed by government, perhaps by making primary education compulsory or free – or both.

Education is often seen as a merit good

Other examples of merit goods are museums, libraries and art galleries. These are goods that are provided or subsidised because someone somewhere thinks that communities should have more of them. Economists are wary of playing the merit good card too often, as it entails such a high normative element. It is also difficult sometimes to disentangle merit good arguments from externality effects.

Demerit goods

In contrast, there is a category of goods that government thinks should not be consumed even if individuals want to do so. These are known as **demerit goods** – or sometimes as 'merit bads'. Obvious examples are hard drugs and tobacco. Here the argument is that individual consumers overvalue the benefits from consuming such a good.

Key term

demerit good: a good that brings less benefit to consumers than they expect, such that society believes that it should not be consumed by individuals regardless of whether they wish to do so

Figure 7.3 shows the market for cocaine. Marginal private benefits (*MPB*) are shown as being much higher than marginal social benefits (*MSB*), so that in a free market too much cocaine is consumed. Society would like to be at Q^*, but ends up at Q_1. In this particular market, the government may see the marginal social benefit from consuming cocaine to be so low (e.g. at *MSB** in the figure) that consumption should be driven to zero.

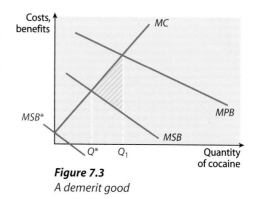

Figure 7.3
A demerit good

Again, this could be interpreted as partly an information problem, in the sense that individual consumers may not perceive the dangers of addiction and thus may overvalue cocaine. In addition, addiction would have the effect of making an individual's demand for the good highly inelastic in the long run. However, it is paternalistic of the government to intervene directly for this reason, although it might wish to correct other externalities — for instance, those imposed on others when addicts steal to fund their habit.

An alternative approach is to try to remove the information failure; clearly, the government has adopted this approach in seeking to educate people about the dangers of tobacco smoking.

Taxing tobacco

This market for tobacco is characterised in Figure 7.4. Demand (*MPB*) represents the marginal private benefit that consumers gain from smoking tobacco. However, the government believes that consumers underestimate the damaging effects of smoking, so that the true benefits are given by *MSB* (marginal social benefit). Given the marginal cost (supply) curve, in an unregulated market consumers will choose to smoke up to Q_1 tobacco. The optimum for society, however, is at Q^*.

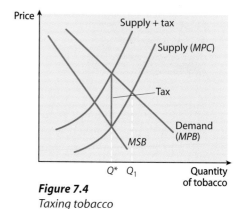

Figure 7.4
Taxing tobacco

One way of tackling this problem is through taxation. If the government imposes a tax shown by the red line in Figure 7.4, this effectively shifts the supply curve to the market, as shown in the figure. This raises the price in the market, so consumers are persuaded to reduce their consumption to the optimal level at Q^*. Notice that because the demand curve (*MPB*) is quite steep (relatively inelastic), a substantial tax is needed in order to reach Q^*. Empirical evidence suggests that the demand for tobacco is relatively inelastic — and therefore tobacco taxes have risen to comprise a large portion of the price of a packet of cigarettes.

Conversely, if the government wishes to encourage the consumption of a merit good, it may do so through subsidies. Thus, the museum service is subsidised, and the ballet and opera have enjoyed subsidies in the past. Figure 7.5 shows how such a subsidy might be used to affect the quantity of museum services provided. Demand (*MPB*) again shows the demand for museum services from the public, which is below the marginal social benefit (*MSB*) that the authorities perceive to be the true value of museum services. Thus the free market equilibrium position is at Q_1, although the government believes that Q^* is the socially optimum position. By providing a subsidy, the supply curve is shifted to the right, and consumers will choose to demand the optimum quantity at the subsidised price P_2.

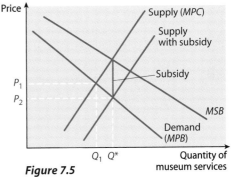

Figure 7.5
Subsidising museums

Information failures

If markets are to be effective in guiding resource allocation, it is important that economic decision-makers receive full and accurate information about market conditions. Consumers need information about the prices at which they can buy and the quality of the products for sale. Producers need to be able to observe how consumers react to prices. Information is thus of crucial significance if markets are to work. However, there are some markets in which not all traders have access to good information, or in which some traders have more or better access to it than others. This is known as a situation of **asymmetric information**, and can be a source of market failure.

Key term

asymmetric information:
a situation in which some participants in a market have better information about market conditions than others

Healthcare

One example of asymmetric information is in healthcare. Suppose you go to your dentist for a check-up. He tells you that you have a filling that needs to be replaced, although you have had no pain or problems with it. In this situation the seller in a market has much better information about the product than the buyer. You as the buyer have no idea whether or not the recommended treatment is needed, and without going to another dentist for a second opinion you have no way of finding out. You might think this is an unsatisfactory situation, as it seems to give a lot of power to the seller relative to the consumer. The situation is even worse where the dentist does not even publish the prices for treatment until after it has been carried out! The Office of Fair Trading criticised private dentists for exactly this sort of practice when they reported on this market in March 2003. Indeed, dentists are now required by law to publish prices for treatment.

The same argument applies in the case of other areas of healthcare, where doctors have better information than their patients about the sort of treatment that is needed.

Exercise 7.2

Ethel, an old-age pensioner, is sitting quietly at home when the doorbell rings. At the door is a stranger called Frank, who tells her that he has noticed that her roof is in desperate need of repair, and if she does not get something done about it very soon, there will be problems in the next rainstorm. Fortunately, he can help — for a price. Discuss whether there is a market failure in this situation, and what Ethel (or others) could do about it.

Education

The market for education is similar. Teachers or government inspectors may know more about the subjects and topics that students need to study than the students do themselves. This is partly because teachers are able to take a longer view and can see education provision in a broader perspective. Students taking economics at university may have to take a course in mathematics and statistics in their first year, and some will always complain that they have come to study economics, not maths. It is only later that they come to realise that competence in maths is crucial these days for the economics that they will study later in their course.

How could this problem be tackled? The answer would seem to be obvious — if the problem arises from an information failure, then the answer should be to improve the information flow, in this case to students. This might be achieved by providing a convincing explanation of why the curriculum has been designed in a particular way. It may also be necessary to provide incentives for students to study particular unpopular subjects, perhaps by making success a requirement for progression to the next stage of the course. By understanding the economic cause of a problem, it is possible to devise a strategy that should go some way towards removing the market failure.

Second-hand cars

One of the most famous examples of asymmetric information relates to the second-hand (or 'pre-owned', by the latest terminology) car market. This is because the first paper that drew attention to the problem of asymmetric information, by Nobel laureate George Akerlof, focused on this market.

Publishing Pictures

Akerlof argued that there are two types of car. Some cars are good runners and are totally reliable, whereas some are continually breaking down and needing parts

The second-hand car market is an example of a market with asymmetric information

and servicing; the latter are known as 'lemons' in the USA (allegedly from fruit machines, where lemons offer the lowest prize). The problem in the second-hand car market arises because the owners of cars (potential sellers) have better information about their cars than the potential buyers. In other words, when a car owner decides to sell a car, he or she knows whether it is a lemon or a good-quality car – but a buyer cannot tell.

In this sort of market, car dealers can adopt one of two possible strategies. One is to offer a high price and buy up all the cars in the market, knowing that the lemons will be sold on at a loss. The problem is that, if the lemons make up a large proportion of the cars in the market, this could generate overall losses for the dealers. The alternative is to offer a low price, and just buy up all the lemons to sell for scrap. In this situation, the market for good-quality used cars is effectively destroyed because owners of good-quality cars will not accept the low price – an extreme form of market failure!

Again, the solution may be to tackle the problem at its root, by finding a way to provide information. In the case of second-hand cars, AA inspection schemes or the offering of warranties may be a way of improving the flow of information about the quality of cars for sale.

Summary

➤ A merit good is one that society believes should be consumed by individuals whether or not they have the means or the willingness to do so.

➤ There is a strong normative element in the identification of merit goods.

➤ Demerit goods (or 'merit bads') are goods that society believes should not be consumed by individuals even if they wish to do so.

➤ In the case of merit and demerit goods, 'society' (as represented by government) believes that it has better information than consumers about these goods, and about what is good (or bad) for consumers.

➤ Information deficiency can lead to market failure in other situations: for example, where some participants in a market have better information about some aspect(s) of the market than others.

➤ Examples of this include healthcare, education and second-hand cars.

Exercise 7.3

The *Guardian* reported on 27 August 2004 that the pharmaceutical company GlaxoSmithKline had been forced to publish details of a clinical trial of one of its leading anti-depressant drugs following a lawsuit that had accused the company of concealing evidence that the drug could be harmful to children. Discuss the extent to which this situation may have led to a market failure because of information problems.

Chapter 8
Government intervention and government failure

Previous chapters have identified various ways in which markets can fail to bring about an efficient allocation of resources in a society. This chapter investigates questions of equity, and discusses whether inequality in the distribution of income requires intervention by government. The chapter also explores how some well-intentioned interventions by government can sometimes produce unintended results.

Learning outcomes

After studying this chapter, you should:

➤ be aware of global inequality in the distribution of income
➤ appreciate that there is also inequality in the distribution of income between different groups within societies
➤ be able to identify areas in which government actions may have unintended distortionary effects
➤ be aware of some sources of government failure
➤ be familiar with the effects of minimum wage legislation and rent controls
➤ be able to analyse the effects of sales taxes and subsidies

Equity

In discussing ways in which markets may fail to lead to an optimal allocation of resources, the focus has been primarily on questions of efficiency. In particular, it has been noted that allocative efficiency will not be attained in circumstances in which there is a divergence between private and social costs or benefits. However, it was noted in Chapter 5 that there is no unique overall equilibrium for a society, and that a different distribution of income between individuals will lead to a different Pareto optimum position.

This highlights the potential importance of issues of *equity*. One aspect of this is whether individuals face equal opportunities, and whether identical people receive identical treatment in economic terms. However, there is also the unavoidable fact that people are not identical, and that different innate abilities and talents command

different rewards. This then raises the question of whether society needs to provide some protection for any of its members who find themselves disadvantaged by the way in which resources are allocated. In other words, do communities need a system whereby resources are transferred from some members of society to others?

This is another area in which normative judgements arise. The government may take the view that everybody in society has the right to some minimum standard of living. This may reflect the government's view of the collective desires of the population. In order to alleviate poverty, therefore, some income may need to be transferred from the relatively rich in society to the relatively poor. The normative judgement arises because of the need to define what constitutes a minimum standard of living, and to determine the extent to which such transfers should be undertaken.

This argument is effectively saying that a free market allocation of resources may produce a distribution of income among individuals that is not acceptable in terms of society's objectives.

The question of income distribution can be explored at a number of levels. You could look at the global distribution — the way in which incomes are distributed between countries. You could also examine income distribution *within* countries — that is, between different groups in society. For example, in the UK the richest 10% of households receive more than ten times the income of the poorest 10% of households.

Some variation in incomes between households is, of course, inevitable. For example, there may be differences in pay between different occupations, or between people producing goods or services that are more highly valued by consumers. There may also be differences in income that arise because of the pattern of distribution of wealth within a society. The extent to which a society wishes government to intervene to influence the pattern of wealth and income distribution is often a prominent issue during electioneering.

Global inequality

It is well known that there is substantial inequality in the distribution of incomes worldwide. Figure 8.1 gives some indication of how unequal it is.

The World Bank classifies countries according to income. Income in this case is defined as gross national income (GNI), which is a similar measure to GDP, which was introduced earlier. Low-income countries (LICs) are those in which average annual income is less than $905 in 2006, middle-income countries (MICs) have an average income between $906 and $11,115; high-income countries (HICs) have average incomes above $11,115. Figure 8.1 shows the distribution of income and people between these broad groups of countries. In 2006 about 37% of the world's population lived in low-income countries, but they received only 3% of the world's GNI. In contrast, the 15.7% of people living in the high-income countries received almost 80% of the world's GNI.

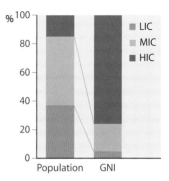

Figure 8.1 *Distribution of world population and GNI, 2006*
Source: *World Development Report 2008.*

There is also substantial inequality *within* many societies. Some inequality is to be expected, as people differ in their innate ability, talents and training. However, it is clear that the degree of inequality varies between countries. In order to examine this more carefully, it is necessary to have a way of measuring inequality.

Measuring income inequality

Table 8.1 presents data for some selected countries. Such data are not collected every year, as it is quite expensive to gather the statistics needed to describe the distribution of income; hence the variety of survey years for the data. As the pattern of income distribution tends not to change dramatically from one year to the next, however, there is still some justification for comparing across countries.

Table 8.1 *Income distribution in selected countries*

Note: countries are listed in ascending order of average incomes.

Sources: *World Development Report, Human Development Report.*

	GNI per capita		Percentage share of income or consumption			
	US$ 2006	Survey year	Poorest 10%	Poorest 20%	Richest 20%	Richest 10%
Ethiopia	180	1999–00	3.9	9.1	39.4	25.5
Sierra Leone	240	1989	0.5	1.1	63.4	43.6
Zimbabwe	340	1995	1.8	4.6	55.7	40.3
Bangladesh	480	2000	3.7	8.6	42.7	27.9
Pakistan	770	2002	4.0	9.3	40.3	26.3
India	820	2004–05	3.6	8.1	45.3	31.1
Bolivia	1,100	2002	0.3	1.5	63.0	47.2
Sri Lanka	1,300	2002	3.0	7.0	48.0	32.7
Indonesia	1,420	2002	3.6	8.4	43.3	28.5
China	2,010	2004	1.6	4.3	51.9	34.9
Belarus	3,380	2002	3.4	8.5	38.3	23.5
Brazil	4,730	2004	0.9	2.8	61.1	44.8
South Africa	5,390	2000	1.4	3.5	62.2	44.7
Malaysia	5,490	1997	1.7	4.4	54.3	38.4
Hungary	10,950	2002	4.0	9.5	36.5	22.2
South Korea	17,690	1998	2.9	7.9	37.5	22.5
Italy	32,020	2000	2.3	6.5	42.0	26.8
France	33,550	1995	2.8	7.2	40.2	25.1
Japan	38,410	1993	4.8	10.6	35.7	21.7
UK	40,180	1999	2.1	6.1	44.0	28.5
USA	44,970	2000	1.9	5.4	45.8	29.9

These data come from surveys conducted on the income levels of individual households. Households are then ranked in ascending order of income levels, and the shares of total income going to groups of households are calculated.

For example, for Ethiopia, the first country listed in the table, it can be seen that the poorest 10% of households receive 3.9% of total household income, and the poorest 20% receive just 9.1%. At the top end of the distribution, the richest 10% receive 25.5% of the total income. This contrasts quite markedly with the second country listed (Sierra Leone), where the data suggest greater inequality in distribution, with the poorest 10% receiving only 0.5% of total household income and the richest 10% getting as much as 43.6%.

Shanty town in a less developed country

Income distribution in the UK

Table 8.1 shows that the UK is neither the most equal nor the most unequal of societies as far as post-tax income is concerned. You can see in the table that the poorest 10% of households receive about 2% of total household income, which is not very different from Italy or the USA; the richest 10% receive 28.5% of income, which again is similar to the levels in Italy and the USA.

Inequality in the UK increased between the mid-1970s and the mid-1990s, especially during the period between 1979 and 1989 when Margaret Thatcher was prime minister. However, things have stabilised since then. On some measures, it would appear that income inequality has changed very little in the UK since 1989. However, this does not mean that government policy has had no impact on inequality. For example, there is some evidence that measures introduced since 1997 have improved the income distribution, in the sense that inequality would have continued to increase without these measures. Some research carried out by the Institute for Fiscal Studies has shown that, in the absence of policies introduced by the government, poverty would have been higher in 2005 than it was in the mid-1990s.

An important issue here is whether the government needs to intervene in order to influence the distribution of income within a society such as the UK — and to what extent such redistribution is desirable for society as a whole. There is a narrow path to be trodden between protecting vulnerable members of society, and giving incentives for people to provide work effort. If richer households are taxed too heavily, it may affect their incentives to work. On the other hand, taxes need to be set at a sufficient level to be able to protect the poor. These issues will be revisited in Part 2.

Regional disparities

One particular aspect of inequality is between regions of the UK. This partly reflects the way in which regions have tended to specialise in different types of economic activity. Then as the pattern of production has changed over time, some areas have gone into decline while others have boomed. This leads to inequality in incomes

because of variations in the unemployment rate between regions. One explanation for the persistence of such patterns through time is related to the immobility of factors of production. People are reluctant to move house in search of jobs, and firms may also be reluctant to move to find workers, because of the costs involved with relocation. In other words, disparities may arise because of *geographical immobility*.

In addition, there may be unemployment that arises because people who are unemployed do not have the sorts of skills for which employers are looking. In other words, there may also be disparities in income that arise because of *occupational immobility*. Such immobility may cause disparities within regions as well as between regions.

There may be a number of market-failure explanations for regional inequality. For example, it may be that one reason why people do not move in search of jobs is a lack of information about job opportunities — in other words, an information failure.

Summary

➤ Allocative efficiency can be achieved in a range of alternative situations, some of which may be more 'equitable' than others.

➤ There may be situations in which the government finds it appropriate to intervene to influence the income distribution within a society.

➤ There is substantial global disparity in the distribution of resources, and significant inequality within countries.

➤ There is also disparity in income levels between regions in the UK.

Exercise 8.1

Examine the data provided in Table 8.1, and identify the countries with the most and least unequal distribution of income. Discuss whether there is an association between the degree of inequality and the level of average income (as measured by GNI per capita — notice that the countries are ranked in ascending order of GNI per capita).

Government failure

Most governments see it as their responsibility to try to correct some of the failures of markets to allocate resources efficiently. This has led to a wide variety of policies being devised to address issues of market failure. Some of these have been discussed already. However, some policies have unintended effects that may not culminate in successful elimination of market failure. Indeed, in some cases government intervention may introduce new market distortions, leading to a phenomenon known as **government failure**. The remainder of this chapter examines some examples of such government failure.

 Key *term*

government failure: a misallocation of resources arising from government intervention

The minimum wage

In 1999 the UK National **Minimum Wage** came into force, designed to protect workers on low pay. To illustrate how this works, Figure 8.2 represents the labour market for office cleaners. Employers demand labour according to the wage rate — the lower the wage, the higher the demand for the labour of office cleaners. On the supply side, more workers will offer themselves for work when the wage rate is relatively high. If the market is unregulated, it will reach equilibrium with a wage rate W^* and quantity of labour L^*.

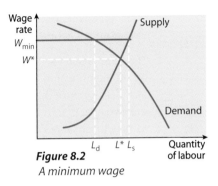

Figure 8.2
A minimum wage

Suppose now that the government comes to the view that W^* is not sufficiently high to provide a reasonable wage for cleaners. One response is to impose a minimum wage, below which employers are not permitted to offer employment — say, W_{min} on the figure. This will have two effects on the market situation. First, employers will demand less labour at this higher wage, so employment will fall to L_d. Second, more workers will be prepared to offer themselves for employment at the higher wage, so labour supply will rise to L_s. However, the net effect of this is that there is an excess supply of labour at this wage and hence unemployment, with more workers offering themselves for work than there are jobs available in the market.

What is happening here is that, with the minimum wage in effect, *some* workers (those who manage to remain in employment) are better off, and now receive a better wage. However, those who are now unemployed are worse off. It is not then clear whether the effect of the minimum wage is to make society as a whole better off — some people will be better off, but others will be worse off.

> **term**
>
> **minimum wage:** a system designed to protect the low paid by setting a minimum wage rate that employers are permitted to offer workers

Notice that this analysis rests on some assumptions that have not been made explicit. In particular, it rests on the assumption that the labour market is competitive. Where there are labour markets in which the employers have some market power, and are able to offer lower wages to workers than would be obtained in a free market equilibrium situation, it is possible that the imposition of a minimum wage will increase employment.

Rent controls

Another market in which governments have been tempted to intervene is the housing market. Figure 8.3 represents the market for rented accommodation. The free market equilibrium would be where demand and supply intersect, with the equilibrium rent being R^* and the quantity of accommodation traded being Q^*.

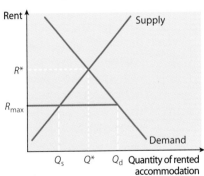

Figure 8.3
Rent controls

If the government regards the level of rent as excessive, to the point where households on low incomes may be unable to afford rented accommodation, then, given that housing is one of life's necessities, it may regard this as unacceptable.

The temptation for the government is to move this market away from its equilibrium by imposing a maximum level of rent that landlords are allowed to charge their tenants. Suppose that this level of rent is denoted by R_{max} in Figure 8.3. Again, there are two effects that follow. First, landlords will no longer find it profitable to supply as much rental accommodation, and so will reduce supply to Q_s. Second, at this lower rent there will be more people looking for accommodation, so that demand for rented accommodation will move to Q_d. The upshot of the rent controls, therefore, is that there is less accommodation available, and more homeless people.

It can be seen that the well-meaning rent control policy, intended to protect low-income households from being exploited by landlords, merely has the effect of reducing the amount of accommodation available. This is not what was supposed to happen.

Sales tax

Governments need to raise funds to finance the expenditure that they undertake. One way of doing this is through expenditure taxes such as value added tax (VAT) or excise duties on such items as alcohol or tobacco. You might think that raising money in this way to provide goods and services that would otherwise not be provided would be a benefit to society. But there is a downside to this action, even if all the funds raised by a sales tax are spent wisely.

The effects of a sales tax can be seen in a demand and supply diagram. An **indirect tax** is paid by the seller, so it affects the supply curve for a product. Figure 8.4 illustrates the case of a *fixed rate* or *specific* tax — a tax that is set at a constant amount per pack of cigarettes. Without the tax, the market equilibrium is at the intersection of demand and supply with a price of P_0 and a quantity traded of Q_0. The effect of the tax is to reduce the quantity that firms are prepared to supply at any given price — or, to put it another way, for any given quantity of cigarettes, firms need to receive the amount of the tax over and above the price at which they would have been prepared to supply that quantity. The effect is thus to move the supply curve upwards by the amount of the tax, as shown in the figure. We get a new equilibrium with a higher price at P_1 and a lower quantity traded at Q_1.

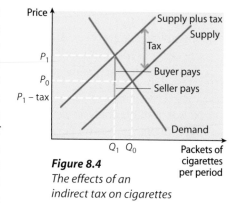

Figure 8.4
The effects of an indirect tax on cigarettes

Key **term**

indirect tax: a tax levied on expenditure on goods or services (as opposed to a direct tax, which is a tax charged directly to an individual based on a component of income)

An important question is: who bears the burden of the tax? If you look at the diagram, you will see that the price difference between the with-tax and without-tax situations (i.e. $P_1 - P_0$) is *less* than the amount of the tax, which is the vertical distance between the with-tax and without-tax supply curves. Although the seller may be responsible for the mechanics of paying the tax, part of the tax is effectively passed on to the buyer in the form of the higher price. In Figure 8.4, the **incidence of the tax** falls partly upon the seller, but most of the tax is borne by the buyer.

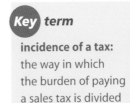

Key term

incidence of a tax: the way in which the burden of paying a sales tax is divided between buyers and sellers

The price elasticity of demand determines the incidence of the tax. If demand were perfectly inelastic, then the sellers would be able to pass the whole burden of the tax on to the buyers through an increase in price equal to the value of the tax, knowing that this would not affect demand. However, if demand were perfectly elastic, then the sellers would not be able to raise the price at all, so they would have to bear the entire burden of the tax.

Exercise 8.2

Sketch demand and supply diagrams to confirm that the statements in the previous paragraph are correct — that is, that if demand is perfectly inelastic, then the tax falls entirely on the buyers, whereas if demand is perfectly elastic, it is the sellers who have to bear the burden of the tax.

If the tax is not a constant amount, but a percentage of the price (known as an *ad valorem* tax), the effect is still on the supply curve, but the tax steepens the supply curve, as shown in Figure 8.5. Here, the free market equilibrium would be where demand equals supply, with price at P_0 and the quantity traded at Q_0. With an *ad valorem* tax in place, the price rises to P_1, with quantity falling to Q_1.

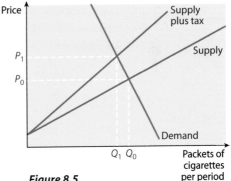

Figure 8.5
The effects of an ad valorem *tax on cigarettes*

In some situations, the government may wish to encourage production of a particular good or service, perhaps because it views a good as having strategic significance to the country. One way it can do this is by giving **subsidies**.

Subsidies were discussed in the previous chapter in the context of merit goods. Here, subsidies are used to encourage producers to increase their output of particular goods. Subsidies have been especially common in agriculture, which is often seen as being of strategic significance. In recent

Key term

subsidy: a grant given by the government to producers to encourage production of a good or service

years, the USA has come under pressure to reduce the subsidies that it grants to cotton producers. Analytically, we can regard a subsidy as a sort of negative indirect tax that shifts the supply curve down – as shown in Figure 8.6. Without the subsidy, market equilibrium is at a price P_0 and the quantity traded is Q_0. With the subsidy in place, the equilibrium price falls to P_1 and quantity traded increases to Q_1.

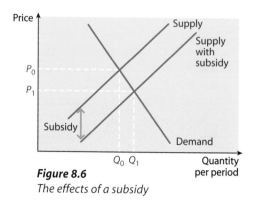

Figure 8.6
The effects of a subsidy

Again, notice that because the price falls by less than the amount of the subsidy, the benefits of the subsidy are shared between the buyers and sellers – depending on the elasticity of demand. If the aim of the subsidy is to increase production, it is only partially successful; the degree of success also depends upon the elasticity of demand.

Extension material

An important question is how a sales tax will affect total welfare in society. Consider Figure 8.7, which shows the market for DVDs. Suppose that the government imposes a specific tax on DVDs. This would have the effect of taking market equilibrium from the free market position at P^* with quantity traded at Q^* to a new position, with price now at P_t and quantity traded at Q_t. Remember that the price rises by less than the amount of the tax, implying that the incidence of the tax falls partly on buyers and partly on sellers. In Figure 8.7 consumers pay more of the tax (the area P^*P_tBE) than the producers (who pay FP^*EG). The effect on society's overall welfare will now be examined.

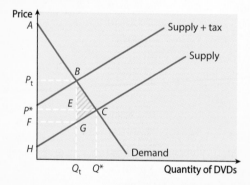

Figure 8.7
A sales tax and economic welfare

Remember that the total welfare that society receives from consuming a product is the sum of consumer and producer surplus. The situation before and after the sales tax is as follows. Before the tax, consumer surplus is given by the area AP^*C and producer surplus is given by the triangle P^*CH. How about afterwards? Consumer surplus is now the smaller triangle AP_tB, and producer surplus is FGH. The area P_tBGF is the revenue raised by the government from the tax, which should be included in total welfare on the assumption that the government

uses this wisely. The total amount of welfare is now *ABGH*. If you compare these total welfare areas before and after the tax, you will realise that they differ by the area *BCG*. This triangle represents a deadweight loss that arises from the imposition of the tax. It is sometimes referred to as the **excess burden** of the tax.

 term

excess burden of a sales tax: the deadweight loss to society following the imposition of a sales tax

So, even where the government intervenes to raise funding for its expenditure — and spends wisely — a distortion is introduced to resource allocation, and society must bear a loss of welfare.

Prohibition

Another example of how government intervention may have unintended effects is when action is taken to prohibit the consumption of a demerit good. Consider the case of a hard drug, such as cocaine. It can be argued that there are substantial social disbenefits arising from the consumption of hard drugs, and that addicts and potential addicts are in no position to make informed decisions about their consumption of them. One response to such a situation is to consider making the drug illegal – that is, to impose **prohibition**.

Key term

prohibition: an attempt to prevent the consumption of a demerit good by declaring it illegal

Figure 8.8 shows how the market for cocaine might look. You may wonder why the demand curve takes on this shape. The argument is that there are two types of cocaine user. There are the recreational users, who will take cocaine if it is available at a reasonable price, but who are not addicts. In addition, there is a hard core of habitual users who are addicts, whose demand for cocaine is highly inelastic. Thus, at low prices demand is relatively elastic because of the presence of the recreational users, who are relatively price-sensitive. At higher prices the recreational users drop away, and demand from the addicts is highly price-inelastic. Suppose that the supply in free market equilibrium is given by S_0; the equilibrium will be with price P_0 and quantity traded Q_0. If the drug is made illegal, this will affect supply. Some dealers will leave the market to trade in something else, and the police will succeed in confiscating a certain proportion of the drugs in the market. However, they are unlikely to be totally successful, so supply could move to, say, S_1.

Figure 8.8 Prohibition

In the new market situation, price rises substantially to P_1, and quantity traded falls to Q_1. However, what has happened is that the recreational users have dropped out of the market, leaving a hard core of addicts who will pay any price for the drug, and who may resort to muggings and robberies in order to finance

their habit. This behaviour clearly imposes a new sort of externality on society. And the more successful the police are in confiscating supplies, the higher the price will be driven. There may thus be disadvantages in using prohibition as a way of discouraging consumption of a demerit good.

Costs of intervention

Some roles are critical for a government to perform if a mixed economy is to function effectively. A vital role is the provision by the government of an environment in which markets can operate effectively. There must be stability in the political system if firms and consumers are to take decisions with confidence about the future. And there must be a secure system of property rights, without which markets could not be expected to work.

In addition, there are sources of market failure that require intervention. This does not necessarily mean that governments need to substitute markets with direct action. However, it does mean that they need to be more active in markets that cannot operate effectively, while at the same time performing an enabling role to encourage markets to work well whenever this is feasible.

Such intervention entails costs. There are costs of administering, and costs of monitoring the policy to ensure that it is working as intended. This includes the need to look out for the unintended distortionary effects that some policies can have on resource allocation in a society. It is therefore important to check that the marginal costs of implementing and monitoring policies do not exceed their marginal benefits.

Summary

➤ Government failure can occur when well-meaning intervention by governments has unintended effects.

➤ In some circumstances a minimum wage intended to protect the low paid may aggravate their situation by increasing unemployment.

➤ Rent controls may have the effect of reducing the amount of accommodation available.

➤ A sales tax imposes an excess burden on society.

➤ Prohibition may also have unintended effects.

Review section

The first module of the AS programme introduces you to the way in which markets can enable resources to be allocated in an economy. This brief review is intended to remind you of the key concepts that have been discussed in each chapter and to provide an overview of the material. This may be especially helpful when you come to the end of the module and want to look back over what has been covered, or when you come to revise in preparation for the examination.

Chapter 1 Introducing economics

Chapter 1 introduced some key themes of economics and set the scene ready for you to begin thinking like an economist. At the heart of economic analysis is the realisation that the world is characterised by **scarcity**, so the fundamental economic problem is how a society allocates its resources to the production of goods and services. A crucial concept here is that of **opportunity cost** – the idea that the cost of any choice is the next best alternative that is forgone. This notion underlies economic analysis.

In the presence of scarcity, society needs to solve the coordination problem; in other words, how is it possible to reconcile the decisions made by different economic agents in a society – firms, consumers, the government and so on? In a **market economy**, this is left to the operation of the **market**; at the other extreme, the state takes on this role in a **centrally planned economy**. In most societies, resources are allocated by a combination of these two systems in a **mixed economy**.

Economists see output as being produced by the **factors of production**, the most important being labour and capital, although other inputs are also essential. The **production possibility curve** is used to show the combinations of two goods (or two kinds of goods) that can be produced by the society's factors of production. In this context, the opportunity cost of producing more of one good is the quantity of the other good that must be sacrificed. For example, if a society wishes to produce more investment goods in order to increase output in the future, the opportunity cost is that fewer consumption goods can be produced. An increase in the productive

capacity of the economy is known as **economic growth**. The total amount of output produced in an economy in a given period can be measured by **gross domestic product (GDP)**.

Specialisation and the **division of labour** can make workers more productive and opens up the possibility of trade, gaining advantage from exploiting differences in opportunity cost.

Chapter 1 also discussed the way in which economic analysis is based on the use of **models** and assumptions in order to be able to explain and understand economic decisions. In addition, the distinction between **microeconomics** (the analysis of individual economic decisions) and **macroeconomics** (the analysis of interactions at the level of the economy as a whole) was noted. Finally, the difference between **positive** and **normative** analysis was noted.

Chapter 2 The nature of demand

Perhaps the most famous model in economics is the demand and supply model. Chapter 2 begins the discussion by introducing the concept of **demand**.

A fundamental insight is that the quantity of a good or service that will be demanded depends on the price of the good and also upon the price of other goods, consumer incomes and preferences, and the number of potential buyers in the market. The **demand curve** focuses on the relationship between the quantity demanded of a good and its price, tracing out the quantity demanded at any given price. When you draw a demand curve, you assume that the other factors that determine demand are held constant – denoted by the Latin phrase **ceteris paribus**. The other factors that influence demand can then be seen to affect the *position* of the demand curve. In other words, a change in any of these things will cause a *shift* in the position of the demand curve, whereas a change in the price of the good will induce a *movement along* the demand curve.

The **law of demand** states that there is an inverse relationship between the quantity demanded of a good and its price, ceteris paribus. In other words, the demand curve slopes downwards.

A good for which the quantity demanded at any price increases when consumer incomes increase is known as a **normal good**. However, there are some goods where the demand is expected to fall at any price if incomes increase – such a good is known as an **inferior good**.

There are some goods which are **substitutes** for each other, whereas others are **complements**.

Chapter 3 The nature of supply

The other key component of the demand and supply model, of course, entails **supply**. Decisions about supply are taken by **firms**, where a firm is seen simply as an organisation that brings together the factors of production in order to produce output of goods and services. In this analysis, it is assumed that firms set out with the objective of maximising profits.

As part of the analysis of the supply side of the demand and supply model, the notion of a **competitive market** was introduced. A key feature of such a market is that firms are not able to influence the price of their product, selling at the going market price. In this situation, profit-maximising firms will supply more output at a higher price. The **supply curve** traces out the quantity that firms are prepared to supply at any given price.

As with the demand curve, there are several influences that will affect the *position* of the supply curve — in other words, influences other than the price of the good. These include firms' costs, technology, taxes and subsidies, the prices of related goods and firms' expectations about future prices. A change in any of these things will cause a *shift* in the position of the supply curve, whereas a change in the price of the good will induce a *movement along* the supply curve.

Chapter 4 Using the demand and supply model

Chapter 4 explored the way in which the demand and supply model can be used to analyse market situations. Bringing the demand and supply curves together allows the **market equilibrium** to be identified. This occurs at the unique price at which the quantity that consumers wish to buy is matched by the quantity that firms wish to supply.

There are many different applications of this model. For example, there are many different types of markets, so the analysis does not only apply in the case of markets for goods and services. It is also possible to use the model to analyse markets for labour, foreign exchange or money. In the case of the labour market, demand and supply analysis may help to explain the occurrence of **unemployment**.

By analysing the effect on market equilibrium of a change in one of the factors that influence the position of either the demand or the supply curve, it is possible to analyse how the market will react to changing market conditions. This form of analysis is common in economics — it is known as **comparative static analysis**.

Of particular interest is the extent to which demand or supply will be sensitive to changes in one of its determinants. This is measured by the **elasticity**, of which there are many forms.

The **price elasticity of demand (*PED*)** measures the sensitivity of the quantity demanded of a good to a change in its price. This has important implications for the way that a firm's revenue will change in response to a change in the price.

The **income elasticity of demand (*YED*)** measures the responsiveness of quantity demanded to a change in consumer incomes. For normal goods, the income elasticity is positive, whereas for inferior goods, it is negative. A good for which the income elasticity of demand is positive and greater than one is known as a **luxury good**.

The **cross-price elasticity of demand (*XED*)** measures the sensitivity of the quantity demanded of a good to a change in the price of some other good. The sign of the XED helps to determine whether two goods are substitutes or complements.

The **price elasticity of supply (*PES*)** measures the responsiveness of the quantity supplied of a good to a change in its price. This is likely to be stronger in the long run than in the short run, as firms are more able to adjust their output in the longer term.

Chapter 5 Prices, resource allocation and market failure

This chapter contains some important material, looking at the way in which a **free market economy** can lead to an allocation of resources that is favourable for society as a whole. This works because prices act as signals to producers about the value that consumers place on the various goods and services available in the economy. Indeed, it may be argued that the demand curve reflects consumers' willingness to pay for a product and may be interpreted as the **marginal social benefit** that society receives from consuming a product. **Consumer surplus** is the value that consumers gain from consuming a good or service over and above the price paid for it.

In a competitive market, the supply curve reflects the **marginal cost** faced by firms — that is, the cost of producing an additional unit of a good. **Producer surplus** is the difference between the price received by firms for a good or service and the price at which they would have been prepared to supply that good or service.

Chapter 5 introduced some different types of efficiency that are important in economic analysis. These include **productive efficiency**, which is attained when a firm operates at minimum **average total cost**, choosing an appropriate combination of inputs (cost efficiency) and producing the maximum output possible from those inputs (technical efficiency). Firms may face a situation in which average total cost falls as output rises; this is known as **economies of scale**.

Equally important is **allocative efficiency**, which is achieved when society is producing an appropriate bundle of goods relative to consumer preferences. Associated with this is the notion of a **Pareto optimum**. An allocation of resources is said to be a Pareto optimum if no reallocation of resources can make an individual better off without making some other individual worse off. Allocative efficiency is attained when price is set equal to marginal cost.

Under the market system known as **capitalism**, there is private ownership of productive resources and individuals are free to pursue their own interests. Adam Smith argued that in such an economy, an **invisible hand** would guide the allocation of resources. This is one description of the way in which price signals operate. A key aspect of this is that there is freedom of entry into and exit from markets.

There are many reasons that may prevent a free market system from reaching allocative efficiency. Such situations are known as **market failure**, for example where for some reason there is a divergence between marginal social benefit and marginal social cost. The chapter introduces a number of reasons for market failure — imperfect competition, the existence of **externalities**, information failure and public goods. It was also noted that there may be issues surrounding the distribution of resources and income within a society.

Chapter 6 Externalities

A significant form of market failure occurs where there is some form of **externality** — a situation in which there is some cost or benefit that is not reflected in market prices. This has the effect of distorting the signals that prices give to decision makers.

Consumption externalities occur when an externality affects the consumption side of a market, whereas **production externalities** affect the production side. Both types of externality may have positive or negative effects. Externalities are common in relation to the environment, for example where producers do not face the full cost of their production activities because of pollution emitted by the firm, that imposes costs on others that they do not have to face. In other words, firms face the direct costs of their production activities — the **private costs** — but may also impose **external costs** on third parties. Examples of externalities are also provided in relation to transport, health, education and tourism.

One way of dealing with an externality is by **internalising the externality** by bringing the external costs or benefits into the price mechanism, for example by forcing firms to face the full costs of their production activities.

It is sometimes the case that you cannot please everyone all the time. Everyone may agree that certain activities need to be undertaken in an economy, but everyone may also feel that they do not want these activities located near their own homes — this is the **NIMBY (not in my backyard)** syndrome.

Chapter 7 Other forms of market failure

Having examined the impact of externalities in Chapter 6, attention now switches to other forms of market failure, any of which may prevent a market economy from achieving full allocative efficiency.

Many goods that are produced and consumed in a society are **private goods**, in the sense that once they have been consumed by one person, they cannot be consumed by somebody else. However, there are some goods which have the characteristics that consumers cannot be excluded from consuming them and that consumption by one person does not prevent the amount of the good available for consumption by others. A good with these characteristics of non-exclusiveness and non-rivalry is known as a **public good**. In a free market environment, too little of such a good will be supplied for society as a result of the **free-rider problem**. If an individual cannot be excluded from consuming a good, there is no incentive to pay for its provision.

There are some goods that the government believes that people should consume, regardless of whether they have the means or the willingness to do so — these are known as **merit goods**. Equally, there are **demerit goods**, where the good brings less benefit to consumers than they expect.

Information failure may also impede the achievement of allocative efficiency, especially where there is **asymmetric information**, that is a situation in which some economic agents have better information than others and can use this to their own advantage.

Chapter 8 Government intervention and government failure

Chapters 6 and 7 explored some ways in which market failure may prevent an economy from reaching allocative efficiency. Although not strictly market failure, there may also be situations in which inequity in the distribution of income and/or resources may produce an allocation of resources that may be unacceptable for society. This may be inequity between individuals or groups within society, between regions within a country, or between nations within the global economy. It may be that governments will wish to intervene to influence the distribution of income.

It is also important to be aware that actions taken by a government in order to address market failure may sometimes have unintended effects, and **government failure** may result in a misallocation of resources. Chapter 8 explores some such situations.

One example is where a government imposes a **minimum wage** in order to protect the low paid. In some markets, this may have the result of increasing the level of unemployment. In a similar way, imposing **rent controls** to protect the poor may lead to a distortion in the housing market.

Governments need to raise revenue in order to finance their expenditure plans. One way of doing this is by imposing an **indirect tax** (such as VAT, for example). The way in which the burden of such a tax is shared between consumers and producers depends upon the price elasticities of demand and supply. This is known as the **incidence of a tax**. Government failure in the form of unintended effects may also result from government action to prohibit the consumption of demerit goods.

The national and international economy

Part 2

Chapter 9
Measuring economic performance

This part of the book switches attention to macroeconomics. Macroeconomics has much in common with microeconomics, but focuses on the whole economy, rather than on individual markets and how they operate. Although the way of thinking about issues is similar, and although similar tools are used, now it is interactions between economic variables at the level of the whole economy that are studied. This process will introduce some of the major concerns of the media, such as unemployment, inflation and economic growth.

Learning outcomes

After studying this chapter, you should:

➤ be aware of the main economic aggregates in a modern economy

➤ understand the distinction between real and nominal variables

➤ be familiar with the use of index numbers and the calculation of growth rates

➤ appreciate the significance of alternative measurements of inflation and unemployment in the context of the UK economy

➤ be familiar with the role and importance of the balance of payments

➤ be aware of the circular flow of income, output and expenditure

➤ understand the meaning of GDP and its use as an indicator in international comparisons

Economic performance

Part 1 of the book emphasised the importance of individual markets in achieving allocative and productive efficiency. In a modern economy, there are so many separate markets that it is difficult to get an overall picture of how well the economy is working. When it comes to monitoring its overall performance, the focus thus tends to be on the **macroeconomic** aggregates. 'Aggregate' here means

Key term

macroeconomics: the study of the interrelationships between economic variables at an aggregate (macroeconomic) level

'totals' — for example, total unemployment in an economy, or total spending on goods and services — rather than, say, unemployed workers in a particular occupation, or spending on a particular good.

There are a number of dimensions in which the economy as a whole can be monitored. One prime focus of economic policy in recent years has been the inflation rate, as it has been argued that maintaining a stable economic environment is crucial to enabling markets to operate effectively. A second focus has been unemployment, which has been seen as an indicator of whether the economy is using its resources to the full — in other words, whether there are factors of production that are not being fully utilised. In addition, of course, there may be concern that the people who are unemployed are being disadvantaged.

Perhaps more fundamentally, there is an interest in economic growth. Is the economy expanding its potential capacity as time goes by, thereby making more resources available for members of society? In fact, it might be argued that this is the most fundamental objective for the economy, and the most important indicator of the economy's performance.

Other concerns may also need to be kept in mind. In particular, there is the question of how the economy interacts with the rest of the world. The UK is an 'open' economy — one that actively engages in international trade — and this aspect of UK economic performance needs to be monitored too. This is done through the balance of payments accounts, which will be examined in Chapter 12.

The importance of data

To monitor the performance of the economy, it is crucial to be able to observe how the economy is functioning, and for this you need data. Remember that economics, especially macroeconomics, is a non-experimental discipline. It is not possible to conduct experiments to see how the economy reacts to various stimuli in order to learn how it works. Instead, it is necessary to observe the economy, and to come to a judgement about whether or not its performance is satisfactory, and whether macroeconomic theories about how the economy works are supported by the evidence.

So, a reliable measure is needed for tracking each of the variables mentioned above, in order to observe how the economy is evolving through time. The key indicators of the economy's performance will be introduced as this chapter unfolds.

Most of the economic statistics used by economists are collected and published by various government agencies. Such data in the UK are published mainly by the Office of National Statistics (ONS). Data on other countries are published by the International Monetary Fund (IMF), the World Bank and the United Nations, as well as national sources. There is little alternative to relying on such sources because the accurate collection of data is an expensive and time-consuming business.

www.imf.org

An IMF meeting

Care needs to be taken in the interpretation of economic data. It is important to be aware of how the data are compiled, and the extent to which they are indicators of what economists are trying to measure. It is also important to remember that the economic environment is ever changing, and that single causes can rarely be ascribed to the economic events that are observed. This is because the ceteris paribus condition that underlies so much economic analysis is rarely fulfilled in reality. In other words, you cannot rely on 'other things remaining constant' when using data about the real world.

It is also important to realise that even the ONS cannot observe with absolute accuracy. Indeed, some data take so long to be assembled that early estimates are provisional in nature and subject to later revision as more information becomes available. Data used in international comparisons must be treated with even greater caution.

Real and nominal measurements

The measurement of economic variables poses many dilemmas for statisticians. Not least is the fundamental problem of what to use as units of measurement. Suppose economists wish to measure total output produced in an economy during successive years. In the first place, they cannot use volume measures. They may be able to count how many computers, passenger cars, tins of paint and cauliflowers the economy produces — but how do they add all these different items together to produce a total?

An obvious solution is to use the money values. Given prices for all the items, it is possible to calculate the money values of all these goods and thus produce a measurement of the total output produced in an economy during a year in terms of pounds sterling. However, this is just the beginning of the problem because, in order to monitor changes in total output between 2 years, it is important to be aware that not only do the volumes of goods produced change, but so too do their prices. In effect, this means that, if pounds sterling are used as the unit of measurement, the unit of measurement will change from one year to the next as prices change.

This is a problem that is not faced by most of the physical sciences. After all, the length of a metre does not alter from one year to the next, so if the length of something is being measured, the unit is fixed. Economists, however, have to make allowance for changing prices when measuring in pounds sterling.

Measurements made using prices that are current at the time a transaction takes place are known as measurements of **nominal values**. When prices are rising, these nominal measurements will always overstate the extent to which an economic variable is growing through time. Clearly, to analyse performance, economists will be more interested in 'real' values — that is, the quantities produced after having removed the effects of price changes. One way in which these real measures can be obtained is by taking the volumes produced in each year and valuing these quantities at the prices that prevailed in some base year. This then enables allowance to be made for the changes in prices that take place, permitting a focus on the real values. These can be thought of as being measured at *constant prices*.

For example, suppose that last year you bought a tub of ice cream for £2, but that inflation has been 10%, so that this year you had to pay £2.20 for the same tub. Your *real* consumption of the item has not changed, but your spending has increased. If you were to use the value of your spending to measure changes in consumption through time, it would be misleading, as you know that your *real* consumption has not changed at all (so is still £2), although its *nominal* value has increased to £2.20.

Index numbers

In some cases there is no apparent unit of measurement that is meaningful. For example, if you wished to measure the general level of prices in an economy, there is no meaningful unit of measurement that could be used. In such cases the solution is to use **index numbers**, which is a form of ratio that compares the value of a variable with some base point.

 terms

nominal value: value of an economic variable based on current prices, taking no account of changing prices through time

real value: value of an economic variable taking account of changing prices through time

index number: a device for comparing the value of a variable in one period or location with a base observation (e.g. the retail price index measures the average level of prices relative to a base period)

For example, suppose the price of a 250g pack of butter last year was 80p, and this year it is 84p. How can the price between the two periods be compared? One way of doing it is to calculate the percentage change:

$100 \times (84 - 80) \div 80 = 5\%$

(Note that this is the formula for calculating any growth rate in percentage terms. The change in the variable is always expressed as a percentage of the initial value, not the final value.)

An alternative way of doing this is to calculate an index number. In the above example, the current value of the index could be calculated as $100 \times 84 \div 80 = 105$. In other words, the current value is divided by the base value and multiplied by 100. The resulting number gives the current value relative to the base value. This turns out to be a useful way of expressing a range of economic variables where you want to show the value relative to a base period.

One particular use for this technique is when you want to show the average level of prices at different points in time. For such a general price index, one procedure is to define a typical basket of commodities that reflects the spending pattern of a representative household. The cost of that bundle can be calculated in a base year, and then in subsequent years. The cost in the base year is set to equal 100, and in subsequent years the index is measured relative to that base date, thereby reflecting the change in prices since then. For example, if in the second year the weighted average increase in prices were 2.5%, then the index in year 2 would take on the value 102.5 (based on year 1 = 100). Such a general index of prices could be seen as an index of the *cost of living* for the representative household, as it would give the level of prices faced by the average household relative to the base year.

The price of a typical basket of commodities can be used as an index of the cost of living

Exercise 9.1

Table 9.1 provides data on consumer prices for the UK, USA and Italy.

	UK consumer price index	USA consumer price index	Italy consumer price index
1996	89.7	91.1	92.2
1997	92.5	93.2	94.1
1998	95.7	94.7	95.9
1999	97.2	96.7	97.5
2000	100.0	100.0	100.0
2001	101.8	102.8	102.8
2002	103.5	104.5	105.3
2003	106.5	106.8	108.1
2004	109.7	109.7	110.5
2005	112.8	113.4	112.7
2006	116.4	117.1	115.1

Table 9.1
Consumer prices
Source: IMF.

a   Calculate the annual inflation rate for each of the countries from 1997–2006.

b   Plot these three inflation series on a graph against time.

c   By what percentage did prices increase in each country over the whole period — that is, between 1996 and 2006?

d   Which economy do you judge to have experienced most stability in the inflation rate?

Summary

> Macroeconomics is the study of the interrelationships between economic variables at the level of the whole economy.

> Some variables are of particular interest when monitoring the performance of an economy — for example, inflation, unemployment and economic growth.

> As economists cannot easily conduct experiments in order to test economic theory, they rely on the use of economic data: that is, observations of the world around them.

> Data measured in money terms need to be handled carefully, as prices change over time, thereby affecting the units in which many economic variables are measured.

> Index numbers are helpful in comparing the value of a variable with a base date or unit.

The consumer price index

The most important general price index in the UK is the **consumer price index** (CPI), which has been used by the government in setting its inflation target since the beginning of 2004. This index is based on the prices of a bundle of about 650 goods and services measured at different points in time. The information is compiled through the *Family Expenditure Survey*, in which data about the prices of goods and services in the bundle are collected on a monthly basis from a sample of 7,000 households across the country. Some prices are observed directly in randomly selected shops; these are then used to create an index based on 1996 = 100. The weights for the items included in the index are set to reflect the typical spending habits of consumers in the economy, based on the share of each component in their total expenditure. These weights are updated each year, as changes in the consumption patterns of households need to be accommodated if the index is to remain representative.

 Key *terms*

consumer price index (CPI): a measure of the general level of prices in the UK, adopted as the government's inflation target since December 2003

inflation: the rate of change of the average price level: for example, the percentage annual rate of change of the CPI

It is important to remember that the CPI provides a measurement of the *level* of prices in the economy. This is not inflation: **inflation** is the *rate of change* of prices, and the percentage change in the CPI provides one estimate of the inflation rate.

Being able to calculate percentage changes is a useful skill. Going back to the example of the ice cream from page 113, remember that you had bought a tub of ice cream for £2 last year, but now have to pay £2.20. The percentage change in the price is obtained by dividing the *change* in price by the original price and multiplying by 100. Thus, the percentage change is $100 \times 0.20/2.00 = 10\%$.

Alternative measurements of inflation

The traditional measure of inflation in the UK for many years was the **retail price index** (RPI), which was first calculated (under another name) in the early twentieth century to evaluate the extent to which workers were affected by price changes during the First World War. When the Blair government first set an explicit inflation target, it chose the RPIX, which is the RPI excluding mortgage interest payments. This was felt to be a better measure of the effectiveness of macro-economic policy. It was argued that if interest rates are used to curb inflation, then including mortgage interest payments in the inflation measure will be misleading.

 Key *term*

retail price index (RPI):
a measure of the average level of prices in the UK

The CPI replaced RPIX partly because it is believed to be a more appropriate indicator for evaluating policy effectiveness. In addition, it has the advantage of being calculated using the same methodology as is used in other countries within the European Union, so that it is more useful than the RPIX for making international comparisons of inflation.

The CPI and RPI are based on a similar approach, although there are some significant differences in the detail of the calculation. Both measures set out to calculate the overall price level at different points in time. Each is based on calculating the overall cost of a representative basket of goods and services at different points in time relative to a base period. Both are produced by combining some 120,000 individual prices, which are collected each month for around 650 representative items. The result of these calculations is an index that shows how the general level of prices has changed relative to the base year. The rate of inflation is then calculated as the percentage rate of change of the price index, whether it be the CPI or the RPI.

The indexes share a common failing, arising from the fixed weights used in calcu-lating the overall index. Suppose the price of a particular item rises more rapidly than other prices during the year. One response by consumers is to substitute an alternative, cheaper, product. As the indexes are based on fixed weights, they do not pick up this substitution effect, and therefore tend to overstate the price level in terms of the cost of living. Some attempt is made to overcome this problem by changing the weights on an annual basis in order to limit the impact of major changes. This includes incorporating new items when appropriate – for example, digital cameras were included in the CPI calculations for the first time in 2004, reflecting a change in consumer spending patterns.

The CPI and RPI differ for a number of reasons, partly because of differences in the content of the basket of goods and services that are included, and partly in terms of the population of people who are covered by the index. For example, in calculating the weights, the RPI excludes pensioner households and the highest-income house-holds, whereas the CPI does not. There are also some other differences in the ways that the calculations are carried out.

Figure 9.1 shows data for the rates of change of the RPI and the CPI since March 1997. These rates have been calculated on a monthly basis, computing the percentage rate of change of each index relative to the value 12 months previously.

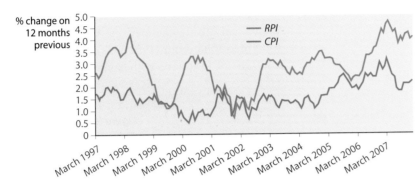

Figure 9.1
Alternative inflation measures in the UK

Source: ONS.

A noticeable characteristic of Figure 9.1 is that for much of the period the CPI has shown a lower rate of change than the RPI. In part this reflects the way in which the prices are combined, but it also reflects the fact that different items and households are covered. The National Statistician, Len Cook, said:

> The CPI's fairly recent development as a macroeconomic indicator of inflation means that it has some distinct advantages over RPIX... Its coverage of spending and households better matches other economic data. The way it combines individual prices also has some clear statistical benefits, and helps us to compare UK inflation with inflation in other countries.

Until the end of 2003, the government's target for inflation was set at 2.5% per annum in the RPIX. After that date, the target for CPI was set at 2% per annum. Since 1997, the Bank of England has had the responsibility of ensuring that inflation remains within one percentage point of this target. You can see from Figure 9.1 that inflation accelerated (on both measures) after March 2006, and in March 2007 the rate of change of CPI went above 3%, thus moving out of the permissible target range for the first time since the inflation target was introduced. You can also see that inflation came back into range very rapidly.

The Bank of England is responsible for ensuring inflation remains on target

Inflation in the UK and throughout the world

Figure 9.2 shows a time path for the rate of change in price levels since 1949. RPI has been used for this purpose, as the CPI was introduced only in 1997, so there is no consistent long-run series for it. The figure provides the backdrop to understanding the way the UK economy evolved during this period. Apart from the period of the Korean War, which generated inflation in 1951–52, the 1950s and early 1960s were typified by a low rate of inflation, with some acceleration becoming apparent in the early 1970s.

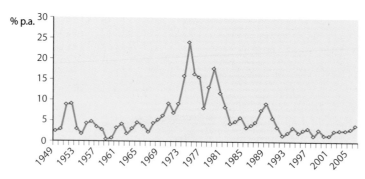

Figure 9.2 *RPI inflation, 1949–2007 (% change over previous year)*

Source: ONS.

The instability of the 1970s was due to a combination of factors. Oil prices rose dramatically in 1973–74 and again in 1979–80, which certainly contributed to rising prices, not only in the UK but worldwide. However, inflation was further fuelled by the abandonment of the fixed exchange rate system under which sterling had been tied to the US dollar until 1972. Under a fixed exchange rate system, the government must dedicate the use of monetary policy to maintaining the value of the currency. However, the transition to a floating exchange rate system freed up monetary policy in a way that was perhaps not fully understood by the government of the day. As you can see in Figure 9.2, prices were allowed to rise rapidly – by nearly 25% in 1974/75. The diagram also shows how inflation was gradually reined in during the 1980s, and underlines the relative stability that has now been achieved, with inflation keeping well within the target range set by the government – with the exception of March 2007, as noted above. The significance of the exchange rate will be explained more fully in Chapter 12.

Figure 9.3 shows something of the extent to which the UK's experience is typical of the pattern of inflation worldwide. You can see from this how inflation in the industrial countries followed a similar general pattern, with a common acceleration in the early 1970s, and a period of gradual control after 1980. However, you can also see that the developing countries in the world experienced inflation at a much higher average level after 1974 because they proved to be less able to bring prices under control after the oil price shocks. Much of this reflects events in Latin America, which suffered especially high rates of inflation in the 1980s and 1990s. This instability in the macroeconomic environment has almost certainly hindered development in the countries affected, and makes it important to understand how inflation is generated and how to curb it. This topic will be revisited in Chapter 13.

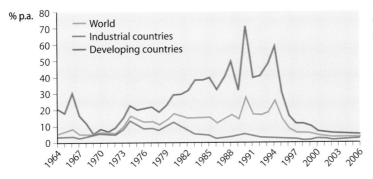

Figure 9.3 *World inflation since 1964 (% change in the consumer price index)*

Source: IMF.

Unemployment

The measurement of unemployment in the UK has also been contentious over the years, and the standard definition used to monitor performance has altered several times, especially during the 1980s, when a number of rationalisations were introduced.

Historically, unemployment was measured by the number of people registered as unemployed and claiming unemployment benefit (the Jobseeker's Allowance (JSA)). This measure of employment is known as the **claimant count of unemployment**. People claiming the JSA must declare that they are out of work, capable of, available for and actively seeking work, during the week in which their claim is made.

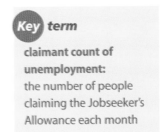

Key term

claimant count of unemployment: the number of people claiming the Jobseeker's Allowance each month

Figure 9.4 shows monthly data on the claimant count since 1971, expressed as a percentage of the workforce. The surge in unemployment in the early 1980s stands out on the graph, when the percentage of the workforce registered as unemployed more than doubled in a relatively short period. Although this seemed to be coming under control towards the end of the 1980s, unemployment rose again in the early 1990s before a steady decline into the new millennium.

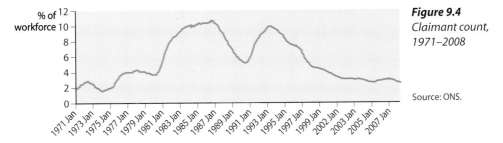

Figure 9.4 *Claimant count, 1971–2008*

Source: ONS.

One of the problems with the claimant count is that although people claiming the JSA must declare that they are available for work, it nonetheless includes some people who are claiming benefit, but are not actually available or prepared for work. It also excludes some people who would like to work, and who are looking for work, but who are not eligible for unemployment benefit, such as women returning to the labour force after childbirth.

Because of these problems, the claimant count has been superseded for official purposes by the so-called **ILO unemployment rate**, a measure based on the *Labour Force Survey*. This identifies the number of people available for work, and seeking work, but without a job. This definition corresponds to that used by the International Labour Organisation (ILO), and is closer to what economists would like unemployment to measure. It defines as being unemployed those people who are:

— without a job, want a job, have actively sought work in the last four weeks and are available to start work in the next two weeks; or

— out of work, have found a job and are waiting to start it in the next two weeks

Labour Market Statistics, September 2004

However, a major difference between the two alternatives from a measurement perspective is that the claimant count is a full count of all those who register, whereas the ILO measure is based on a sample. Figure 9.5 shows both the claimant and ILO measures for the period since 1984. You can see that the difference between the two measures is narrower when unemployment is relatively high, and wider when unemployment is falling. This may be partly because low unemployment encourages more people who are not eligible for unemployment benefit to look for jobs, whereas they withdraw from the workforce when unemployment rises and they perceive that finding a job will be difficult. This is said to affect women in particular, who may not be eligible for the Jobseeker's Allowance because of their partner's earnings.

 term

ILO unemployment rate: measure of the percentage of the workforce who are without jobs, but are available for work, willing to work and looking for work

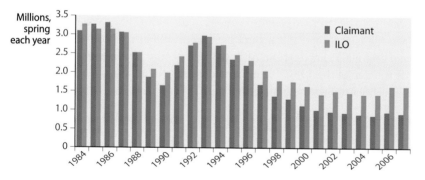

Figure 9.5
Alternative measures of unemployment in the UK, 1984–2007

Note: numbers unemployed in March–May each year (average).

Source: ONS.

Summary

➤ The retail price index (RPI) is the best-known measure of the average price level in the UK.

➤ In December 2003 the government adopted the consumer price index (CPI) as its preferred measure of the price level, and inflation is now monitored through the rate of change of CPI.

➤ Unemployment is measured in two ways. The claimant count is based on the number of people claiming Jobseeker's Allowance. However, the ILO measure, based on the *Labour Force Survey*, is more meaningful.

The circular flow of income, expenditure and output

Chapter 1 introduced the notion of *gross domestic product* (GDP), which was described as the total output of an economy. It is now time to examine this concept more closely, and to see how it may be measured.

Consider a simplified model of an economy. Assume for the moment that there are just two types of economic agent in an economy: households and firms. In other words, ignore the government and assume there is no international trade. (These agents will be brought back into the picture soon.) We also assume that all factors of production are owned and supplied to firms by households.

In this simple world, assume that firms produce goods and hire labour and other factor inputs from households. Also assume that they buy investment goods from other firms, for which purpose they need to borrow in a financial market. Households supply their labour (and other factor inputs) and buy consumer goods. In return for supplying factor inputs, households receive income, part of which they spend on consumer goods and part of which they save in the financial market.

If you examine the monetary flows in this economy, you can see how the economy operates. In Figure 9.6 the blue arrow shows the flow of income that goes from firms to households as payment for their factor services (labour, land and capital). The red arrows show what happens to the output produced by firms: part of it goes to households in the form of consumer goods (C); the rest flows back to other firms as investment goods (I). The green arrows show the expenditure flows back to firms, part of which is for consumer goods (C) from households, and part for investment goods (I) from firms. The circle is closed by households' savings, by which part of their income is invested in the financial market; this is then borrowed by firms to finance their purchases of investment goods. These flows are shown by the orange arrows. This model is sometimes known as the circular flow model.

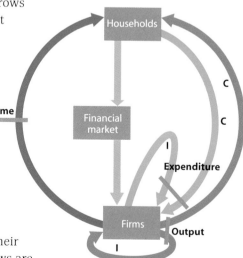

Figure 9.6 *The circular flow of income, expenditure and output*

As this is a closed system, these flows must balance. This means that there are three ways in which the total amount of economic activity in this economy can be measured: by the incomes that firms pay out, by the total amount of output that is produced, or by total expenditure. Whichever method is chosen, it should give the same result.

An economy such as the UK's is more complicated than this, so it is also necessary to take into account the economic activities of government and the fact that the UK engages in international trade, so that some of the output produced is sold abroad and some of the expenditure goes on foreign goods and services. However, the principle of measuring total economic activity is the same: GDP can be measured in three ways.

In practice, when the ONS carries out the measurements the three answers are never quite the same, as it is impossible to measure with complete accuracy. The published data for GDP are therefore calculated as the average of these three measures, each of which gives information about different aspects of a society's total resources.

The expenditure-side estimate describes how those resources are being used, so that it can be seen what proportion of society's resources is being used for consumption and what for investment etc.

The income-side estimate reports on the way in which households earn their income. In other words, it tells something about the balance between rewards to labour (e.g. wages and salaries), capital (profits), land (rents), enterprise (self-employment) and so on.

The output-side estimate focuses on the economic structure of the economy. One way in which countries differ is in the balance between primary production such as agriculture, secondary activity such as manufacturing, and tertiary activity such as services. Service activity has increased in importance in the UK in recent years, with financial services in particular emerging as a strong part of the UK's comparative advantage.

Figure 9.7 traces real GDP in the UK since 1948. In some ways this is an unhelpful way of presenting the data, as the trend component of the series is so strong. In other words, real GDP has been increasing steadily throughout the period. There are one or two periods in which there was a movement away from the trend, but these are relatively rare and not easy to analyse. This reflects the nature of economic variables such as GDP, where the fluctuations around trend are small relative to the trend, but can seem substantial when the economy is experiencing them.

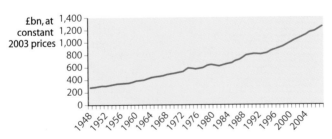

Figure 9.7 *Real GDP, 1948–2006 (£bn)*
Source: ONS.

The ratio of nominal to real GDP is a price index, known as the **GDP deflator**. This is defined as:

$$\text{price index} = 100 \times \frac{\text{GDP at current prices}}{\text{GDP at constant prices}}$$

This provides another measure of the average level of prices in the economy.

Key term

GDP deflator: an implicit price index showing the relationship between real and nominal measures of GDP, providing an alternative measure of the general level of prices in the economy

It is also sometimes useful to be able to convert nominal measurements into real terms. This can be done by dividing the nominal measurement by the price index, a process known as *deflating* the nominal measure.

Figure 9.8 converts the data into annual growth rates, which in some ways are more revealing. This certainly makes it more straightforward to identify the main periods of fluctuation, in particular periods of negative growth: that is, when the economy contracted. It is also apparent from this graph that the economy has been relatively stable since 1995.

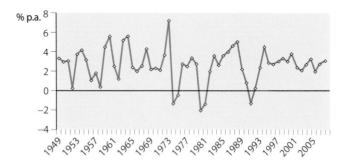

Figure 9.8 *Growth of real GDP, 1949–2007 (% change over previous year)*
Source: ONS.

It should be noted that the measure of GDP has not been without its critics. In particular, economists have questioned whether it provides a reasonable measure of the standard of living enjoyed by the residents of a country, and whether its rate of change is therefore informative about economic growth.

The business cycle

In the past it has not been uncommon for economies to go through a regular **business cycle**, where the level of economic activity has varied around an underlying trend. Figure 9.9 shows an economy in which real GDP is trending upwards over time but fluctuating around the trend, so that actual GDP follows a regular cycle around the trend. The point of maximum growth is often referred to as the *peak* of the cycle — or a *boom* period — whereas the low point is known as the *trough* of the cycle. If the growth rate is negative for two consecutive quarters, the economy is considered to be in *recession*.

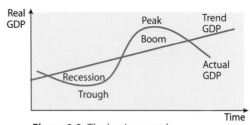

Figure 9.9 *The business cycle*

Key term

business cycle: a phenomenon whereby GDP fluctuates around its underlying trend, following a regular pattern

Figure 9.10 illustrates this in a different way, by showing the growth rates of real GDP in the UK over a cycle from 1984 to 1994. There was evidence in Figure 9.8 that the fluctuations have been less marked in the later years shown.

A number of explanations have been advanced to explain the business cycle. One suggestion is that some governments engineer the cycle, taking the economy into a boom in the lead-up to an election, only to slow it down again once elected. This has become known as the *political business cycle.* Another suggestion is that cycles arise because of the lagged impact of policy measures on the economy: in other words, it takes time for policies to take effect — sometimes so long that they can destabilise the economy by having unintended effects.

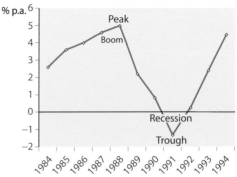

Figure 9.10 *Profile of a cycle: growth of real GDP, 1984–94 (% change over previous year)*
Source: *Economic Trends Annual Supplement.*

In the past, considerable effort has gone into trying to predict the turning points of the business cycle by looking for *leading indicators* that turn in advance of the cycle — for example, the CBI quarterly survey of business optimism, which is designed to gather firms' views about the cycle. Changes in the number of new dwellings started and changes in consumer borrowing are also seen as leading indicators. In contrast, *coincident indicators* move in step with the current state of the business cycle — for example, real GDP or the volume of retail sales. On the other hand, unemployment tends to be a *lagging indicator*, as firms may not reduce their labour force right at the start of a recession, preferring first to ensure that it is not a temporary blip. In Chapter 15 it will be seen that there are some responses within the economy that tend to dampen the business cycle automatically; these are known as *automatic stabilisers.*

The volume of retail sales moves in step with the business cycle

Summary

➤ The circular flow of income, expenditure and output describes the relationship between these three key variables.

➤ The model suggests that there are three ways in which the total level of economic activity in an economy during a period of time can be measured: by total income, by total expenditure, and by total output produced.

➤ In principle, these should give the same answers, but in practice data measurements are not so accurate.

➤ GDP is a measure of the total economic activity carried out in an economy during a period by residents living on its territory.

➤ Economies tend not to grow according to a constant trend, but to fluctuate around the underlying trend, creating the business cycle.

Exercise 9.3

Table 9.2 provides data on real GDP for the period 2000–06. Convert the series to an index based on 1999 = 100. Calculate the growth rate of GDP for each year from 2000/01 to 2005/06. In which year was growth at its highest and in which year was it at its lowest?

Table 9.2
Real GDP in the UK, 2000–2006 (£bn)

2000	1,035
2001	1,060
2002	1,081
2003	1,110
2004	1,147
2005	1,169
2006	1,201

Chapter 10
Aggregate demand

Now that you are familiar with the main macroeconomic aggregates, it is time to start thinking about how economic analysis can be used to explore the way in which these variables interact. The starting point is to consider the components of aggregate demand. The way in which the levels of these components are determined in practice is an important key to the operation of the economy when considered at the aggregate level.

Learning outcomes

After studying this chapter, you should:
➤ understand what is meant by aggregate demand
➤ be able to identify the components of aggregate demand and their determinants
➤ be aware of the possibility of multiplier effects
➤ be familiar with the notion of the aggregate demand curve

The components of aggregate demand

Chapter 9 introduced the notion of the circular flow of income, expenditure and output. If aggregate demand were considered in that model, it would comprise the combined spending of households (on consumer goods) and firms (on investment goods). It was noted that in the real world it is also necessary to include international trade (exports and imports) and spending by government in this measure. The full version of aggregate expenditure can be written as:

$$AD = C + I + G + X - M$$

where AD denotes aggregate demand, C is consumption, I is investment, G is government spending, X is exports and M is imports.

Figure 10.1 shows the expenditure-side breakdown of real GDP in the UK in 2006. This highlights the relative size of the components of aggregate demand. Consumption is by far the largest component, amounting to more than 64% of real GDP in 2006.

Government current expenditure accounted for about 20%, but you should realise that this somewhat under-states the importance of government in overall spending, as it excludes public spending on invest-ment, which is treated together with private sector investment in the data. Combined public and private sector investment made up just over 18% of total GDP; this includes changes in the inventory holdings of firms. Notice that imports were rather higher than exports, indicating a negative balance of trade in goods and services.

In the circular flow model it was noted that total expenditure should be the same as total income and total output if all were measured fully. This seems to suggest that the macroeconomy is always in a sort of equilibrium, in the sense that expenditure and output are always the same. However, this is misleading. Although when you observe the economy, you should find that expenditure and output are the same *after* the event, this does not mean that equilibrium holds in the sense that all economic agents will have found that their plans were fulfilled. In other words, it is not necessarily the case that *planned* expenditure equals *planned* output.

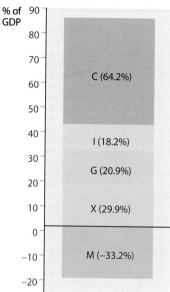

Figure 10.1
The breakdown of real GDP in 2006

Note: C includes spending by non-profit institutions serving households; I includes changes in inventory holdings; the statistical discrepancy is not shown.
Source: ONS.

This is the significance of the inclusion of inventory changes as part of investment. If firms find that they have produced more output than is subsequently purchased, their inventory holdings increase. Thus, although after the event expenditure always equals output, this is because any disequilibrium is reflected in unplanned inventory changes.

Exercise 10.1

Suppose there is an economy in which the values in Table 10.1 apply (all measured in $ million):

Consumption	75
Profits	60
Investment	30
Government expenditure	25
Exports	50
Private saving	50
Imports	55

Table 10.1
Values for an economy

a Calculate the level of aggregate demand.
b Calculate the trade balance.

When in the next chapter you come to consider the conditions under which a macroeconomy will be in equilibrium, you will need to think in terms of the factors that will influence *ex ante* (planned) aggregate demand. The first step is to consider each component in turn.

Consumption

Consumption is the largest single component of aggregate demand. What factors could be expected to influence the size of total spending by households? John Maynard Keynes, in his influential book *The General Theory of Employment, Interest and Money*, published in 1936, suggested that the most important determinant is **disposable income**. In other words, as real incomes rise, households will tend to spend more. However, he also pointed out that they would not spend all of an increase in income, but would save some of it. Remember that this was important in the circular flow model. Keynes defined the **average propensity to consume** as the *ratio* of consumption to income, and the **marginal propensity to consume** as the proportion of an *increase* in disposable income that households would devote to consumption.

J. M. Keynes's hugely influential book The General Theory of Employment, Interest and Money *was published in 1936*

However, income will not be the only influence on consumption. Consumption may also depend partly on the *wealth* of a household. Notice that income and wealth are not the same. Income accrues during a period as a reward for the supply of factor services, such as labour. Wealth, on the other hand, represents the stock of accumulated past savings. If you like, wealth can be thought of in terms of the asset holdings of households. If households experience an increase in the value of their asset holdings, this may influence their spending decisions.

 terms

disposable income: the income that households have to devote to consumption and saving, taking into account payments of direct taxes and transfer payments

average propensity to consume: the proportion of income that households devote to consumption

marginal propensity to consume: the proportion of additional income devoted to consumption

Later writers argued that consumption does not necessarily depend upon current income alone. For example, Milton Friedman put forward the *permanent income hypothesis*, which suggested that consumers take decisions about consumption based on a notion of their permanent, or normal, income levels — that is, the income that they expect to receive over a 5- or 10-year time horizon. This suggests that households do not necessarily vary their consumption patterns in response to changes in income that they perceive to be only transitory. An associated theory is the *life-cycle hypothesis*, developed by Ando Modigliani, who suggested that households smooth their consumption over their lifetimes, on the basis of their expected lifetime incomes. Thus, people tend to borrow in their youth against future income; then in middle age, when earning more strongly, they pay off their debts and save in preparation to fund their consumption in retirement. Consumption thus varies by much less than income, and is based on expected lifetime earnings rather than on current income.

Furthermore, if part of household spending is financed by borrowing, the rate of interest may be significant in influencing the total amount of consumption spending. An increase in the rate of interest that raises the cost of borrowing may deter consumption. At the same time it may encourage saving, as the return on saving is higher when the interest rate is higher. The rate of interest may also have an indirect effect on consumption through its effect on the value of asset holdings. In addition, households may be influenced in their consumption decisions by their expectations about future inflation. Notice that some of these effects may not be instantaneous: that is, consumption may adjust to changes in its determinants only after a time lag.

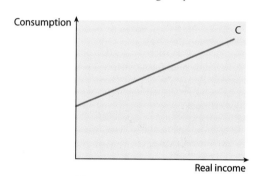

Figure 10.2
The consumption function

This **consumption function** can be portrayed as a relationship between consumption and income. This is shown in Figure 10.2, which focuses on the relationship between consumption and household income, ceteris paribus: in other words, in drawing the relationship between consumption and income, it is assumed that the other determinants of consumption, such as wealth and the interest rate, remain constant. A change in any of these other influences will affect the *position* of the line. Notice that the marginal propensity to consume (*MPC*) is the slope of this line. For example, if the *MPC* is 0.7, this means that for every additional £100 of income received by households, £70 would be spent on consumption and the remaining £30 would be saved.

 term

consumption function: the relationship between consumption and disposable income; its position depends upon the other factors that affect how much households spend on consumption

In practice, it is not expected that the empirical relationship between consumption and income will reveal an exact straight line, if only because over a long time period there will be changes in the other influences on consumption, such as interest rates and expected inflation. However, Figure 10.3 shows that the hypothesis is not totally implausible.

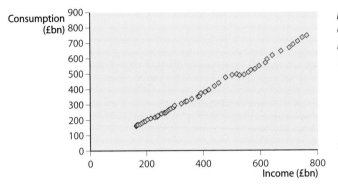

Figure 10.3
Consumption and income in the UK, 1948–2006

Source: ONS.

Investment

The rate of interest is also likely to be influential in affecting firms' decisions about investment spending. Again, this is because the interest rate represents the cost of borrowing; so, if firms need to borrow in order to undertake **investment**, they may be discouraged from spending on investment goods when the rate of interest is relatively high.

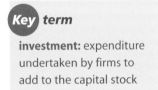

Key *term*

investment: expenditure undertaken by firms to add to the capital stock

Investment leads to an increase in the productive capacity of the economy, by increasing the stock of capital available for production. This capital stock comprises plant and machinery, vehicles and other transport equipment, and buildings, including new dwellings, which provide a supply of housing services over a long period.

Although important, the rate of interest is not likely to be the only factor that determines how much investment firms choose to undertake. First, not all investment has to be funded from borrowing – firms may be able to use past profits for this purpose. However, if firms choose to do this, they face an opportunity cost. In other words, profits can be used to buy financial assets that will provide a rate of return dependent on the rate of interest. The rate of interest is thus still important, as it represents the opportunity cost of an investment project.

In considering an investment project, firms will need to form expectations about the future stream of earnings that will flow from the investment. Their expectations about the future state of the economy (and of the demand for their products) will thus be an important influence on current investment. This is one reason why it is argued that inflation is damaging for an economy, as a high rate of inflation increases uncertainty about the future and may dampen firms' expectations about future demand, thereby discouraging investment.

Figure 10.4 shows the relationship between investment and the rate of interest. The investment demand function I_{D0} is downward sloping because investment is relatively low when the rate of interest is relatively high. An improvement in business confidence for the future would result in more investment being undertaken at any given interest rate, so the investment function would move from I_{D0} to I_{D1}.

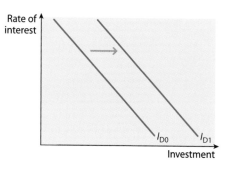

Figure 10.4
Investment and the rate of interest

Government expenditure

By and large, you might expect government expenditure to be decided by different criteria from those influencing private sector expenditures. Indeed, some aspects of government expenditure might be regarded as part of macroeconomic policy, as will be seen in Chapter 15. Some other aspects of government expenditure may vary automatically with variations in the overall level of economic activity over time. For example, unemployment benefit payments are likely to increase during recessionary periods. The effects of this will be examined in Chapter 15.

From the point of view of investigating macroeconomic equilibrium, however, government expenditure can be regarded as mainly *autonomous*: that is, independent of the variables in the model that will be constructed in this chapter.

Trade in goods and services

Finally, there are the factors that may influence the level of exports and imports. One factor that will affect both of these is the exchange rate between sterling and other currencies. This affects the relative prices of UK goods and those produced overseas. Other things being equal, an increase in the sterling exchange rate makes UK exports less competitive and imports into the UK more competitive.

However, the demand for exports and imports will also depend upon the relative prices of goods produced in the UK and the rest of the world. If UK inflation is high relative to elsewhere, again, this will tend to make UK exports less competitive and imports more competitive. These effects will be examined more carefully in Chapter 12, when it will be shown that movements in the exchange rate tend to counteract changes in relative prices between countries.

In addition, the demand for imports into the UK will depend partly upon the level of domestic aggregate income, and the demand for UK exports will depend partly upon the level of incomes in the rest of the world. Thus, a recession in the European Union will affect the demand for UK exports.

The multiplier

In his *General Theory*, Keynes pointed out that there may be **multiplier** effects in response to certain types of expenditure. Suppose that the government increases its expenditure by £1 billion, perhaps by increasing its road-building programme. The effect of this is to generate incomes for households — for example, those of the contractors hired to build the road. Those contractors then spend part of the additional income (and save part of it). By spending part of the extra money earned, an additional income stream is generated for shopkeepers and café owners, who in turn spend part of *their* additional income, and so on. Thus, the original increase in government spending sparks off further income generation and spending, causing the multiplier effect. In effect, equilibrium output may change by more than the original increase in expenditure.

> **Key term**
>
> **multiplier:** the ratio of a change in equilibrium real income to the autonomous change that brought it about; it is defined as 1 divided by the marginal propensity to withdraw

The size of this multiplier effect depends on a number of factors. Most importantly, it depends upon the size of *withdrawals* or *leakages* from the system. In particular, it depends upon how much of the additional income is saved by households, how much is spent on imported goods, and how much is returned to the government in the form of direct taxes. These items constitute withdrawals from the system, in the sense that they detract from the multiplier effect. For example, if households save a high proportion of their additional income, then this clearly reduces the multiplier effect, as the next round of spending will be that much lower. This seems to go against the traditional view that saving is good for the economy.

However, there are also *injections* into the system in the form of autonomous government expenditure, investment and exports. One condition of macro-economic equilibrium is that total withdrawals equal total injections. The fact that injections can have this multiplied effect on equilibrium output and income seems to make the government potentially very powerful, as by increasing its expenditure it can have a multiplied effect on the economy.

Government spending on road building may increase spending in other areas of the economy due to the multiplier effect

Extension point

A numerical value for the multiplier can be calculated with reference to the withdrawals from the circular flow. First, define the *marginal propensity to withdraw* (*MPW*) as the sum of the marginal propensities to save, tax and import. The multiplier formula is then 1 divided by the marginal propensity to withdraw (1/*MPW*). If the value of the multiplier is 2, then for every £100 million injection into the circular flow, there will be a £200 million increase in equilibrium output.

It is worth noting that the size of the leakages may depend in part upon the domestic elasticity of supply. If domestic supply is inflexible, and therefore unable to meet an increase in demand, more of the increase in income will spill over into purchasing imports, and this will dilute the multiplier effect.

Exercise 10.2

Identify each of the following as an injection or a leakage, and state whether it increases or decreases the impact of the multiplier:

a   saving by households

b   expenditure by central government

c   spending by UK residents on imported goods and services

d   expenditure by firms on investment

e   spending by overseas residents on UK goods and services

f   income tax payments

The aggregate demand curve

The key relationship to carry forward is the **aggregate demand (*AD*) curve**, which shows the relationship between aggregate demand and the overall price level. Formally, this curve shows the total amount of goods and services demanded in an economy at any given overall level of prices.

It is important to realise that this is a very different sort of demand curve from the micro-economic demand curves that were introduced in Chapter 2, where the focus was on an individual product and its relationship with its own price. Here the relationship is between the *total* demand for goods and services and the overall price level. Thus, aggregate demand is made up of all the components discussed above, and price is an average of all prices of goods and services in the economy.

 term

aggregate demand (*AD*) curve: the relationship between the level of aggregate demand and the overall price level; it shows planned expenditure at any given possible overall price level

Figure 10.5 shows an aggregate demand curve. The key question is why it slopes downwards. To answer this, it is necessary to determine the likely influence of the price level on the various components of aggregate demand that have been discussed in this chapter, as prices have not been mentioned explicitly (except for how expectations about inflation might influence consumer spending). First, however, the discussion needs to be cast in terms of the price *level*.

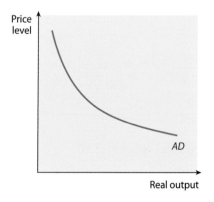

Figure 10.5
An aggregate demand curve

When the overall level of prices is relatively low, the purchasing power of income is relatively high. In other words, low overall prices can be thought of as indicating relatively high real income. Furthermore, when prices are low, this raises the real value of households' wealth. For example, suppose a household holds a financial asset such as a bond with a fixed money value of £100. The relative (real) value of that asset is higher when the overall price level is relatively low. From the above discussion, this suggests that, ceteris paribus, a low overall price level means relatively high consumption.

A second argument relates to interest rates. When prices are relatively low, interest rates also tend to be relatively low, which, it was argued, would encourage both investment and consumption expenditure, as interest rates can be seen as representing the cost of borrowing.

A third argument concerns exports and imports. It has been argued that, ceteris paribus, when UK prices are relatively low compared with the rest of the world, this will increase the competitiveness of UK goods, leading to an increase in foreign demand for UK exports, and a fall in the demand for imports into the UK as people switch to buying UK goods and services.

All of these arguments support the idea that the aggregate demand curve should be downward sloping. In other words, when the overall price level is relatively low, aggregate demand will be relatively high, and when prices are relatively high, aggregate demand will be relatively low.

Other factors discussed above will affect the *position* of the *AD* curve. This point will be explored after the introduction of the other side of the coin — the aggregate supply curve.

Summary

➤ Aggregate demand is the total demand in an economy, made up of consumption, investment, government spending and net exports.

➤ Consumption is the largest of these components and is determined by income and other influences, such as interest rates, wealth and expectations about the future.

➤ Investment leads to increases in the capital stock and is influenced by interest rates, past profits and expectations about future demand.

➤ Government expenditure may be regarded as largely autonomous.

➤ Trade in goods and services (exports and imports) is determined by the competitiveness of domestic goods and services compared with the rest of the world, which in turn is determined by relative inflation rates and the exchange rate. Imports are also affected by domestic income, and exports are affected by incomes in the rest of the world.

➤ Autonomous spending, such as government expenditure, may give rise to a magnified impact on equilibrium output through the multiplier effect.

➤ The aggregate demand curve shows the relationship between aggregate demand and the overall price level.

Chapter 11
Aggregate supply and macroeconomic equilibrium

Having seen what is meant by aggregate demand, it is now time to investigate aggregate supply and the factors that will influence it. This chapter explores the notion of macroeconomic equilibrium. As in microeconomics, this relates to the process by which balance can be achieved between the opposing forces of demand and supply. However, there are some important differences in these concepts when applied at the macroeconomic level.

Learning outcomes

After studying this chapter, you should:

➤ understand what is meant by aggregate supply
➤ be able to identify the factors that influence aggregate supply
➤ be familiar with the notion of the aggregate supply curve
➤ understand the nature of equilibrium in the macroeconomy
➤ be able to undertake comparative static analysis of external shocks affecting aggregate demand and aggregate supply

The aggregate supply curve

The previous chapter discussed the notion of aggregate demand and introduced the aggregate demand curve. In order to analyse the overall macroeconomic equilibrium, it is necessary to derive a second relationship: that between aggregate supply and the price level. It is important to remember that the level of aggregate supply covers the output of all sorts of goods and services that are produced within an economy during a period of time. However, it is not simply a question of adding up all the individual supply curves from individual markets. Within an individual market, an increase in price may induce higher supply of a good because firms will switch from other markets in search of higher profits. What you now need to be looking for is a relationship between the *overall* price level and the total amount supplied, which is a different kettle of fish.

The total quantity of output supplied in an economy over a period of time depends upon the quantities of inputs of factors of production employed: that is, the total amounts of labour, capital and other factors used. The ability of firms to vary output in the short run will be influenced by the degree of flexibility the firms have in varying inputs. This suggests that it is necessary to distinguish between short-run and long-run aggregate supply.

In the short run, firms may have relatively little flexibility to vary their inputs. Money wages are likely to be fixed, and if firms wish to vary output, they may need to do so by varying the intensity of utilisation of existing inputs. For example, if a firm wishes to expand output, the only way of doing so in the short run may be by paying its existing workers overtime, and it will be prepared to do this only in response to higher prices. This suggests that in the short run, aggregate supply may be upward sloping, as shown in Figure 11.1, where *SAS* represents **short-run aggregate supply**.

Figure 11.1
Aggregate supply in the short run

Firms will not want to operate in this way in the long run. It is not good practice to be permanently paying workers overtime. In the long run, therefore, firms will adjust their working practices and hire additional workers to avoid this situation.

What factors influence the position of aggregate supply? Given that aggregate supply arises from the use of inputs of factors of production, one important influence is the availability and effectiveness of factor inputs.

As far as labour is concerned, an increase in the *size* of the workforce will affect the position of aggregate supply. In practice, the size of the labour force tends to change relatively slowly unless substantial international migration is taking place. However, another important factor is the *level of skills* in the workforce. An increase in the skills that workers have will increase the amount of aggregate output that can be produced and lead to a shift in the aggregate supply curve.

For example, in Figure 11.2 aggregate supply was originally at SAS_0. An increase in the skills of the workforce means that firms are prepared to supply more output at any given overall price level, so the aggregate supply curve moves to SAS_1.

> **Key term**
>
> **short-run aggregate supply curve:**
> a curve showing how much output firms would be prepared to supply in the short run at any given overall price level

Figure 11.2
A shift in aggregate supply

An increase in the efficiency of capital, perhaps arising from improvements in technology, would have a similar effect, enabling greater aggregate supply at any given overall price level, and raising the productive capacity of the economy.

An increase in the quantity of capital will also have this effect, by increasing the capacity of the economy to produce. However, such an increase requires firms to have undertaken investment activity. In other words, the balance of spending between consumption and investment may affect the position of the aggregate supply curve in future periods.

Macroeconomic equilibrium

Bringing aggregate demand and aggregate supply together, the overall equilibrium position for the macroeconomy can be identified. In Figure 11.3, with aggregate supply given by *SAS* and aggregate demand by *AD*, equilibrium is reached at the real output level *Y*, with the price level at *P*.

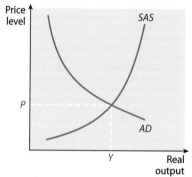

Figure 11.3
Macroeconomic equilibrium

This is an equilibrium, in the sense that if nothing changes then firms and households will have no reason to alter their behaviour in the next period. At the price *P*, aggregate supply is matched by aggregate demand.

Can it be guaranteed that the macroeconomic equilibrium will occur at the full employment level of output? For example, suppose that in Figure 11.4 the output level Y^* corresponds to the full employment level of output — that is, the level of output that represents productive capacity when all factors of production are fully employed. It may be possible to produce more than this in the short run, but only on a temporary basis, perhaps by the use of overtime. If aggregate demand is at AD^*, the macroeconomic equilibrium is at this full employment output Y^*. However, if the aggregate demand curve is located at AD_1 the equilibrium will occur at Y_1, which is below the full employment level, so there is surplus capacity in the economy.

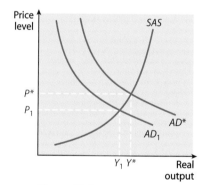

Figure 11.4
Will macroeconomic equilibrium be at full employment?

Summary

➤ The aggregate supply (*SAS*) curve shows the relationship between aggregate supply and the overall price level.

➤ Macroeconomic equilibrium is reached at the intersection of *AD* and *AS*.

Exercise 11.1

For each of the following, state whether the aggregate supply curve would shift to the left or to the right:

a The discovery of a new source of a raw material, reducing its price.

b An increase in the rate of migration from a country.

c An increase in the exchange rate.

d Improvements to the transportation system in a country.

e A technological advance that improves efficiency.

f An increase in investment by firms.

An increase in aggregate demand

Having identified macroeconomic equilibrium, it is possible to undertake some comparative static analysis. The position of the aggregate demand curve depends on the components of aggregate demand: consumption, investment, government spending and net exports. Factors that affect these components will affect the position of aggregate demand.

Consider Figure 11.5. Suppose that the economy begins in equilibrium with aggregate demand at AD_0. The equilibrium output level is Y_0, and the price level is at P_0. An increase in government expenditure will affect the position of the aggregate demand curve, shifting it to AD_1. The economy will move to a new equilibrium position, with higher output level Y_1 and a higher price level P_1.

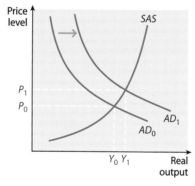

Figure 11.5
A shift in aggregate demand

This seems to suggest that the government can always reach full employment, simply by increasing its expenditure. However, you should be a little cautious in reaching such a conclusion, as the effect on equilibrium output and the price level will depend upon how close the economy is to the full employment level. Notice that the aggregate supply curve becomes steeper as output and the price level increase. In other words, the closer the economy is to the full employment level, the smaller is the elasticity of supply, so an increase in aggregate demand close to full employment will have more of an effect on the price level (and hence potentially on inflation) than on the level of real output.

Indeed, it might be argued that the aggregate supply curve becomes vertical at some point, as there is a maximum level of output that can be produced given the availability of factors of production. Such a curve is shown in Figure 11.6, where Y^* represents the full employment level of real output. In this case, the economy has settled into an equilibrium that is below potential capacity output. We may regard this as a longer-run aggregate supply curve (AS), since the only way that real output can be beyond Y^* is through the temporary use of overtime, which could not be sustained in the long run.

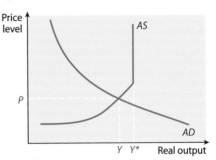

Figure 11.6
Macroeconomic equilibrium revisited

The effect of a supply shock

The AD/AS model can also be used to analyse the effects of an external shock that affects aggregate supply. For example, suppose there is an increase in oil prices arising from a disruption to supplies in the Middle East. This raises firms' costs, and leads to a reduction in aggregate supply. Comparative static analysis can again be employed to examine the likely effects on equilibrium.

Figure 11.7 analyses the situation using the long-run AS curve. The economy begins in equilibrium with output at Y_0 and the overall level of prices at P_0. The increase in oil prices causes a movement of the aggregate supply curve from AS_0 to AS_1, with aggregate demand unchanged at AD. After the economy returns to equilibrium, the new output level has fallen to Y_1 and the overall price level has increased to P_1.

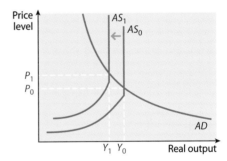

Figure 11.7 *A supply shock*

At the time of the first oil price crisis back in 1973/74, the UK government of the day tried to maintain the previous level of real output by stimulating aggregate demand. This had the effect of pushing up the price level, but did not have any noticeable effect on real output. Such a result is not unexpected, given the steepness of the aggregate supply curve. Indeed, in Figure 11.7 the previous output level Y_0 cannot be reached with aggregate supply in its new position. You can see the effects of the oil shock on the UK economy by looking back at Figures 9.2 and 9.8.

The cost of oil drove up world prices of goods in the 1970s

Exercise 11.2

For each of the following, decide whether the change affects aggregate demand or aggregate supply, and sketch a diagram to illustrate the effects on equilibrium real output and overall price level. Undertake this exercise first for a starting position in the steep part of the *AS* curve, and then repeat the exercise for an initial position further to the left, where *AS* is more elastic:

a an advancement in technology that improves the efficiency of capital

b a financial crisis in Asia that reduces the demand for UK exports

c an improvement in firms' expectations about future demand, such that investment expenditure increases

d the introduction of new health and safety legislation that raises firms' costs

Shifts of and movements along *AD* and *AS*

It is important to be aware of the distinction between shifts *of* the *AD* and *AS* curves, and movements *along* them. Typically, if a shock affects the position of one of the curves, it will lead to a movement *along* the other. For example, if the *AS* curve shifts as a result of a supply shock, the response is a movement *along* the *AD* curve, and vice versa. Thus, in trying to analyse the effects of a shock, the first step is to think about whether the shock affects *AD* or *AS*, and the second is to analyse whether the shock is positive or negative: that is, which way the relevant curve will shift. The move towards a new equilibrium can then be investigated.

Exercise 11.3

For each of the changes that you analysed in Exercise 11.2, indicate whether the result is a shift of or a movement along the *AD* and *AS* curves.

Summary

➤ Comparative static analysis can be used to analyse the effects of changes in the factors that influence aggregate demand and aggregate supply.

➤ Changes in the components of aggregate demand shift the aggregate demand curve. Within the vertical segment of *AS*, changes in *AD* affect only the overall price level, but below full employment both price and real output will be affected.

➤ Changes in the factors affecting aggregate supply alter the long-run potential productive capacity of the economy.

Chapter 12
The balance of payments and the exchange rate

The UK economy is an open economy — it engages in international trade, exporting and importing goods and services. This chapter analyses these transactions and explores ways in which the domestic economy can be influenced by the international environment. This requires discussion of the balance of payments and the exchange rate.

Learning outcomes

After studying this chapter, you should:
- ➤ be able to outline the structure of the current account of the balance of payments
- ➤ be familiar with the role and importance of the balance of payments
- ➤ be able to explain how a deficit or surplus on the current account of the balance of payments may arise
- ➤ be aware of the consequences of a surplus or deficit on the current account of the balance of payments
- ➤ understand how exchange rates are determined
- ➤ be aware of how changes in the exchange rate influence the macroeconomy through export and import prices and aggregate demand

The balance of payments

The **balance of payments** is a set of accounts that monitors the transactions that take place between UK residents and the rest of the world. For an individual household it is important to monitor incomings and outgoings, as items purchased must be paid for in some way — either by using income or savings, or by borrowing. In a similar way, a country has to pay for goods, services or assets that are bought from other countries. The balance of payments accounts enable the analysis of such international transactions.

 Key *term*

balance of payments: a set of accounts showing the transactions conducted between residents of a country and the rest of the world

As with the household, transactions can be categorised as either incoming or outgoing items. For example, if a car made in the UK is exported (i.e. purchased by a non-resident of the UK), this is an 'incoming' item, as the payment for the car is a credit to the UK. On the other hand, the purchase of a bottle of Italian wine (an import) is a debit item.

Similarly, all other transactions entered into the balance of payments accounts can be identified as credit or debit items, depending upon the direction of the payment. In other words, when money flows into the country as the result of a transaction, that is a credit; if money flows out, it is a debit. As all items have to be paid for in some way, the overall balance of payments when everything is added together must be zero. However, individual components can be positive or negative.

In line with international standards, the accounts are divided into three categories. The **current account** identifies transactions in goods and services, together with income payments and international transfers. Income payments here include the earnings of UK nationals from employment abroad and payments of investment income. Transfers are mainly transactions between governments — for example, between the UK government and EU institutions — which make up the largest component. Flows of bilateral aid and social security payments abroad are also included here.

 terms

current account of the balance of payments: account identifying transactions in goods and services between the residents of a country and the rest of the world

financial account of the balance of payments: account identifying transactions in financial assets between the residents of a country and the rest of the world

capital account of the balance of payments: account identifying transactions in (physical) capital between the residents of a country and the rest of the world

The **financial account** measures transactions in financial assets, including investment flows and central government transactions in foreign exchange reserves.

The **capital account** is relatively small. It contains capital transfers, the largest item of which is associated with migrants. When a person changes status from a non-resident to resident of the UK, any assets owned by that person are transferred to being UK-owned.

Figure 12.1 shows the relative size of the main accounts since 1980. Notice that these data are in current prices, so no account has been taken of changing prices during the period. This has the effect of compressing the apparent magnitude of the variables in the early part of the period (when prices were relatively low) and exaggerating the size towards the end of the period. Expressing these nominal values as a percentage of nominal GDP (as in Figure 12.2 for a longer period) provides a less misleading picture.

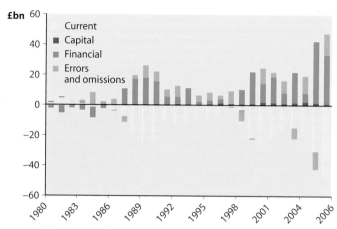

Figure 12.1 *The UK balance of payments, 1980–2006*
Source: ONS.

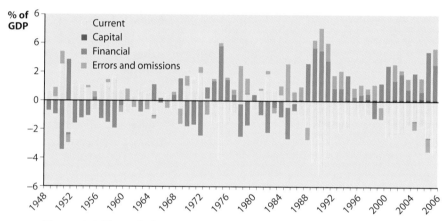

Figure 12.2 *The UK balance of payments, 1948–2006*
Source: ONS.

As the total balance of payments must always be zero, the surplus (positive) components above the line must always exactly match the deficit (negative) items below the line. However, both graphs indicate that the magnitudes of the three major accounts vary through time.

The current account

Commentators often focus on the current account. Three main items appear on this account. First, there is the balance of trade in goods and services — in other words, the balance between UK exports and imports of such goods and services. If UK residents buy German cars, this is an import and counts as a negative entry on the current account; on the other hand, if a German resident buys a British car, this is an export and constitutes a positive entry. The trade in goods is normally negative overall for the UK. However, this is partly balanced by a normally positive flow in trade in services, where the UK earns strong credits from its financial services.

German BMW cars ready for export

The second item in the current account is income. Part of this represents employment income from abroad, but the major item of income is made up of profits, dividends and interest receipts arising from UK ownership of overseas assets.

Finally, there are international transfers — either transfers through central government or transfers made or received by private individuals. This includes transactions with and grants from international organisations or the EU. The current balance combines these items.

The current account has been in deficit every year since 1984. The recorded current account surpluses in 1980–83 were associated with North Sea oil, which was then just coming on stream. There followed a phase in which the deficit grew to record levels, peaking in 1989. During the 1990s, the deficit fell until 1999, at which time the UK economy entered a period in which the current account was consistently in substantial deficit and the financial account in surplus.

Figure 12.3 shows the components of the current account. You can see that until the early 1990s the overall balance on the current account (CBAL) tracked closely the trade in goods. More recently, however, the trade in goods has moved further into deficit, although this has been partially offset by a gradual increase in the trade in services and (except in 1999) by an increase in income — which is made up mainly of investment income.

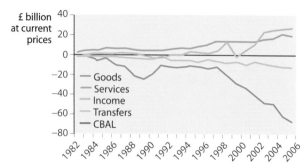

Figure 12.3 *The composition of the current account, 1982–2006 (balances)*
Source: IMF.

It is important to realise that the overall balance on the current account arises from combining the balances on all of these items. An overall current account deficit arises when the deficit items outweigh the surplus items in the accounts. Figure 12.3 clearly shows that it is the strong deficit on trade in goods that has resulted in the long-standing overall deficit.

Trade in goods (sometimes known as **visible trade**) has traditionally shown a deficit for the UK — it has shown a surplus in only 6 years since 1900. As reserves of oil in the North Sea run down, the UK is likely to become a net importer of oil, but up to 2004 it continued to be a net exporter of oil: in other words, the oil part of the trade in goods was in surplus. However, imports of cars and other consumer goods have persistently exceeded exports. A summary for 2006 is presented in Table 12.1, with data for 1996 also provided for comparison. You should be aware that these data are in current prices, so you need to focus on the relative sizes rather than the absolute values. It is interesting to note that in 2006, the only category of goods to show a surplus was chemicals. An important question is whether this needs to be a cause for concern for the UK economy. In order to evaluate this, it is important to consider the extent to which services can be relied upon to help to balance the deficit in trade in goods. In addition, the question of the long-term balance between the current account and the financial account is pertinent, as will be explained later in the chapter.

Item	2006	1996
Food, beverages and tobacco	−6,094	−14,016
Basic materials	−3,755	−2,994
Oil	4,810	−3,905
Coal, gas and electricity	−516	−2,843
Semi-manufactured goods:		
Chemicals	4,071	5,481
Precious stones and silver	−21	−1,139
Other	−5,537	−8,786
Finished manufactured goods:		
Motor cars	−2,528	−6,257
Other consumer goods	−5,271	−22,078
Intermediate goods	−3,757	−10,420
Capital goods	3,108	−14,082
Ships and aircraft	1,580	−1,821
Commodities not classified	188	−771
Total	**−13,722**	**−83,631**

Table 12.1 UK trade in goods (balances), 1996 and 2006 (£m in current prices)

Source: ONS.

Key terms

visible trade: trade in goods

invisible trade: trade in services

In fact, trade in services has recorded a surplus in every year since 1966. This is sometimes referred to as **invisible trade**. Table 12.2 shows the component items in 1996 and 2006 — again measured in current prices, so that no allowance has been made for the effects of inflation.

As you can see, the largest deficit items in trade in services are transportation (especially air transport services, which have shown a deficit every year since the mid-1980s) and travel, where again the deficit has grown significantly since the late 1980s. The main reason for this is the increasing number of UK residents travelling abroad. However, these negative items are more than compensated by the surplus components, especially financial services, which have grown steadily, as have computer and information services. You can see that 'other business' also makes a significant contribution. This category comprises trade-related services such as merchanting and consultancy services, which include advertising, engineering and legal services and operational leasing.

Item	2006	1996
Transportation	−1,001	−2,722
Travel	−2,951	−15,978
Communications	−283	290
Construction	53	129
Insurance	2,089	2,565
Financial	6,594	22,575
Computer and information	757	3,831
Royalties and licence fees	211	1,974
Other business	6,725	15,849
Personal, cultural and recreational	218	1,285
Government	−1,208	−604
Total	**11,204**	**29,194**

Table 12.2 *UK trade in services (balances), 1996 and 2006 (£m in current prices)*
Source: ONS.

An important item on the current account is investment income, which represents earnings on past investment abroad. This item has shown strong growth since 1999 (when there was a deficit). The largest item in this part of the account is earnings from direct investment, although there is also an element of portfolio investment − earnings from holdings of bonds and other securities. The final category is current transfers. This includes taxes and social contributions received from non-resident workers and businesses, bilateral aid flows and military grants. However, the largest item is transfers with EU institutions, which has been in persistent deficit.

In Figure 12.3 the size of the current account balance is shown in current prices. This is a bit misleading in considering the pattern over time. Figure 12.4 shows the size of the current account balance as a percentage of GDP. This is helpful because it removes the effects of prices changes, showing the size of the current account balance relative to GDP. A key question here is whether it is a question of concern to see these persistent deficits being sustained over long periods of time.

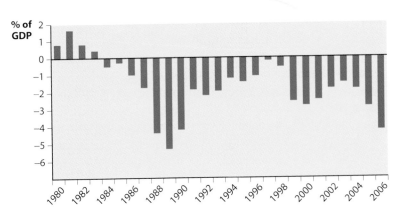

Figure 12.4
*The current
account of
the UK balance
of payments*

Source: ONS.

One perspective on this is to realise that a deficit on the current account must be balanced by a surplus on the financial and capital accounts. In the short run, it may be possible to finance the trade deficit by selling UK financial assets to foreigners or by borrowing from overseas. However, this might not be regarded as being desirable in the longer term, if this affects the overall ownership pattern of British assets. For this reason, the current account cannot be viewed in isolation from the rest of the balance of payments.

The financial account

The trend towards globalisation means that both inward and outward investment increased substantially during the 1990s, although there was a dip after 2000. However, Figure 12.2 shows that the financial account has been in strong surplus in the early part of the twenty-first century. This is in part forced by the deficit on the current account. In other words, if an economy runs a current account deficit, it can do so only by running a surplus on the financial account. Effectively, what is happening is that, in order to fund the current account deficit, the UK is selling assets to foreign investors and borrowing abroad.

An important question is whether this practice is sustainable in the long run. Selling assets or borrowing abroad have future implications for the current account, as there will be outflows of investment income and debt repayments in the future following today's financial surplus. It also has implications for interest rate policy. If the authorities hold interest rates high relative to the rest of the world, this will tend to attract inflows of investment, again with future implications for the current account.

The capital account

The capital account is relatively small. The largest item relates to the flows of capital associated with migration. If someone migrates to the UK, that person's status changes from being a non-resident to being a resident. His or her property then becomes part of the UK's assets and a transaction has to be entered in the balance of payments accounts. There are also some items relating to various EU transactions. This account has been in surplus for 20 years.

Summary

➤ The balance of payments is a set of accounts that contains details of the transactions that take place between the residents of an economy and the rest of the world.

➤ The accounts are divided into three sections: the current, financial and capital accounts.

➤ The current account identifies transactions in goods and services, together with some income payments and international transfers.

➤ The financial account measures transactions in financial assets, including investment flows and central government transactions in foreign reserves.

➤ The capital account, which is relatively small, contains capital transfers.

➤ The overall balance of payments must always be zero.

➤ The current account has been in persistent deficit since 1984, reflecting a deficit in trade in goods that is partly offset by a surplus in invisible trade.

➤ The financial account has been in strong surplus — as is required to balance the current account deficit.

Exercise 12.1

Allocate each of the following items to the current, financial or capital account and calculate the balances for each account. Check that (together with errors and omissions) the total is zero. All data refer to 2005, at current prices in £ billion.

a	Trade in goods	−68.79
b	Migrants' transfers	+1.94
c	Total net direct investment	+57.80
d	Investment income	+26.35
e	Current transfers	−12.01
f	Transactions in reserve assets	+0.43
g	Trade in services	+24.61
h	Other capital transfers	−0.45
I	Compensation of employees	−0.61
j	Net portfolio investment	−29.46
k	Other transactions in financial assets	+11.91
l	Errors and omissions	−11.95

The exchange rate and international competitiveness

Closely associated with the balance of payments is the **exchange rate** — the price of one currency in terms of another. The exchange rate is important because it influences the prices that domestic consumers must pay for imported goods, services and assets and also the price that

 Key *term*

exchange rate: the price of one currency in terms of another

foreigners pay for UK goods, services and assets. Chapter 4 introduced the notion of the demand and supply of foreign currency, shown in Figure 12.5. The demand for pounds arises from overseas residents (e.g. in the euro area) wanting to purchase UK goods, services or assets, whereas the supply of pounds emanates from domestic residents wanting to purchase overseas goods, services or assets. The connection is that the balance of payments accounts itemise these transactions, which entail the demand for and supply of pounds. Chapter 4 also pointed out that the demand for currency is a *derived demand* – thus pounds are demanded when people holding dollars or other currencies want to buy British. Similarly, pounds are supplied when people holding sterling want to buy foreign goods, services or assets.

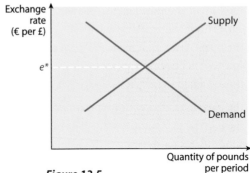

Figure 12.5
The market for pounds sterling

In analysing the balance of payments, the relative competitiveness of UK goods and services is an important issue. If the UK persistently shows a deficit on the current account, does that imply that UK goods are uncompetitive in international markets?

The demand for UK exports in world markets depends upon a number of factors. In some ways, it is similar to the demand for a good. In general, the demand for a good depends on its price, on the prices of other goods and on consumer incomes and preferences. In a similar way, you can think of the demand for UK exports as depending on the price of UK goods, the price of other countries' goods, incomes in the rest of the world and foreigners' preferences for UK goods over those produced elsewhere. However, in the case of international transactions the exchange rate is also relevant, as this determines the purchasing power of UK incomes in the rest of the world. Similarly, the demand for imports into the UK depends upon the relative prices of domestic and foreign goods, incomes in the UK, preferences for foreign and domestically produced goods and the exchange rate. These factors will all come together to determine the balance of demand for exports and imports.

The exchange rate plays a key role in influencing the levels of both imports and exports. Figure 12.6 shows the time path of the US$/£ exchange rate since 1971. It shows some fluctuations between 1971 and the late 1980s, around a declining trend. Since then the exchange rate seems to have remained fairly steady.

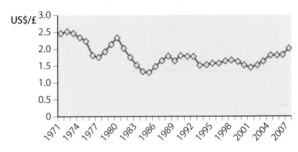

Figure 12.6
The nominal exchange rate, US$/£, 1971–2007
Source: Bank of England.

Nonetheless, there was a fall from a peak of $2.50 to the pound in 1972 to $1.50 some 30 years later. Other things being equal, this suggests an improvement in the competitiveness of UK products. In other words, Americans wanting to buy UK goods got more pounds for their dollars in 2002 than in 1972 and thus would have tended to find UK goods more attractive.

However, some care is needed because other things do not remain equal. In particular, remember that the competitiveness of UK goods in the US market depends not only on the exchange rate but also on movements in the prices of goods over time, so this needs to be taken into account — which is why Figure 12.6 refers to the *nominal exchange rate*. In other words, if the prices of UK goods have risen more rapidly than prices in the USA, this will have partly offset the downward movement in the exchange rate.

The exchange rate on the day the pound reached its highest rate against the dollar in 11 years

Figure 12.7 shows the nominal exchange rate again, but also the ratio of UK/US consumer prices (plotted using the right-hand scale). This reveals that between 1971 and 1977 UK prices rose much more steeply than those in the USA and continued to rise relative to the USA until the 1990s. Thus, the early decline in the nominal exchange rate was offset by the movement in relative prices.

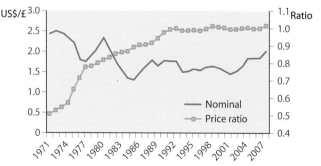

Figure 12.7 *The nominal exchange rate, US$/£, and the ratio of UK/US prices, 1971–2007*

Sources: Bank of England, IMF.

In order to assess the overall competitiveness of UK goods compared with the USA, it is necessary to calculate the **real exchange rate**, which is defined as the nominal exchange rate multiplied by the ratio of relative prices.

The real exchange rate is shown in Figure 12.8. The real exchange rate also shows some fluctuations, especially between about 1977 and 1989. However, there does not seem to be any strong trend to the series, although the real rate was higher at the end of the period than at the beginning.

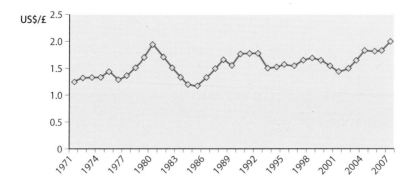

Figure 12.8 *The real exchange rate, US$/£, 1971–2007*
Source: calculated from data shown in Figure 12.7.

Notice that the series in Figure 12.8 relates only to competitiveness relative to the USA, as it is the real US$/£ exchange rate. An alternative measure is the sterling **effective exchange rate**, shown in Figure 12.9. This shows the strength of sterling relative to a weighted average of exchange rates of the UK's trading partners.

 Key terms

real exchange rate: the nominal exchange rate adjusted for differences in relative inflation rates between countries

effective exchange rate: the exchange rate for a country relative to a weighted average of currencies of its trading partners

Figure 12.9 *The sterling effective exchange rate, 1980–2007*
Source: ONS.

Exercise 12.2

Table 12.3 provides data for the €/£ exchange rate, together with the consumer price index for the euro area and for the UK. Use these data to calculate the real exchange rate for the period and comment on the effect that any movement will have had on the competitiveness of UK goods and services relative to the euro area.

	Nominal exchange rate (€/£)	Consumer price index (2000 = 100)	
		UK	Euro area
1998	1.4796	97.9	96.6
1999	1.5189	99.2	97.7
2000	1.6456	100.0	100.0
2001	1.6087	101.8	102.1
2002	1.5909	103.5	104.4
2003	1.4456	106.5	106.6
2004	1.4739	109.7	108.9
2005	1.4629	112.8	111.2

Table 12.3
Competitiveness of the UK compared to the euro area

Sources: OECD, IFS.

The exchange rate and the financial account

The discussion is still incomplete. The exchange rate is influenced by the demand and supply for sterling relative to other currencies, which reflects the demand from foreigners for UK goods, services and assets and the supply of pounds from UK residents wanting to buy foreign goods, services and assets. So far the discussion has focused on the current account — that is, on the demand and supply of goods and services. However, it is also important to be aware that international transactions in financial assets also influence (and are influenced by) the exchange rate.

Suppose that interest rates in the UK are high relative to those that prevail in the USA. American investors looking for a good return may be attracted by the prospect of investing in the UK, so there will thus tend to be an inflow of funds into the UK. This will then lead to an increase in the financial account surplus, helping to fund a current account deficit.

A further twist in the story is that if high interest rates do attract such financial inflows, this means that there is an increase in the demand for pounds, because foreign investors have to buy pounds in order to pay for the British assets that they want to acquire. This will then put upward pressure on the exchange rate, which in turn affects the international competitiveness of UK goods and services. There is therefore a link between movements in the exchange rate and the level of aggregate demand in the economy.

This close interrelationship between the current account, the financial account and the exchange rate is critical in the design of macroeconomic policy, which will be considered in the next chapter.

part 2

Summary

➤ The exchange rate is the price of one currency in terms of another.

➤ The level of the exchange rate is one influence on the competitiveness of British goods, services and assets in international markets, but this also depends upon relative prices in the UK and the rest of the world.

➤ The real exchange rate is a measure of the international competitiveness of an economy's goods.

➤ The effective exchange rate measures the relative strength of sterling compared with a weighted average of the exchange rates of the UK's trading partners.

➤ There is a complex, but important, interrelationship between the exchange rate and the current and financial accounts of the balance of payments.

Exercise 12.3

Discuss why the authorities may need to be aware of the balance of payments when designing macroeconomic policy.

Chapter 13
Macroeconomic policy objectives

Inevitably, there is a policy dimension to the study of the performance of the macroeconomy. Indeed, in evaluating such performance, it is the success of macroeconomic policy that is under scrutiny. However, the success of macroeconomic policy can be judged only if you are aware of what it is that the policy is trying to achieve. This chapter introduces and analyses the main objectives of policy at the macroeconomic level.

Learning outcomes

After studying this chapter, you should:
➤ be familiar with the principal objectives of macroeconomic policy
➤ understand the reasons for setting these policy objectives
➤ be aware of some potential obstacles that may inhibit the achievement of the targets
➤ appreciate that the targets may sometimes conflict with each other

Targets of policy

Chapter 9 introduced a number of ways in which economists try to monitor and evaluate the performance of the economy at the macroeconomic level. If macroeconomic performance is found to be wanting in some way, then it is reasonable to ask whether some policy intervention might improve the situation. This chapter considers aspects of the macroeconomy that might be regarded as legitimate targets for policy action. Chapter 15 analyses the policy actions that might be introduced, and evaluates their possible effectiveness.

Chapter 9 discussed some key measures of an economy's performance, particularly inflation, unemployment, the balance of payments and GDP; the significance of the balance of payments and the exchange rate was examined in Chapter 12. In addition, Chapter 8 raised questions about whether governments should be concerned about inequality of income distribution within a society. These are all policy questions that need to be addressed. Furthermore, there is a growing concern about the need to preserve the environment in which we live; Chapter 6 pointed out

that an externality element in connection with the environment may be a cause of market failure, and commented that there may be international externalities that need to be considered. As this issue has a macroeconomic dimension to it, it will also need to be analysed in conjunction with the discussion of macroeconomic policy. Each of these objectives will now be considered in turn.

Price stability

One of the most prominent objectives of macroeconomic policy in recent years has been the need to control inflation. Indeed, this has been at the heart of governments' stated policy objectives since 1976.

Causes of inflation

As we saw in Chapter 9, inflation occurs when there is a rise in the general price level. However, it is important to distinguish between a one-off increase in the price level and a sustained rise over a long period of time. For example, a one-off rise in the price of oil may have an effect on the price level by shifting aggregate supply, thus affecting the equilibrium price level — as shown in Figure 13.1 (reproducing Figure 11.7). However, this takes the economy to a new equilibrium price level, and if nothing else were to change, there would be no reason for prices to continue to rise beyond P_1.

Nonetheless, this is one reason why prices may begin to increase. Inflation thus may be initiated on the supply side of the macroeconomy, arising from an increase in the costs faced by firms. This is sometimes referred to as **cost-push inflation**, as the increase in the overall level of prices is cost-driven.

In terms of the AD/AS model, it is clear that an alternative explanation of a rise in the general price level could come from the demand side, where an increase in aggregate demand leads to a rise in prices, especially if the AS curve becomes so steep in the long run as to become vertical, as some macroeconomists believe. This is shown in Figure 13.2, where the increase in aggregate demand from AD_0 to AD_1 leads to a rise in the overall price level from P_0 to P_1 with no change at all in real output. An increase in the price level emanating from the demand side of the macro-economy is sometimes referred to as **demand-pull inflation**.

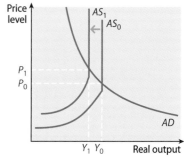

Figure 13.1 A supply shock

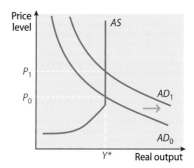

Figure 13.2 An increase in aggregate demand

Key terms

cost-push inflation: inflation initiated by an increase in the costs faced by firms, arising on the supply side of the economy

demand-pull inflation: inflation initiated by an increase in aggregate demand

But why should there be *persistent* increases in prices over time? One-off movements in either aggregate demand or aggregate supply may lead to one-off changes in the overall price level, but unless the movements continue in subsequent periods there is no reason to suppose that inflation will continue. One explanation is provided by changes in the supply of money circulating in an economy.

Persistent inflation can take place only when the **money stock** grows more rapidly than real output. This can be shown in terms of aggregate demand and aggregate supply. If the money supply increases, firms and households in the economy find they have excess cash balances: that is, for a given price level they have more purchasing power than they expected to have. Their impulse will thus be to increase their spending, which will cause the aggregate demand curve to move to the right. They will probably also save some of the excess, which will tend to result in lower interest rates — which will then reinforce the increase in aggregate demand. However, as the *AD* curve moves to the right, the equilibrium price level will rise, returning the economy to equilibrium.

Key *term*

money stock:
the quantity of money in the economy

If the money supply continues to increase, the process repeats itself, with prices then rising persistently. One danger of this is that people will get so accustomed to the process that they speed up their spending decisions, which simply accelerates the whole process.

To summarise, the analysis suggests that, although a price rise can be triggered on either the supply side or the demand side of the macroeconomy, persistent inflation can arise only through persistent excessive growth in the money stock, which can be seen in terms of persistent movements of the aggregate demand curve.

Prices continually change in every economy, normally upwards

Costs of inflation

A crucial question is why it matters if an economy experiences inflation. The answer is that very high inflation gives rise to a number of costs.

The fact that firms have to keep amending their price lists raises the costs of undertaking transactions. These costs are often known as the *menu costs* of inflation; however, this should not be expected to be significant unless inflation really is very

high. A second cost of very high inflation is that it discourages people from holding money because, at the very high nominal interest rates that occur when inflation is high, the opportunity cost of holding money becomes great. People therefore try to keep their money in interest-bearing accounts for as long as possible, even if it means making frequent trips to the bank — for which reason these are known as the *shoe leather costs* of inflation.

This reluctance to use money for transactions may inhibit the effectiveness of markets. For example, there was a period in the early 1980s when inflation in Argentina was so high that some city parking fines had to be paid in litres of petrol rather than in cash. Markets will not work effectively when people do not use money and the economy begins to slip back towards a barter economy. The situation may be worsened if taxes or pensions are not properly indexed so that they do not keep up with inflation.

However, these costs are felt mainly when inflation reaches the *hyperinflation* stage. This has been rare in developed countries in recent years, although many Latin American economies were prone to hyperinflation for a period in the 1980s, and some of the transition economies also went through very high inflation periods as they began to introduce market reforms; one example of this was the Ukraine, where inflation reached 10,000% per year in the early 1990s. Another example is the African country of Zimbabwe, where *The Economist* in February 2008 claimed that inflation had reached 150,000%.

However, there may be costs associated with inflation even when it does not reach these heights, especially if inflation is volatile. If the rate of change of prices cannot be confidently predicted by firms, the increase in uncertainty may be damaging, and firms may become reluctant to undertake the investment that would expand the economy's productive capacity.

Furthermore, as Chapter 5 emphasised, prices are very important in allocating resources in a market economy. Inflation may consequently inhibit the ability of prices to act as reliable signals in this process, leading to a wastage of resources and lost business opportunities.

It is these last reasons that have elevated the control of inflation to one of the central planks of UK government macroeconomic policy. However, it should be noticed that the target for inflation has not been set at zero. During the period when the inflation target was set in terms of RPIX (as explained in Chapter 9), the inflation target was 2.5%; from 2004 the target for CPI inflation was 2%. The reasoning here is twofold. One argument is that it has to be accepted that measured inflation will overstate actual inflation, partly because it is so difficult to take account of quality changes in products such as PCs, where it is impossible to distinguish accurately between a price change and a quality change. Second, wages and prices tend to be sticky in a downward direction: in other words, firms may be reluctant to lower prices and wages. A modest rate of inflation (e.g. 2%) thus allows relative prices to change more readily, with prices in some sectors rising by more than in others. This may help price signals to be more effective in guiding resource allocation.

Summary

➤ The control of inflation has been the major focus of macroeconomic policy in the UK since about 1976.

➤ Inflation can be initiated on either the supply side of an economy or the demand side.

➤ However, sustained inflation can take place only if there is also a sustained increase in money supply.

➤ High inflation imposes costs on society and reduces the effectiveness with which markets can work.

➤ Low inflation reduces uncertainty, and may encourage investment by firms.

Exercise 13.1

Suppose that next year inflation in the UK economy suddenly takes off, reaching 60% per annum — in other words, prices rise by 60% — but so do incomes. Discuss how this would affect your daily life. Why would it be damaging for the economy in the future?

Full employment

For an economy to be operating on the production possibility curve, the factors of production need to be fully employed. From society's point of view, surplus capacity in the economy represents waste. In the macroeconomic policy arena, attention in this context focuses on unemployment. For example, Figure 13.3 shows that it is possible for the economy to be in macroeconomic equilibrium at a level of output Y_1 that is below the potential full employment level at Y^*. This may be seen as an unnecessary waste of potential output. In addition, there may be a cost suffered by the people who are unemployed in this situation and who could have been productively employed.

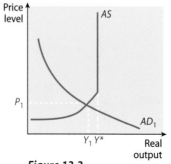

Figure 13.3
Macroeconomic equilibrium below full employment

Causes of unemployment

There will always be some unemployment in a dynamic economy. At any point in time, there will be workers transferring between jobs. Indeed, this needs to happen if the pattern of production is to keep up with changing patterns of consumer demand and relative opportunity cost. In other words, in a typical period of time there will be some sectors of an economy that are expanding and others that are in decline. It is crucial that workers are able to transfer from those activities that are in decline to those that are booming. Accordingly, there will be some unemployment while this transfer takes place, and this is known as **frictional unemployment**.

Key term

frictional unemployment: unemployment associated with job search: that is, people who are between jobs

In some cases, this transfer of workers between sectors may be quite difficult to accomplish. For example, coal mining may be on the decline in an economy, but international banking may be booming. It is clearly unreasonable to expect coal miners to turn themselves into international bankers overnight. In this sort of situation there may be some longer-term unemployment while workers retrain for new occupations and new sectors of activity. Indeed, there may be workers who find themselves redundant at a relatively late stage in their career and for whom the retraining is not worthwhile, or who cannot find firms that will be prepared to train them for a relatively short payback time. Such unemployment is known as **structural unemployment**. It arises because of the mismatch between the skills of workers leaving contracting sectors and the skills required by expanding sectors in the economy.

Figure 13.3 showed a different form of unemployment, one that arises because the economy is trapped in an equilibrium position that is below full employment. This is sometimes referred to as **demand-deficient unemployment** — and a solution to it might be to boost aggregate demand. This possibility will be discussed in Chapter 15.

A further reason for unemployment concerns the level of wages. Figure 13.4 shows a labour market in which a free market equilibrium would have wage W^* and quantity of labour L^*. If for some reason wages were set at W_0, there would be disequilibrium between labour supply (at L_s) and labour demand (at L_d). Expressing this in a different way, here is a situation in which there are more workers seeking employment at the going wage (L_s) than there are firms prepared to hire at that wage (L_d). The difference is unemployment.

Key terms

structural unemployment: unemployment arising because of changes in the pattern of economic activity within an economy

demand-deficient unemployment: unemployment that arises because of a deficiency of aggregate demand in the economy, so that the equilibrium level of output is below full employment

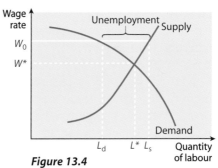
Figure 13.4
Unemployment in a labour market

There are a number of reasons why this situation might arise. Trade unions may have been able to use their power and influence to raise wages above the equilibrium level, thereby ensuring higher wages for their members who remain in employment, but denying jobs to others. Alternatively, it could be argued that wages will be inflexible downwards. Thus, a supply shock that reduced firms' demand for labour could leave wages above the equilibrium, and they may adjust downwards only slowly. Chapter 8 mentioned that in some situations the imposition of a minimum wage in a low-wage competitive labour market could also have the effect of institutionally setting the wage rate above its equilibrium level.

Finally, if unemployment benefits are set at a relatively high level compared with wages in low-paid occupations, some people may choose not to work, thereby creating some **voluntary unemployment**. From the point of view of those individuals, they are making a rational choice on the basis of the options open to them. From society's point of view, however, there needs to be a balance between providing appropriate social protection for those unable to obtain jobs and trying to make the best use of available resources for the benefit of society as a whole.

Costs of unemployment

The costs of unemployment were mentioned earlier. From society's perspective, if the economy is operating below full capacity, then it is operating within the production possibility curve, and therefore is not making the best possible use of society's resources. In other words, if those unemployed workers were in employment, society would be producing more aggregate output; the economy would be operating more efficiently overall.

Furthermore, there may be costs from the perspective of prospective workers, in the sense that **involuntary unemployment** carries a cost to each such individual in terms of forgone earnings and the need to rely on social security support. At the same time, the inability to find work and to contribute to the family budget may impose a cost in terms of personal worth and dignity.

 terms

voluntary unemployment: situation arising when an individual chooses not to accept a job at the going wage rate

involuntary unemployment: situation arising when an individual who would like to accept a job at the going wage rate is unable to find employment

Summary

➤ Full employment occurs when an economy is operating on the production possibility curve, with full utilisation of factors of production.

➤ An economy operating below full capacity is characterised by unemployment.

➤ Some unemployment in a dynamic economy is inevitable, as people may have to undergo short spells of unemployment while between jobs — this is known as frictional unemployment.

➤ Structural unemployment occurs when there is a mismatch between the skills that workers have to offer and the skills that employers want. This occurs when the economy is undergoing structural change, with some sectors expanding and some contracting.

➤ Demand-deficient unemployment may occur if the macroeconomy is in equilibrium below full employment.

➤ If wages are held above the equilibrium level — for example, by minimum wage legislation or trade union action — then unemployment may occur.

➤ High levels of unemployment benefit may encourage some workers not to accept jobs as the opportunity cost of not working is low.

Exercise 13.2

Classify each of the following types of unemployment as arising from frictional, structural, demand-deficient or other causes, and decide whether they are voluntary or involuntary:

a unemployment arising from a decline of the coal mining sector and the expansion of financial services

b a worker leaving one job to search for a better one

c unemployment that arises because the real wage rate is held above the labour market equilibrium

d unemployment arising from slow adjustment to a fall in aggregate demand

e unemployment arising because workers find that low-paid jobs are paying less than can be obtained in unemployment benefit

The balance of payments

Lists of macroeconomic policy objectives invariably include equilibrium on the balance of payments as a key item. Unlike inflation and unemployment, it is not so obvious why disequilibrium in the balance of payments is a problem that warrants policy action.

Figure 13.5 shows the market for pounds relative to euros. Here the demand for pounds arises from residents in the euro area wanting to buy UK goods, services and assets, whereas the supply arises from UK residents wanting to buy goods, services and assets from the euro area. If the exchange rate is at its equilibrium level, this implies that the demand for pounds (i.e. the foreign demand for UK goods, services and assets) is equal to the supply of pounds (i.e. the domestic demand for goods, services and assets from the euro area).

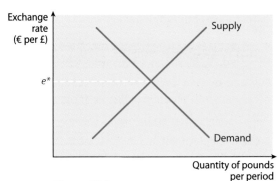

Figure 13.5
The market for pounds sterling

In a free foreign exchange market, the exchange rate can be expected to adjust in order to bring about this equilibrium position. Even under a fixed exchange rate system in which the government pledges to hold the exchange rate at a particular level, any discrepancy between the demand and supply of pounds would have to be met by the monetary authorities buying or selling foreign exchange reserves. Thus, the overall balance of payments is always in equilibrium. So why might there be a problem?

The problem arises not with the *overall* balance of payments, but with an imbalance between components of the balance of payments. In particular, attention focuses on the balance of the current account, which shows the balance in the trade in goods and services together with investment income flows and current transfers.

If the current account is in deficit, UK residents are purchasing more in imports of goods and services than the economy is exporting. In other words, UK earnings from exports are not sufficient to pay for UK imports. This is a bit like a household spending beyond its income, which can be sustained only by selling assets or by borrowing.

The concern for the economy is that a large and sustained deficit on the current account implies that the financial account must be in a large and sustained surplus. This in turn means that the UK is effectively exporting assets. And this means that overseas residents are buying up UK assets, which in turn may mean a leakage of investment income in the future. Alternatively, overall balance could be achieved through the sale of foreign exchange reserves. This soaks up the excess supply of pounds that arises because UK residents are supplying more pounds in order to buy imports than overseas residents are demanding in order to buy UK exports.

However the current account deficit is financed, a large deficit cannot be sustained indefinitely. This begs the question of what is meant by a 'large' deficit. Figure 12.4 showed the current account balance as a percentage of GDP, which gives some idea of the relative magnitude of the deficit. This shows that, although the current account has been in deficit every year since 1984, the deficit has been less than 3% of GDP since 1990. This might be regarded as tolerable.

A critical issue is whether UK assets remain attractive to foreign buyers. Running a sustained deficit on current account requires running a surplus on financial account. If foreign buyers of UK assets become reluctant to buy, UK interest rates might have to rise in order to make UK assets more attractive. A by-product of this would be a curb in spending by UK firms and consumers. Given that part of this reduction in spending would have an impact on imports, this would begin to reduce the current account deficit.

One way in which the balance of payments is important from a policy perspective occurs when a government wishes to stimulate the economy, perhaps because it regards the level of unemployment as being excessive. An expansionary policy may be intended to increase domestic aggregate demand. However, in designing such a policy it is vital to remember that some of the increased demand will go not on domestic goods, but on imports, which is likely to dilute the effect of the expansion.

A major concern during the early years of the twenty-first century has been the large and persistent current account deficit being run by the US economy. This has been associated in part with the sizeable government spending of the Bush administration, which was forecast to reach a level that could have global repercussions.

Causes of a deficit on current account

In Chapter 12 it was argued that the quantity of exports of goods and services from the UK depends partly on income levels in the rest of the world and partly on the competitiveness of UK goods and services, which in turn depends partly on the sterling exchange rate and partly on relative price levels in the UK and elsewhere. Similarly, the level of imports depends partly on domestic income and partly on the international competitiveness of UK and foreign goods and services.

This suggests that a fundamental cause of a deficit on the current account is a lack of competitiveness of UK goods and services, arising from an overvalued exchange rate or from high relative prices of UK goods and services. Alternatively, UK incomes may be rising more rapidly than those in the rest of the world.

Summary

➤ If the exchange rate is free to reach its equilibrium value, the overall balance of payments will always be zero.

➤ However, a deficit on the current account of the balance of payments must always be balanced by a corresponding surplus on the financial account.

➤ A persistent deficit on the current account means that in the long run domestic assets are being sold to overseas buyers, or that foreign exchange reserves are being run down. Neither situation can be sustained in the long run.

➤ A key cause of a deficit on the current account is the lack of competitiveness of domestic goods and services.

Economic growth

If the ultimate aim of a society is to improve the well-being of its citizens, then in economic terms this means that the resources available within the economy need to expand through time in order to widen people's choices. This requires a process of economic growth, which as we saw in Chapter 1 is an increase in the productive capacity of the economy.

From a theoretical point of view, economic growth can be thought of as an expansion of the productive capacity of an economy. If you like, it is an expansion of the potential output of the economy.

Wide choice for high-street shoppers is a sign of economic growth

This is such an important policy objective for an economy that the whole of Chapter 14 is devoted to it. For now, note that the nearest measure that economists have of the resources available to members of a society is GDP; so in looking for economic growth, they are looking for sustained growth in GDP over time.

In many ways, economic growth may be regarded as the most fundamental of all macroeconomic policy objectives, with other policy objectives being subsidiary to it. For example, one of the key reasons for maintaining low inflation is to encourage firms to undertake investment — because this enables economic growth. Maintaining full employment ensures the best possible use of a society's resources, enabling it to reach the production possibility curve — and failure to do this may have indirect consequences for economic curve. Running a sustained current account deficit on the balance of payments that requires the sale of UK assets may limit the future growth prospects of the economy.

Concern for the environment

International externalities pose problems for policy design because they require coordination across countries. If pollution caused by the UK manufacturing sector causes acid rain elsewhere in Europe, the UK is imposing costs on other countries that are not fully reflected in market prices. Furthermore, there may be effects that cross generations. If the environment today is damaged, it may not be enjoyed by future generations — in other words, there may be intergenerational externality effects.

There is a macroeconomic dimension to these issues. If policy were only designed to achieve economic growth, regardless of the consequences for the environment, these externality effects could be severe, and for this reason they cannot be tackled solely at the microeconomic level of individual markets.

Income redistribution

The final macroeconomic policy objective to be considered concerns attempts to influence the distribution of income within a society. This may entail transfers of income between groups in society — that is, from richer to poorer — in order to protect the latter. Income redistribution may work through progressive taxation (whereby those on high incomes pay a higher proportion of their income in tax) or through a system of social security benefits such as the Jobseeker's Allowance or Income Support.

Causes of inequality

Some degree of inequality in the income distribution within a society is inevitable. People have different innate talents and abilities, and choose to undergo different types and levels of education and training, such that they acquire different sets of skills. Market forces imply that different payments will be made to people in different sectors of economic activity and different occupations. Income inequality also arises because of inequality in the ownership of assets. However, people in

identical circumstances and with identical skills and abilities *may* receive identical income. This notion is sometimes known as *horizontal equity*, which most people would agree is desirable.

One category of policy measures is designed to encourage horizontal equity. Equal opportunities legislation tries to ensure that members of society do not suffer discrimination that might deny them equal pay for equal work, or equal access to employment. Nonetheless, there remain significant differences in earnings and employment between ethnic groups and between men and women.

Equal opportunities legislation tries to ensure equal pay for equal work

Setting this aside, the key question remaining is the extent to which the government needs to intervene at the macroeconomic level in order to influence the distribution of income and protect vulnerable groups by redistributing from richer to poorer. Indeed, are there economic effects of inequality suggesting that redistribution of income is needed for reasons other than the purely humanitarian objective of alleviating poverty and protecting the vulnerable?

The costs of inequality

In a society where there is substantial inequality in the distribution of income, there are likely to be groups of people who are disadvantaged in various ways: for example, they may find it more difficult to obtain education for themselves or for their children. In the UK it remains the case that a lower proportion of students from low-income families go to university. It may also be that some potential entrepreneurs find it more difficult to obtain the credit needed to launch their business ideas.

If this is so, it suggests that there are people in society who are inhibited from developing their productive potential – which in turn implies that economic growth in the future will be lower than it might be. This could provide a justification for redistributing income – or at least for trying to ensure that there is equality of opportunity for all members of society. However, it might be argued that redistribution can be taken too far. If the higher-income groups in society face too high a marginal tax rate on their income – in other words, if additions to income are very heavily taxed for the rich – this could remove their incentive to exploit income-earning opportunities, which could have a damaging impact on economic growth.

Too much inequality may also lead to high crime rates and social discontent, which in turn may lead to political instability in a society. This could affect the security of property rights and inhibit economic growth.

There is some evidence that inequality has been widening in many countries in recent years. In particular, the way that technology has been progressing places a higher premium on skills, so that the gap between the earnings of skilled and unskilled workers has been widening.

Policy conflicts

In evaluating these policy options, it is important to realise that there may sometimes be potential conflicts and trade-offs between the targets. For example, a policy that pursued full employment, perhaps through increasing government expenditure, might endanger the achievement of price stability. The pursuit of economic growth may need to be tempered by the need to conserve the environment.

Summary

➤ Economic growth is the most important long-run macroeconomic policy objective, as this enables improvements in the well-being of society's citizens.

➤ However, there may be a need to moderate the pursuit of economic growth in order to protect the environment.

➤ Macroeconomic policy may also encompass the redistribution of income within society, on grounds of equity and also because extreme inequality may inhibit economic growth.

Exercise 13.3

Discuss which of the objectives of macroeconomic policy *you* think to be of most importance.

Chapter 14
Economic growth

One of society's prime responsibilities is to provide a reasonable standard of living for its citizens and to promote their well-being. Hence one of the major objectives for economic policy in the long run is to enable improvements in well-being, and in order to do this it is first necessary to expand the resources available within society. A key element in this process is to achieve economic growth, which is the subject of this chapter. However, there may be more to well-being than just growth, and the chapter also explores some of the limitations of a strategy that aims to maximise GDP growth.

Learning outcomes

After studying this chapter, you should:

➤ be able to understand the meaning of economic growth and productivity
➤ be familiar with factors that can affect the rate of economic growth, in particular the role of investment
➤ appreciate the strengths and weaknesses of GDP as a measure of the standard of living in comparisons across time and between countries
➤ be aware of differences in growth rates between countries and of the explanations that have been advanced to explain them
➤ evaluate the importance to a society of economic growth and the costs that such growth may impose
➤ understand the meaning and significance of sustainable growth

Defining economic growth

From a theoretical point of view, **economic growth** can be thought of as an expansion of the productive capacity of an economy. If you like, it is an expansion of the potential output of the economy.

 Key *term*

economic growth: the expansion of the productive capacity of an economy

There are two ways in which this has been presented in earlier chapters. The first is in terms of the production possibility curve (*PPC*), which was introduced in Chapter 1. Figure 14.1 is a reminder, and reproduces Figure 1.4, where economic growth was characterised as an outward movement of the production possibility curve from PPC_0 to PPC_1. In other words, economic growth enables a society to produce more goods and services in any given period as a result of an expansion in its resources.

A second way of thinking about economic growth is to use the *AD/AS* model introduced in Chapters 10 and 11. In Figure 14.2, an increase in the skills of the workforce will enable firms to produce more output at any given price, so that the aggregate supply curve will shift outwards from AS_0 to AS_1. This entails an increase in full employment output (or capacity output) from Y^* to Y^{**}. This again can be characterised as economic growth. Chapter 15 investigates policies that might be introduced to affect aggregate supply. In this chapter the focus is on a broader perspective within which long-run growth can be achieved.

If economists try to measure economic growth using the rate of change of GDP as an indicator, they are not necessarily measuring what they want to. GDP growth measures the *actual* rate of change of output rather than the growth of the *potential* output capacity of the economy.

In Figure 14.3, a movement from *A* to *B* represents a move to the *PPC*. This is an increase in actual output resulting from using up surplus capacity in the economy, but it is *not* economic growth in our theoretical sense, as moving from *A* to *B* does not entail an increase in productive capacity. On the other hand, a movement of the *PPC* itself, enabling the move from *B* to *C*, *does* represent economic growth. However, when economists observe a change in GDP they cannot easily distinguish between the two sorts of effect, especially if the economy is subject to a business cycle — in other words if the economy is not always operating at full capacity. It is therefore better to think of economic growth in terms of the underlying trend rate of growth of real GDP.

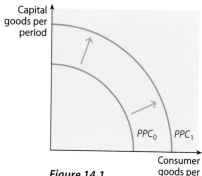

Figure 14.1
Economic growth

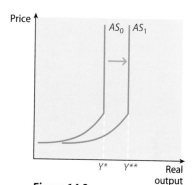

Figure 14.2
A shift in aggregate supply

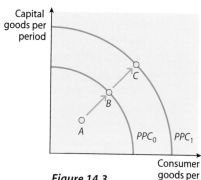

Figure 14.3
Economic growth?

Figure 14.4 helps to illustrate this. It shows the annual growth rate of real GDP in the UK since 1949. You can see that it is quite difficult to determine the underlying trend because the year-to-year movements are so volatile. Figure 14.5 takes 5-yearly average growth rates over the same period, with the horizontal red line showing the underlying trend rate of growth.

Figure 14.4
Growth of real GDP 1949–2007 (% change over previous year)
Source: ONS.

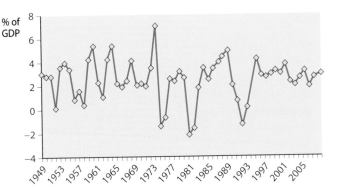

Figure 14.5
Average annual growth rates in the UK since 1950

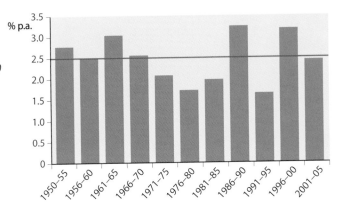

Sources of economic growth

At a basic level, production arises from the use of factors of production — capital, labour, entrepreneurship and so on. Capacity output is reached when all factors of production are fully and efficiently utilised. From this perspective, an increase in capacity output can come either from an increase in the quantity of the factors of production, or from an improvement in their efficiency or productivity. **Productivity** is a measure of the efficiency of a factor of production. For example, **labour productivity** measures output per worker, or output per hour worked. The latter is the more helpful measure, as clearly total output is affected by the number of hours worked, which does vary somewhat across countries. **Capital productivity** measures output per unit of capital.

 terms

productivity: measure of the efficiency of a factor of production

labour productivity: measure of output per worker, or output per hour worked

capital productivity: measure of output per unit of capital

Total factor productivity refers to the average productivity of all factors, measured as the total output divided by the total amount of inputs used.

An increase in productivity raises aggregate supply and the potential capacity output of an economy, and thus contributes to economic growth.

Capital

Capital is a critical factor in the production process. An increase in capital input is thus one source of economic growth. In order for capital to accumulate and increase the capacity of the economy to produce, **investment** needs to take place.

Notice that in economics 'investment' is used in this specific way. In common parlance the term is sometimes used to refer to investing in shares or putting money into a deposit account at the bank. Do not confuse these different concepts. In economics 'investment' relates to a firm buying new capital, such as machinery or factory buildings. If you put money into a bank account, that is an act of saving, not investment.

In the national accounts, the closest measurement that economists have to investment is 'Gross Fixed Capital Formation'. This covers net additions to the capital stock, but it also includes **depreciation**. Some of the machinery and other capital purchased by firms is to replace old, worn-out capital, i.e. to offset depreciation. It does not therefore represent an addition to capital stock. As depreciation cannot be observed easily, the convention in the accounts is to measure gross investment (i.e. including depreciation) and then make an adjustment for depreciation to arrive at **net investment**.

Capital stock includes machinery, a critical factor in the production process

Figure 14.6 shows the time path for gross investment in the UK since 1950, expressed as a percentage of GDP. You can see that the share of investment in GDP has fluctuated a little over the years, but it has settled at about 17% in recent years, which is relatively high by historical standards.

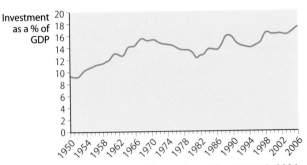

Figure 14.6 *Gross fixed capital formation in the UK, 1950–2006*
Source: ONS.

The choice that any society makes here is between using resources for current consumption and using resources for investment. Investment thus entails sacrificing present consumption in order to have more resources available in the future.

Different countries give investment very different priorities. Something of this can be seen in Figure 14.7, which shows gross capital formation in a selection of countries around the world. The diversity is substantial, ranging from just 12% in Côte d'Ivoire to 41% in China. Given this high rate of investment, it is perhaps not surprising to discover that China is among the fastest growing economies in the world in the early twenty-first century — but it must also be remembered that there is a cost to this, as it means sacrificing present consumption in China.

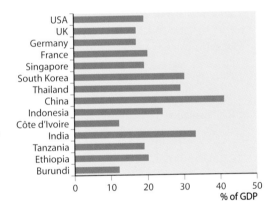

Figure 14.7 *Gross capital formation, selected countries, 2006 (% of GDP)*
Note: countries are in descending order of GNI per capita.
Source: *World Development Report 2008*.

The contribution of capital to growth is reinforced by technological progress, as the productivity of new capital is greater than that of old capital that is being phased out. For example, the speed and power of computers has increased enormously over recent years, which has had a great impact on productivity. Effectively, this means that technology is increasing the contribution that investment can make towards enlarging capacity output in an economy.

Innovation can also contribute, through the invention of new forms of capital and new ways of using existing capital, both of which can aid economic growth.

Labour
Capital has sometimes been seen as the main driver of growth, but labour too has a key contribution to make. There is little point in installing a lot of high-tech equipment unless there is the skilled labour to operate it.

There is relatively little scope for increasing the size of the labour force in a country, except through international migration. (Encouraging population growth is a rather long-term policy.) Nonetheless, the size of the workforce does contribute to the size of capacity output. A number of sub-Saharan African countries have seen this effect in reverse in recent years, with the impact of HIV/AIDS. The spread of this epidemic has had a devastating impact in a number of countries in the region; in some countries the percentage of adults affected is over 30% — nearly 40% in Botswana. This has a serious impact on capacity output, because the disease affects people of working age disproportionately, diminishing the size of the workforce and the productivity of workers.

The quality of labour input is more amenable to policy action. Education and training can improve the productivity of workers, and can be regarded as a form of investment in **human capital**.

Chapter 6 discussed how education and healthcare may have associated externalities. In particular, individuals may not perceive the full social benefits associated with education, training and certain kinds of healthcare, and thus may choose to invest less in these forms of human capital than is desirable from the perspective of society as a whole. Another such externality is the impact of human capital formation on economic growth as a justification for viewing education and healthcare as being merit goods — which were discussed in Chapter 7.

 term

human capital:
the stock of skills and expertise that contribute to a worker's productivity; can be increased through education and training

For many developing countries, the provision of healthcare and improved nutrition can be seen as additional forms of investment in human capital, since such investment can lead to future improvements in productivity.

Summary

➤ Economic growth is the expansion of an economy's productive capacity.

➤ This can be envisaged as a movement outwards of the production possibility curve, or as a rightward shift of the aggregate supply curve.

➤ Economic growth can be seen as the underlying trend rate of growth in real GDP.

➤ Economic growth can stem from an increase in the inputs of factors of production, or from an improvement in their productivity, i.e. the efficiency with which factors of production are utilised.

➤ Investment contributes to growth by increasing the capital stock of an economy, although some investment is to compensate for depreciation.

➤ The contribution of capital is reinforced by the effects of technological progress.

➤ Labour is another critical factor of production that can contribute to economic growth; for instance, education and training can improve labour productivity. This is a form of human capital formation.

Exercise 14.1

Which of the following represent genuine economic growth, and which may just mean a move to the PPC?

a   an increase in the rate of change of potential output

b   a fall in the unemployment rate

c   improved work practices that increase labour productivity

d   an increase in the proportion of the population joining the labour force

e   an increase in the utilisation of capital

f   a rightward shift in the aggregate supply curve

GDP and growth

Chapter 9 introduced GDP as a way of measuring the total output of an economy over a period of time. Although this measure can provide an indicator of the quantity of resources available to citizens of a country in a given period, as an assessment of the standard of living it has its critics.

GDP does have some things going for it. First, it is relatively straightforward and thus is widely understood. Second, it is a well-established indicator and one that is available for almost every country in the world, so that it can be used to compare income levels across countries. For this purpose, it naturally helps to adjust for population size by calculating GDP per person (GDP *per capita*, as it is known). This then provides a measure of average income per head.

Figure 14.8 provides data on GDP per capita for the same countries that appeared in Figure 14.7. The extreme differences that exist around the globe are immediately apparent from the data. GDP per capita in Burundi was just $100 in 2006, whereas in the USA the figure was $44,970. Luxembourg heads this particular league table, with average income of $76,040 in 2006.

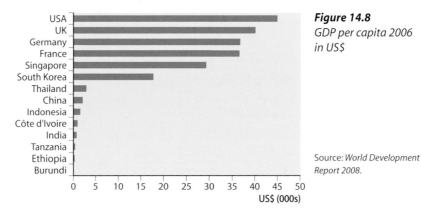

Figure 14.8
GDP per capita 2006 in US$

Source: *World Development Report 2008.*

In trying to interpret these data, there are a number of issues that need to be borne in mind, as the comparison is not as straightforward as it looks.

OCR AS Economics

Inequality in income distribution

One important point to notice is that looking at the average level of income per person may be misleading if there are wide differences in the way in which income is distributed within countries. In other words, it cannot be assumed that every person living in Burundi receives $100, or that every Luxembourgian receives $76,040. If income is more unequally distributed in some countries, this will affect one's perception of what the term 'average' means. For example, Brazil and Bulgaria had similar GDP per capita levels in 2006, but the income distribution in Bulgaria was far more equitable than in Brazil.

The informal sector and the accuracy of data

A further problem with undertaking international comparisons is that it is never absolutely certain that the accuracy with which data are collected is consistent across countries. Definitions of GDP and other variables are now set out in a clear, internationally agreed form, but even when countries are working to the same definitions, some data collection agencies may be more reliable than others.

One particular area in which this is pertinent relates to the informal sector. In every economy there are some transactions that go unrecorded. In most economies, there are economic activities that take place that cannot be closely monitored because of their informal nature. This is especially prevalent in many developing countries, where often substantial amounts of economic activity take place without an exchange of money. For example, in many countries subsistence agriculture remains an important facet of economic life. If households are producing food simply for their own consumption, there is no reason for a money transaction to take place with regard to its production, and thus such activity will not be recorded as a part of GDP. Equally, much economic activity within the urban areas of less-developed countries comes under the category of the 'informal sector'.

In many developing countries, substantial economic activity may take place without an exchange of money.

Where such activity varies in importance between countries, comparing incomes on the basis of measured GDP may be misleading, as GDP will be a closer indicator of the amount of real economic activity in some countries than in others.

Exchange rate problems

The data presented in Figure 14.8 were expressed in terms of US dollars. This allows economists to compare average incomes using a common unit of measurement. At the same time, however, it may create some problems.

Economists want to compare average income levels so that they can evaluate the standard of living, and compare standards across countries. In other words, it is important to be able to assess people's command over resources in different societies, and to be able to compare the purchasing power of income in different countries.

GDP is calculated initially in terms of local currencies, and subsequently converted into US dollars using official exchange rates. Will this provide information about the relative local purchasing power of incomes? Not necessarily.

One reason for this is that official exchange rates are sometimes affected by government intervention. Indeed, in many of the less-developed countries exchange rates are pegged to an international currency — usually the US dollar. In these circumstances exchange rates are more likely to reflect the government's policy and actions than the relative purchasing power of incomes in the countries under scrutiny.

Where exchange rates are free to find their own equilibrium level, exchange rates are likely to be influenced strongly by the price of internationally traded goods — which is likely to be a very different combination of goods than that typically consumed by residents in these countries. Again, it can be argued that the official exchange rates may not be a good reflection of the relative purchasing power of incomes across countries.

The United Nations International Comparison Project has been working on this problem for many years. It now produces an alternative set of international estimates of GDP based on purchasing power parity (PPP) exchange rates, which are designed to reflect the relative purchasing power of incomes in different societies more accurately. Figure 14.9 shows estimates for the same set of countries.

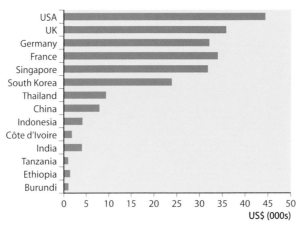

Figure 14.9
GDP per capita 2006 in PPP$

Source: *World Development Report 2008.*

OCR AS Economics

Comparing this with Figure 14.8, you will notice that the gap between the low-income and high-income countries seems less marked when PPP dollars are used as the unit of measurement. In other words, the US dollar estimates exaggerate the gap in living standards between rich and poor countries. This is a general feature of these measurements — that measurements in US dollars tend to understate real incomes for low-income countries and overstate them for high-income countries compared with PPP-dollar data. Put another way, people in the lower-income countries have a stronger command over goods and services than is suggested by US-dollar comparisons of GDP per capita. You can also see that the relative rankings of countries in PPP dollars are different in some cases — for example, compare India with Côte d'Ivoire.

Social indicators

A final question that arises is whether GDP can be regarded as a reasonable indicator of a country's standard of living. You have seen that GDP provides an indicator of the total resources available within an economy in a given period, calculated from data about total output, total incomes or total expenditure. This focus on summing the transactions that take place in an economy over a period can be seen as a rather narrow view of what constitutes the 'standard of living'. After all, it may be argued that the quality of people's lives depends on more things than simply the material resources that are available.

For one thing, people need to have knowledge if they are to make good use of the resources that are available. Two societies with similar income levels may nonetheless provide very different quality of life for their inhabitants, depending on the education levels of the population. Furthermore, if people are to benefit from consuming or using the available resources, they need a reasonable lifespan coupled with good health. So, good standards of health are also crucial to a good quality of life.

It is important to remember that different societies tend to set different priorities on the pursuit of growth and the promotion of education and health. This needs to be taken into account when judging relative living standards through a comparison of GDP per capita, as some countries have higher-than-average levels of health and education as compared with other countries with similar levels of GDP per capita.

A reasonable environment in which to live may be seen as another important factor in one's quality of life, and there may be a trade-off between economic growth and environmental standards.

There are some environmental issues that can distort the GDP measure of resources. Suppose there is an environmental disaster — perhaps an oil tanker breaks up close to a beautiful beach. This reduces the overall quality of life by degrading the landscape and preventing enjoyment of the beach. However, it does not have a negative effect on GDP; on the contrary, the money spent on clearing up the damage actually adds to GDP, so that the net effect of an environmental disaster may be to *increase* the measured level of GDP!

Summary

➤ GDP is a widely used measure of the total amount of economic activity in an economy over a period of time.

➤ The trend rate of change of GDP may thus be an indicator of economic growth.

➤ GDP is a widely understood and widely available measure, but it does have some drawbacks.

➤ Average GDP per person neglects the important issue of income distribution.

➤ There may be variation in the effectiveness of data collection agencies in different countries, and variation in the size of the informal sector.

➤ Converting from a local currency into US dollars may distort the use of GDP as a measure of the purchasing power of local incomes.

➤ GDP may neglect some important aspects of the quality of life.

Exercise 14.2

Below are some indicators for two countries, A and B. Discuss the extent to which GDP (here measured in PPP$) provides a good indication of relative living standards in the two countries. (All data are for 2005. Data are taken from the *Human Development Report 2006*.)

	Country A	Country B
GDP per capita (PPP$)	10,276	11,192
Life expectancy (in years at birth)	73.4	47.0
Adult literacy rate (%)	88.7	82.4
People living with HIV/AIDS (% of adults aged 15–49)	0.5	18.8
Infant mortality rate (per 1,000 live births)	12	54
% of population living on less than $1 per person per day	2.0	10.7

Discuss what other indicators might be useful in this evaluation.

Economic growth: international experience

The growth performance of different regions around the world has shown contrasting patterns in recent years. As early as the 1950s, a gap had opened up between the early developing countries in North America, Western Europe and Japan and the late developers in sub-Saharan Africa and Latin America.

Between 1960 and 1980 this gap began to widen, except for a small group of countries, mainly in East Asia, that had begun to close it. Figure 14.10 gives some data for countries in different regions. Tanzania and Ethiopia (in sub-Saharan Africa), together with Sri Lanka and India (in South Asia) grew relatively slowly in this period, with only Sri Lanka achieving an average growth rate above 2% per annum. Latin America showed a diverse experience: the examples shown in the figure are Colombia, which grew at about 3% per annum, and Brazil, which achieved growth of above 5% per annum. However, East Asia (represented here by

South Korea and Singapore) took off during this period, growing at an average rate of 7% per year and more, achieved partly through exporting to world markets. Japan also grew rapidly at this time, while the UK and the USA grew at a more sedate pace of just above 2% per annum.

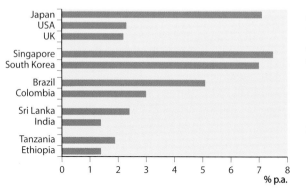

Figure 14.10
Growth of GDP per capita, selected countries, 1960–1980

Sources: World Bank, *World Development Report 1982.*

Figure 14.11 presents some more recent data, this time by region, for the period 1975–2005 (and for 1990–2005). This reveals some important patterns. The high-income OECD member countries continued to grow at a rather sedate rate of around 2% per annum, and less in the 1990s. Countries in East Asia and the Pacific maintained their impressive high growth of nearly 6% per annum, but again slowed a bit in the 1990s. South Asia showed some improvement, and even accelerated in the 1990s, as indeed did Latin America and the Caribbean. However, sub-Saharan African countries went through a dismal period in which their GDP per capita growth was negative – in other words, GDP per capita was lower in 2005 than it had been in 1975. This is serious indeed.

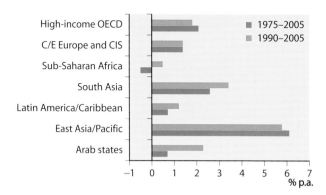

Figure 14.11
Growth of GDP per capita

Note: data represent growth rates of real GDP per capita measured in local currency.
Source: UNDP.

The importance of economic growth

Expanding the availability of resources in an economy enables the standard of living of the country to increase. For developing countries this may facilitate the easing of poverty, and may allow investment in human capital that will improve standards of living further in the future. In the industrial economies, populations have come to expect steady improvements in incomes and resources.

Thus for any society economic growth is likely to be seen as a fundamental objective – perhaps even the most important one. As was argued in Chapter 13, other policy objectives may be regarded as subsidiary to the growth target. In other words, the control of inflation, the maintenance of full employment and the achievement of stability in the current account of the balance of payments are all seen as important short-run objectives, because their achievement facilitates long-run economic growth.

In some less-developed countries the perspective may be different, and there has been a long-running debate about whether a society in its early stages of development should devote its resources to achieving the growth objective or to catering for basic needs. By making economic growth the prime target of policy, it may be necessary in the short run to allow inequality of incomes to continue, in order to provide the incentives for entrepreneurs to pursue growth. With such a 'growth-first' approach, it is argued that eventually, as growth takes place, the benefits will trickle down; in other words, growth is necessary in order to tackle poverty and provide for basic needs. However, others have argued that the first priority should be to deal with basic needs, so that people gain in human capital and become better able to contribute to the growth process.

For the industrial countries, growth has become embedded as the main long-run objective of the economy, although the short-run objective of inflation control sometimes dominates media discussion. Nonetheless, the long-run growth rate of GDP is monitored on a regular basis, to assess how the UK is performing relative to other countries. If you would like to see how the UK is doing, Figure 14.12 shows some growth rates for 2001–06 for a selected group of OECD countries.

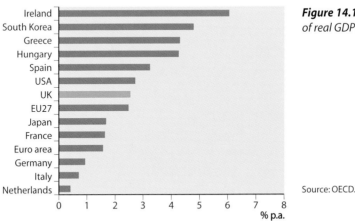

Figure 14.12 Growth of real GDP 2001–06

Source: OECD.

The costs of economic growth

Economic growth also brings costs, perhaps most obviously in terms of pollution and degradation of the environment. In designing long-term policy for economic growth, governments need to be aware of the need to maintain a good balance between enabling resources to increase and safeguarding the environment.

Pollution reduces the quality of life, so pursuing economic growth without regard to this may be damaging. This means that it is important to consider the long-term effects of economic growth — it may even be important to consider the effects not only for today's generation of citizens, but also for future generations.

This thinking has led to the important notion of **sustainability**, which is of increasing concern in the twenty-first century. The idea has come to the fore with the realisation that the planet does not have unlimited supplies of resources, and that today's generation has a responsibility to approach economic growth in a way that does not endanger the quality of life for future generations that will follow. For example, it may be possible to generate income for today's generation by clearing Indonesia's rainforests for timber, but this could have devastating effects in the future — effects that may not be confined to Indonesia.

sustainable development: 'development that meets the needs of the present without compromising the ability of future generations to meet their own needs' (Brundtland Commission, 1987)

These costs have been highlighted in recent years by the growing concerns that have been expressed about global climate change and the pressures on nonrenewable resources such as oil and natural gas. For example, the rapid growth rates being achieved by large emerging economies such as China and India have raised questions about the sustainability of economic growth in the long run. China in particular has experienced a period of unprecedented growth since 1978, which is shown in Figure 14.13. This shows the average growth between 1978 and 1985 (when reforms began to affect the economy), and for each five-year period afterwards. No other economy in recent history has been able to achieve an average growth rate of 9.64% per annum over a 27-year period.

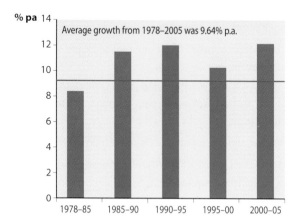

Figure 14.13 *China's average growth of GDP per capita*

Source: calculated from IMF data.

These concerns have led to research into the development of renewable energy sources, but progress in promoting sustainability is impeded because of international externality effects. Where there are externality effects that cross international borders, it becomes difficult to ensure regulation or control.

A coal-fired power plant in Shenyang, China. Rapid economic growth may not be sustainable in the long run

Exercise 14.3

Discuss with your fellow students the various benefits and costs associated with economic growth, and evaluate their relative importance.

Summary

➤ The experience of economic growth has varied substantially in different regions of the world.

➤ There is a gap in living standards between countries that industrialised early and countries that are now classified as being less developed.

➤ A few countries, mainly in East Asia, went through a period of rapid growth from the 1960s that has allowed them to close the gap. This was achieved partly through export-led growth, although other factors were also important.

➤ However, countries in sub-Saharan Africa have stagnated, and remain on very low incomes.

➤ Economic growth remains important for all countries, at whatever stage of development.

➤ There may be costs attached to economic growth, particularly in respect of the environment.

Chapter 15
Macroeconomic policy instruments

Previous chapters have shown that there may be a range of macroeconomic policy objectives, from economic growth, full employment, the control of inflation and equilibrium on the current account of the balance of payments, to concerns for the environment and for the distribution of income. Attention now turns to the sorts of policy that might be implemented to try to meet these targets. Policies at the macroeconomic level are designed to affect either aggregate demand or aggregate supply, and each will be examined in turn.

Learning outcomes

After studying this chapter, you should:
➤ understand and be able to evaluate policies that affect aggregate demand, including fiscal, monetary and exchange rate policies
➤ understand and be able to evaluate policies that affect aggregate supply
➤ be able to appraise the relative merits of policies applied to the demand and supply sides of the macroeconomy
➤ be familiar with how macroeconomic policy has been conducted in the UK in recent years

Macroeconomic policy objectives revisited

Chapter 13 identified a number of objectives that might be seen as desirable for the macroeconomy. These can be interpreted in terms of Figure 15.1, which shows an economy in macroeconomic equilibrium.

Price stability

The first objective discussed related to the control of inflation, where it was pointed out that prices can increase because of shifts in either aggregate demand or aggregate supply. However, it was also pointed out that *persistent* inflation would arise only in a situation in which money stock was growing more rapidly than real output. This seems to suggest that one policy response to control persistent inflation would be to control the growth of the money stock.

An increase in money stock affects aggregate demand, shifting the aggregate demand curve to the right and causing prices to rise in an attempt to regain macroeconomic equilibrium. Thus, attempts to control inflation can be interpreted as attempts to create stability in the overall equilibrium price level.

Full employment

A second macroeconomic policy objective is full employment, which occurs at Y^* in Figure 15.1. If the aggregate demand curve is positioned well to the left in Figure 15.1, macroeconomic equilibrium occurs at less than the full employment level of real output. This suggests that, to restore full employment, policy should be aimed at altering the position of the aggregate demand curve in order to bring the economy back to Y^*.

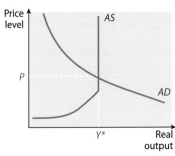

Figure 15.1
Macroeconomic policy objectives

Balance of payments

Policy-makers need to be aware of the dangers of a prolonged and substantial deficit on the balance of payments current account, which can have long-run effects on the ownership pattern of UK assets. If these assets are sold to foreigners, their sale will have a long-run effect on the aggregate supply curve. However, the deficit is caused by an imbalance between the components of aggregate demand, so in a sense the current account objective is related to both aggregate supply and aggregate demand. In effect, the need to achieve current account balance acts as a constraint on attempts to meet other policy objectives, so the trade-offs between objectives are of the greatest importance in this case.

Economic growth

The achievement of economic growth is a long-term objective, the aim of which is to increase the economy's productive capacity. With respect to Figure 15.1, this can be interpreted in terms of policies affecting the *position* of the long-run aggregate supply curve. Economic growth occurs when the aggregate supply curve moves to the right. Thus, in order to influence the economic growth rate of a country, economists need to look for policies that can affect aggregate supply.

Demand-side policies

Policies that aim to influence an economy's aggregate demand are designed either to stabilise the level of output and employment or to stabilise the price level. The prime focus is thus on the short-run position of the macroeconomy. The two major categories of policy are fiscal policy and monetary policy.

Fiscal policy

The term **fiscal policy** covers a range of policy measures that affect government expenditures and revenues. For example, an expansionary fiscal policy would be seen as an increase in government spending (or reduction in taxes) that shifts the aggregate demand curve to the right.

fiscal policy: decisions made by the government on its expenditure, taxation and borrowing

In Figure 15.2 macroeconomic equilibrium is initially at the intersection of aggregate supply (*AS*) and the initial aggregate demand curve (*AD*$_0$), so that real output is at Y_0, which is below the full employment level of output at Y^*. As government expenditure is one of the components of aggregate demand, an increase in such expenditure shifts the aggregate demand curve from AD_0 to AD_1. In response, the economy moves to a new equilibrium, in which the overall price level has risen to P_1 but real output has moved to Y_1, which is closer to the full employment level Y^*.

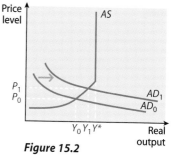

Figure 15.2
The use of fiscal policy

In this scenario, government expenditure is treated as an injection into the circular flow, and it will be reinforced by a multiplier effect. In the present context, an increase in government expenditure is effective in raising the level of real output in the economy, although some of the increase is dissipated in the form of an increase in the overall level of prices. Notice that such a move cannot be interpreted as 'economic growth' per se, as this term is reserved for a situation in which there is an increase in the full employment (potential capacity) level of real output. It is also important to be aware that, if the multiplier is relatively low, the reinforcement of fiscal policy through this route will also be relatively weak.

This kind of policy is effective only if the aggregate demand curve intersects the aggregate supply curve in the upward-sloping segment of *AS*. If the economy is already at the full employment level of output, an increase in aggregate demand merely results in a higher overall level of prices. The effective use of such policy thus requires policy-makers to have good information about the current state of the economy; in particular, they need to know whether the economy is at or below full employment. Otherwise, the results could be damaging for the price stability target. In other words, there is a danger that an expansionary fiscal policy will lead to inflation, but not affect output very much if the *AS* curve is relatively steep.

The effect on the balance of payments must also be borne in mind. Part of an increase in aggregate demand is likely to be spent on imports, but there is no immediate reason for exports to change, so in the short run there is likely to be an increase in the current account deficit on the balance of payments.

Although the focus of the discussion so far has been on government expenditure, fiscal policy also refers to taxation. In fact, the key issue in considering fiscal policy is the *balance* between government expenditure and government revenue, as it is this balance that affects the position of aggregate demand directly.

An increase in the **government budget deficit** (or a decrease in the **government budget surplus**) moves the aggregate demand curve to the right. The budget deficit may arise either from an increase in expenditure or from a decrease in taxation, although the two have some differential effects.

To a certain extent, the government budget deficit changes automatically, without active intervention from the government. If the economy goes into a period of recession, unemployment benefit payments will rise, thereby increasing government expenditure. At the same time, tax revenues will decrease, partly because people who lose their jobs no longer pay income tax. In addition, people whose income is reduced — perhaps because they no longer work overtime — also pay less tax. This is reinforced by the progressive nature of the income tax system, which means that people pay lower rates of tax at lower levels of income. Furthermore, VAT receipts will fall if people are spending less on goods and services.

The government budget deficit will change regardless of government intervention

The opposite effects will be evident in a boom period, preventing the economy from overheating. For example, tax revenues will tend to increase during the boom, and the government will need to make fewer payments of social security benefits. By such **automatic stabilisers,** government expenditure automatically rises during a recession and falls during a boom.

Key *terms*

government budget deficit (surplus): the balance between government expenditure and revenue

automatic stabilisers: effects by which government expenditure adjusts to offset the effects of recession and boom without the need for active intervention

In the past there was a tendency for governments to use fiscal policy in a *discretionary* way in order to influence the path of the economy. A government might use its discretion to increase government expenditure to prevent a recession, for example. Indeed, there have been accusations that governments have sometimes, in some countries, used fiscal policy to create a 'feel-good' factor in the run-up to a general election, by allowing the economy to boom as the election approaches, only to impose a clampdown afterwards.

Such intervention has been shown to be damaging to the long-run path of the economy because of its effect on inflation. Furthermore, there are other problems with using fiscal policy in this way. Apart from anything else, it takes time to collect data about the performance of the economy, so its *current* state is never known for

certain. Because the economy responds quite sluggishly to policy change, it is often the case that the policy comes into effect just when the economy is already turning around of its own accord. This is potentially destabilising, and can do more harm than good.

Exercise 15.1

Use *AD/AS* analysis to consider the effect of an expansionary fiscal policy on the equilibrium level of real output and the overall price level. Undertake this exercise with different initial positions along the aggregate supply curve, first analysing an economy that begins at full employment and then one in which aggregate demand creates an equilibrium that is below full employment. Discuss the differences in your results.

Fiscal policy in the UK

If the government spends more than it raises in revenue, the resulting deficit has to be financed in some way. The government deficit is the difference between public sector spending and revenues, and is known as the *public sector net cash requirement* (PSNCR), which until 1999 was known as the *public sector borrowing requirement* (PSBR). Part of the PSNCR is covered by borrowing, and the government closely monitors its *net borrowing*. Over time, such borrowing leads to *net debt*, which is the accumulation of past borrowing. Figure 15.3 shows public sector net debt as a percentage of GDP. The Labour government has aimed to keep this below 40% – and has been successful in achieving this after 1998.

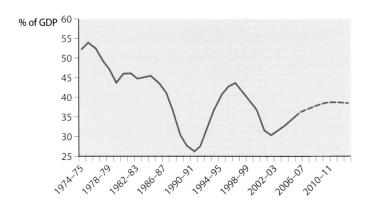

Figure 15.3
Public sector net debt (% of GDP)

Source: HM Treasury (projections from 2006/07 onwards).

In 1998 the UK government issued its *Code for Fiscal Stability*, which established its objectives for fiscal policy and the rules under which it would operate. The Treasury set these out in the *Budget 2004* statement as follows:

> The Government's fiscal policy objectives are:
> ➤ over the medium term, to ensure sound public finances and that spending and taxation impact fairly within and between generations; and
> ➤ over the short term, to support monetary policy and, in particular, to allow the automatic stabilisers to help smooth the path of the economy

This highlights two major concerns of the government that represent a change in practice. First, there is a concern for the long-run effects of policy on spending and borrowing. It has come to be recognised that sustainable economic growth has to take into account the needs of future generations. The government therefore has taken the view that its current spending should be met out of current revenues, and that only investment for the future should be met through borrowing.

The second important commitment is to use fiscal policy as a *support* to monetary policy. In other words, monetary policy is seen as the most important way of influencing the macroeconomy, and, although the automatic stabilisers are allowed to cut in, there is no intention of using discretionary policy. This clear statement is intended to increase the credibility of government policy by indicating its refusal to take action that could destabilise the macroeconomy.

This suggests that fiscal policy has two kinds of effect. In the first place, the automatic stabilisers help to regulate the economy over the cycle by allowing aggregate demand to be affected by changes in the government budget deficit during the cycle.

The second one is a supply-side effect. By improving the credibility of government policy, and by ensuring that the macroeconomy is not destabilised by inappropriate interventions, it is hoped that the private sector will have more confidence in the future state of the economy. Such confidence may then affect the amount of investment that firms will be prepared to undertake. Furthermore, if the government has to borrow less, this will allow interest rates to be lower. As this reduces the cost of borrowing by firms, this will also encourage investment. This would shift aggregate supply in the long run.

Summary

➤ Fiscal policy is concerned with the decisions made by government about its expenditure, taxation and borrowing.

➤ As government expenditure is an autonomous component of aggregate demand, an increase in expenditure will shift the *AD* curve to the right.

➤ If *AD* intersects *AS* in the vertical segment of *AS*, the effect of the increase in aggregate demand is felt only in prices.

➤ However, if the initial equilibrium is below the full employment level, the shift in *AD* will lead to an increase in both equilibrium real output and the overall price level.

➤ In fact, it is net spending that is important, so government decisions on taxation are also significant.

➤ The government budget deficit (surplus) is the difference between government expenditure and revenue.

➤ The budget deficit varies automatically through the business cycle because of the action of the automatic stabilisers.

➤ If the government runs a budget deficit, it may need to undertake net borrowing, which over time affects the net debt position.

Monetary policy

Monetary policy is the approach currently favoured by the UK government to stabilise the macroeconomy. It entails the use of monetary variables such as the money supply and interest rates to influence aggregate demand.

Key term

monetary policy: the decisions made by government regarding monetary variables such as the money supply or the interest rate

The prime instrument of monetary policy in recent years has been the interest rate. Through the interest rate, monetary policy affects aggregate demand. At higher interest rates, firms undertake less investment expenditure and households undertake less consumption expenditure. This is partly because when the interest rate is relatively high, the cost of borrowing becomes high and people are discouraged from borrowing for investment or consumption purposes. There are reinforcing effects that operate through the exchange rate if UK interest rates are high relative to elsewhere in the world. If the exchange rate rises because of high interest rates, this will reduce the competitiveness of UK goods.

Suppose the government believes that the economy is close to full employment and is in danger of overheating. Overheating could push prices up without any resulting benefit in terms of higher real output. An increase in the interest rate will lead to a fall in aggregate demand, thereby relieving the pressure on prices. This is illustrated in Figure 15.4, where the initial position has aggregate demand relatively high at AD_0, real output at the full employment level Y_0 and the overall price level at P_0. The increase in interest rates shifts aggregate demand to the left, to AD_1. Real output falls slightly to Y_1 and the equilibrium price level falls to P_1.

A meeting of Monetary Policy Committee of the Bank of England

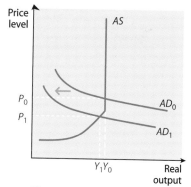

Figure 15.4 The use of monetary policy

Monetary policy in the UK

One of the first steps taken by Tony Blair's government after it was first elected in 1997 was to devolve the responsibility for monetary policy to the Bank of England, which was given the task of achieving the government's stated inflation target, initially set at 2.5% for RPIX inflation. As noted in Chapter 9, the target was amended in 2004, when it became 2% per annum as measured by the CPI.

According to this arrangement, the **Monetary Policy Committee** (MPC) of the Bank of England sets interest rates in order to achieve the target rate of inflation. If inflation moves beyond 1 percentage point above or below the target, the Bank has to write an open letter to the chancellor of the exchequer to explain why the target has not been met. Such a letter became necessary for the first time in March 2007, when CPI inflation touched 3.1%.

 Key *terms*

Monetary Policy Committee: body within the Bank of England responsible for the conduct of monetary policy

bank rate: the interest rate that is set by the Monetary Policy Committee of the Bank of England in order to influence inflation

Operationally, the MPC sets the interest rate which it pays on commercial bank reserves. This is known as the **bank rate**. The commercial banks tend to use this rate as their own base rate, from which they calculate the rates of interest that they charge to their borrowers. Thus, if the MPC changes the bank rate, the commercial banks soon adjust the rates they charge to borrowers. These will vary according to the riskiness of the loans; thus credit cards are charged at a higher rate than mortgages, but all the rates are geared to the base rate set by the commercial banks, and hence indirectly to the bank rate set by the Bank of England.

Figure 15.5 shows the target rates for RPIX up to December 2003 and for the CPI thereafter, together with the outcomes. The bank rate is also shown. As you can see, inflation has remained within the 1% band throughout the period, apart from in March 2007. The association between the bank rate and movements in the inflation rate does not seem very close. This is partly because the relationship between them is obscured to some extent by other influences; it also reflects the fact that the MPC takes into account a wide range of factors when deciding whether to move the bank rate or to leave it as it was in the previous month.

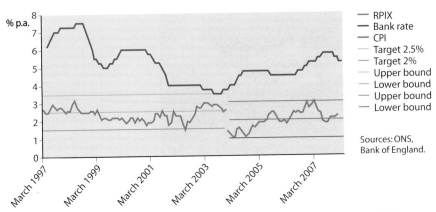

Figure 15.5 UK interest rates and the inflation target, 1997– January 2008

For example, at the August 2007 meeting the MPC discussed financial markets developments, the international economy, money, credit, demand and output, and costs and prices. In other words, the inflation target is considered within the broad

context of developments in various aspects of the economy, and all of these factors were discussed in some detail before taking a decision on what the bank rate should be. In the event, the MPC at this meeting unanimously decided to maintain the bank rate at its existing level of 5.75%, to which it had been raised in the previous meeting in July. At this point in time, the MPC's central projection for inflation was that it would settle around the 2% target during the second half of 2007, but it also recognised there was substantial uncertainty surrounding the projections.

Similar discussions take place every month, and in the interests of transparency, the minutes of the regular MPC meetings are published on the internet – you can see them at **http://www.bankofengland.co.uk/mpc**. This means that you can readily check recent developments in the economy.

By influencing the level of aggregate demand, the MPC can affect the rate of inflation so as to achieve the target, although the effects of a change in the bank rate are not likely to take immediate effect. One reason for giving the Bank of England such independence is that it increases the credibility of the policy. If firms and households realise that the government is serious about controlling inflation, they will have more confidence in its actions, and will be better able to form expectations about the future path the economy will take. In particular, firms will be encouraged to undertake more investment, and this will have a supply-side effect, shifting the aggregate supply curve to the right in the long run.

Exercise 15.2

Visit the Bank of England website and check whether the MPC chose to change the interest rate at their most recent meeting. Take a look at the minutes of the meeting to see the factors that were considered in taking this decision.

Summary

➤ Monetary policy is concerned with the decisions made by government on monetary variables such as money supply and the interest rate.

➤ A change in the interest rate influences the level of aggregate demand through the investment expenditure of firms, the consumption behaviour of households and (indirectly) net exports.

➤ Since 1997, the Bank of England has been given independent responsibility to set interest rates in order to meet the government's inflation target.

➤ The Monetary Policy Committee (MPC) of the Bank sets the bank rate, which is then used as a base rate by the commercial banks and other financial institutions.

➤ Giving independence to the Bank of England in this way increases the credibility of monetary policy.

➤ If this encourages investment, there may be a long-run impact on aggregate supply.

Policies affecting aggregate supply

Demand-side policies have been aimed primarily at stabilising the macroeconomy in the relatively short run, but with the intention of affecting aggregate supply in the long run, by influencing firms' and households' confidence in the future path of the economy. However, there are also a number of policies that can be used to influence the aggregate supply curve directly.

Chapter 11 indicated that the position of the aggregate supply curve depends primarily on the quantity of factor inputs available in the economy, and on the efficiency of those factors. **Supply-side policies** thus focus on affecting these determinants of aggregate supply in order to shift the *AS* curve to the right.

Investment is one key to this in the long run, and this chapter has already shown how demand-side policies that stabilise the macroeconomy in the short run may also have long-run effects on aggregate supply by encouraging investment.

Key *term*

supply-side policies: range of measures intended to have a direct impact on aggregate supply — and specifically the potential capacity output of the economy

Education and training

Investment is also needed in human capital, and one form that this can take is education and training. An important supply-side policy therefore takes the form of encouraging workers (and potential workers) to undertake education and training to improve their productivity.

This takes place partly through education in schools and colleges in preparation for work. It is important, therefore, that the curriculum is designed to provide key skills that will be useful in the workplace. However, this does not mean that all education has to be geared directly to providing skills; problem-solving and analytical skills, for example, can be developed through the study of a wide range of disciplines.

Investment in human capital can increase productivity

Adult education is also important. When the structure of the economy is changing, retraining must be made available to enable workers to move easily between sectors and occupations. This is crucial if structural unemployment is not to become a major problem. For any society — whether industrialised or less developed and needing to reduce its dependence on agriculture — education and skills are necessary to enable workers to switch into new activities in response to structural changes in the economy.

Figure 15.6 shows how such a policy can affect the aggregate supply curve, moving it from AS_0 to AS_1. This move enables an increase in the potential output capacity of the economy, and it need not be inflationary. Indeed, in the figure the overall price level falls from P_0 to P_1 following the shift in aggregate supply, with real output increasing from Y^* to Y^{**}.

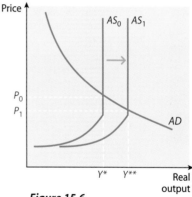

Figure 15.6
A shift in aggregate supply

Flexibility of markets

The rationale for including retraining as a supply-side policy rests partly on the argument that this provides for greater flexibility in labour markets, enabling workers to switch between economic activities to improve the overall workings of the economy.

There are other ways of improving market flexibility. One is to limit the power of the trade unions, whose actions can sometimes lead to inflexibility in the labour market, either through resistance to new working practices that could improve productivity or by pushing up wages so that the level of employment is reduced.

Indeed, maintaining the flexibility of markets is one way in which the macro-economic stability promoted by disciplined fiscal and monetary policy can improve aggregate supply. Macroeconomic stability enables price signals to work more effectively, as producers are better able to observe changes in relative prices. This can promote allocative efficiency.

Promotion of competition

If firms gain dominance in a market, the pursuit of profits may lead them to use their market position to restrict output and raise prices. Such market dominance arises because of a lack of competition. In addition, it is possible that in some markets the lack of competition will produce complacency, depriving firms of the incentive to operate at maximum efficiency. This was especially true in the UK for the formerly nationalised industries such as electricity and gas supply, which were widely believed to have operated with widespread productive inefficiency.

Policies that promote competition may thus lead to improvements in both alloca-tive and productive efficiency. This was one of the motivations behind the privatisation drive that began in the 1980s under Margaret Thatcher. However, it should be noted that there is not wholesale agreement on whether privatisation has invariably led to improvements in efficiency in industries such as the railways or water supply.

Unemployment benefits

An important influence on labour supply, particularly for low-income workers, is the level of unemployment benefit. If unemployment benefit is provided at too high a level, it may inhibit labour force participation, in that some workers may opt to live on unemployment benefit rather than take up low-skilled (and low-paid)

employment. In such a situation, a reduction in unemployment benefit may induce an increase in labour supply, which again will shift the aggregate supply curve to the right.

However, such a policy needs to be balanced against the need to provide protection for those who are unable to find employment. It is also important that unemployment benefit is not reduced to such a level that workers are unwilling to leave their jobs to search for better ones, as this may inhibit the flexibility of the labour market.

Incentive effects

Similarly, there are dangers in making the taxation system too progressive. Most people accept that income tax should be progressive — that is, that those on relatively high incomes should pay a higher rate of tax than those on low incomes — as a way of redistributing income within society and preventing inequality from becoming extreme. However, there may come a point at which marginal tax rates are so high that a large proportion of additional income is taxed away, reducing incentives for individuals to supply additional effort or labour. This could also have an effect on aggregate supply. Again, however, it is important to balance these incentive effects against the distortion caused by having too much inequality in society.

Exercise 15.3

For each of the following policies, identify whether it is an example of fiscal, monetary or supply-side policy. Discuss how each policy affects either aggregate demand or aggregate supply (or both), and examine its effects on equilibrium real output and the overall price level:

a   an increase in government expenditure

b   a decrease in the rate of unemployment benefit

c   a fall in the rate of interest

d   legislation limiting the power of trade unions

e   encouragement for more students to attend university

f   provision of retraining in the form of adult education

g   a reduction in the highest rate of income tax

h   measures to break up a concentrated market

i   an increase in the bank rate

Relative merits

In the context of the aggregate demand/aggregate supply model, it is clear that demand- and supply-side policies are aimed at achieving rather different objectives.

The primary rationale for monetary and fiscal policies is to stabilise the macro-economy. In this, fiscal policy has come to take on a subsidiary role, supporting monetary policy. This was not always the case, and there have been periods in which fiscal policy has been used much more actively to try to stimulate the economy. There are still some countries in which such policies are very much the vogue: for example, it has been suggested that much of Latin America's problem with high inflation has stemmed from fiscal indiscipline, although not all Latin American economists accept this argument. The fact that fiscal policy has not always been well implemented does not mean that such policies cannot be valuable tools — but it does warn against misuse.

In the UK, the use of monetary policy with the support of fiscal policy seems to be working reasonably effectively in the early twenty-first century. Furthermore, it seems to be operating in such a way as to complement the supply-side policies. When a stable macroeconomic environment is created, microeconomic markets are able to operate effectively and investment is encouraged, thereby leading to a boost in aggregate supply.

Supply-side policies aim to influence aggregate supply directly, either raising the supply of factor inputs or improving productivity and efficiency.

Summary

➤ Policies to shift the aggregate supply curve may be used to encourage economic growth.

➤ Education and training can be viewed as a form of investment in human capital, which is designed to improve the productivity of workers.

➤ Measures to improve the flexibility of labour and product markets may lead to an overall improvement in productivity and thus may affect aggregate supply.

➤ Promoting competition can also improve the effectiveness of markets in the economy.

➤ Incentive effects are an important influence on aggregate supply. For example, if unem-ployment benefits are set too high, this may discourage labour force participation. An over-progressive income taxation structure can also have damaging incentive effects.

➤ Demand-side and supply-side policies have different objectives. Demand-side policies such as fiscal and monetary policy are aimed primarily at stabilising the economy. Supply-side policies are geared more towards promoting economic growth.

➤ However, effective stabilisation of the economy may also have long-term effects on aggregate supply.

Chapter 16
The international economy

The world economy is becoming increasingly integrated, and it is no longer possible to think of any single economy in isolation. The UK economy is no exception. It relies on international trade, engaging in exporting and importing activity, and many UK firms are increasingly active in global markets. This situation has created opportunities for UK firms to expand and become global players, and for UK consumers to have access to a wider range of goods and services. However, there is also a downside: global shocks, whether caused by increases in oil prices, financial crises or the emergence of China as a world economic force, can reverberate throughout economies in all parts of the world. It is also apparent that, although economic analysis suggests that there are potential gains to be reaped from international trade, it is still the case that many countries interfere with freedom of trade and try to protect their domestic markets. These are some of the issues that will be explored in this chapter.

Learning outcomes

After studying this chapter, you should:
➤ appreciate the importance of trade and exchange between nations
➤ realise how countries may be able to gain from engaging in international trade
➤ be aware of the risks that come from overspecialisation
➤ understand what is meant by globalisation, and be aware of the factors that have given rise to this phenomenon
➤ be familiar with the arguments for trade liberalisation as opposed to protectionism

Gains from international trade

Chapter 1 highlighted the importance of specialisation, by which, it was argued, workers could become more productive. This same principle can be applied in the context of international trade. Suppose there are two countries — call them Anywhere and Somewhere. Each country can produce combinations of agricultural goods and manufactured goods. However, Anywhere faces lower opportunity cost in producing manufactured goods, and Somewhere has lower opportunity cost in producing agricultural goods. Their respective *PPC*s are shown in Figure 16.1.

The pattern of opportunity cost is reflected in the different slopes of the countries' *PPC*s. If the countries each produce some of each of the goods, one possibility (chosen for simplicity) is that they produce at point *A*, which is the intersection of the two *PPC*s. At this point each country produces 20 units of manufactured goods and 20 units of agricultural goods. Total world output is thus 40 units of manufactured goods and 40 units of agricultural goods — this point is marked on the figure.

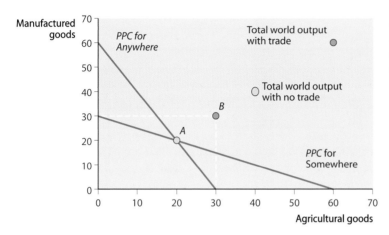

Figure 16.1
PPCs for Anywhere and Somewhere

However, suppose each country were to specialise. Anywhere could produce 60 units of manufactured goods, and Somewhere could produce 60 units of agricultural goods. Then if they were to engage in trade, one possible outcome is point *B*, where they would each now have 30 units of each good, leaving them both unequivocally better off: they would each have more of both commodities. The figure shows that total world output of each type of good has increased by 20 units.

It can be seen that in this situation trade may be mutually beneficial. Notice that this particular result of trading has assumed that the countries exchange the goods on a one-to-one basis. Although this exchange rate makes both better off, it is not the only possibility. It is possible that exchange will take place at different prices for the goods, and clearly, the prices at which exchange takes place will determine which of the countries will gain most from the trade that occurs.

Exercise 16.1

Next time you go shopping, make a list of the goods that you see on offer that have been imported from elsewhere in the world. See if you can detect any patterns in the sorts of goods that come from different parts of the world.

Exercise 16.2

Figure 16.2 shows production possibility curves for two countries, each of which produces both coats and scooters. The countries are called 'Here' and 'There'.

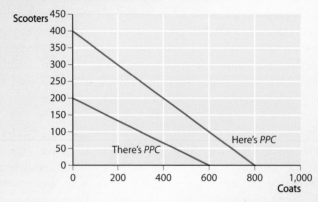

Figure 16.2
Coats and scooters

a Suppose that Here produces 200 scooters and There produces 100: how many coats are produced in each country?

b Now suppose that 300 scooters and 200 coats are produced by Here, and that There produces only coats. What has happened to total production of coats and scooters?

In the above examples and exercises, specialisation and trade are seen to lead to higher overall production of goods. Although the examples have related to goods, you should be equally aware that services too may be a source of specialisation and trade. This is potentially important for an economy such as the UK's, where there is a comparative advantage in the provision of financial services.

Who gains from international trade?

Specialisation can result in an overall increase in total production. However, one of the fundamental questions of economics is 'for whom?' So far nothing has been said about which of the countries will gain from trade. It is possible that exchange can take place between countries in such a way that both countries are better off. But whether this will happen in practice depends on the prices at which exchange takes place. After analysing the way in which prices come to be determined in various markets, this question will be revisited, as the rate at which commodities are exchanged between nations will have important implications for determining who gains from trade.

In particular, specialisation may bring dangers and risks, as well as benefits. One obvious way in which this may be relevant is that, by specialising, a country allows some sectors to run down. For example, suppose a country came to rely on imported food and allowed its agricultural sector to waste away. If the country then became involved in a war, or for some other reason was unable to import its food, there would clearly be serious consequences if it could no longer grow its own food-stuffs. For this reason, many countries have in place measures designed to protect

their agricultural sectors — or other sectors that are seen to be strategic in nature. This is a contentious area, and there has been considerable criticism of the European Common Agricultural Policy — especially from the vantage point of developing countries, which argue that they are disadvantaged by the overprotection of European agriculture.

Overreliance on some commodities may also be risky. For example, the development of artificial substitutes for rubber had an enormous impact on the demand for natural rubber; this was reflected in falls in its price, which caused difficulties for countries that had specialised in producing rubber.

Trade between nations

Countries all around the world engage in international trade. This is partly for obvious reasons: for example, the UK is not a sensible place to grow bananas on a commercial scale, but people living in the UK like to eat bananas. International trade enables individuals to consume goods that cannot be easily produced domestically. It makes sense for bananas to be produced in countries where the relative opportunity cost is low.

The extent to which countries engage in international trade varies enormously, as can be seen in Figure 16.3, which shows total trade (exports plus imports) as a percentage of GDP. In some cases, the extent of dependence on trade reflects the availability of natural resources in a country, but it may also reflect political attitudes towards trade.

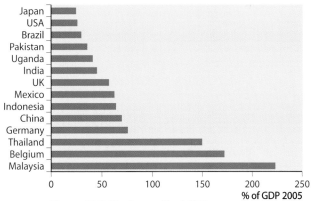

Figure 16.3 *Trade as a % of GDP*
Source: *Human Development Report 2007/08.*

The USA has a large and diverse economy, with a wealth of natural resources, and does not depend so heavily on trade. Brazil, India and Pakistan have a similar level of dependence, but this partly reflects a conscious policy over many years to limit the extent to which their economies have to rely on external trade. At the other extreme, countries such as Malaysia and Thailand have followed policies that promote exports, believing that this will allow more rapid economic growth. China is in a process of transition, having been

The extent to which countries trade varies enormously

closed to international trade for a long period and now not only opening up, but also relying heavily on exporting in order to stimulate economic growth. The share of trade in GDP for China is expanding rapidly. You may be curious as to how it is possible for a country to display a ratio of trade to GDP that is greater than 100%. The reason is that exports include re-exports, i.e. goods that are imported, perhaps as components for other goods, and then exported again. In other words, there is some double-counting going on here.

Moves towards closer integration between countries have strongly affected the pattern of world trade. For example, the moves towards European integration have made Western Europe a major player in world trade. Something of this can be seen in Figure 16.4(a), which shows the destination of world exports in 2005 (i.e. the percentage of the world's exports *imported* by each region). You can see that more than 40% of the world's exports head for Western Europe and 22% to North America. Asia has also become an important part of the world trade scene, with China expanding its trading at an unprecedented rate in recent years.

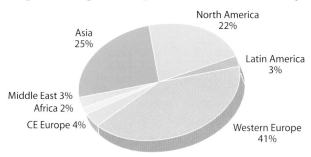

Figure 16.4(a) *Destination of world exports, 2005*
Note: 'CE Europe' is Central and Eastern Europe, the Baltic and the CIS.
Source: World Trade Organization.

Figure 16.4(b) shows the origin of world imports (i.e. the percentage of the world's imports *exported* by each region). Notice that North America has a much smaller share in this diagram, indicating that it is exporting far less than it is importing. On the other hand, Asia and Western Europe were exporting more than they were importing in 2005. Given the size of its population, Africa contributes very little to world trade.

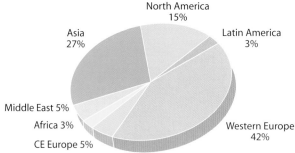

Figure 16.4(b) *Origin of world imports, 2005*
Note: 'CE Europe' is Central and Eastern Europe, the Baltic and the CIS.
Source: World Trade Organization.

Globalisation

The term '**globalisation**' has been much used in recent years, especially by the protest groups that have demonstrated against it. It is therefore important to be clear about what the term means before seeking to evaluate the strengths and weaknesses of the phenomenon.

Ann Krueger, the first deputy managing director of the IMF, defined globalisation as 'a phenomenon by which economic agents in any given part of the world are much more affected by events elsewhere in the world'. Joseph Stiglitz, the Nobel laureate and former chief economist at the World Bank, defined it as follows:

> Fundamentally, [globalization] is the closer integration of countries and peoples of the world which has been brought about by the enormous reduction of costs of transportation and communication, and the breaking down of artificial barriers to the flows of goods, services, capital, knowledge, and (to a lesser extent) people across borders.
>
> J. Stiglitz, *Globalization and its Discontents* (Penguin, 2004)

On this basis, globalisation is crucially about the closer integration of the world's economies. Critics have focused partly on the environmental effects of rapid global economic growth, and partly on the opportunities that powerful nations and large corporations have for exploiting the weak.

The quotation from the book by Joseph Stiglitz not only defines what is meant by globalisation, but also offers some reasons for its occurrence.

Transportation costs

One of the contributory factors to the spread of globalisation has undoubtedly been the rapid advances in the technology of transportation and communications.

Improvements in transportation have enabled firms to fragment their production process to take advantage of varying cost conditions in different parts of the world. For example, it is now possible to site labour-intensive parts of a production process in areas of the world where labour is relatively plentiful, and thus relatively cheap. This is one way in which **multinational corporations** (MNCs) arise, in some cases operating across a wide range of countries.

Furthermore, communications technology has developed rapidly with the growth of the worldwide web and e-commerce, enabling firms to compete more easily in global markets.

 terms

globalisation: a process by which the world's economies are becoming more closely integrated

multinational corporation: a company whose production activities are carried out in more than one country

These technological changes have augmented existing economies of scale and scope, enabling firms to grow. If the size of firms were measured by their gross turnover, many of them would be found to be larger in size than a lot of the countries in which they operate (when size is measured by GDP): for instance, on this basis General Motors is bigger than Hong Kong or Norway.

Reduction of trade barriers

A second factor that has contributed to globalisation has been the successive reductions in trade barriers during the period since the Second World War, first under the auspices of the **General Agreement on Tariffs and Trade (GATT)**, and later under the **World Trade Organization (WTO)**, which replaced it.

In addition to these trade-liberalising measures, there has been a trend towards the establishment of free trade areas and customs unions in various parts of the world, with the European Union being just one example.

 Key *terms*

General Agreement on Tariffs and Trade (GATT): the precursor of the WTO, which organised a series of 'rounds' of tariff reductions

World Trade Organization (WTO): a multilateral body now responsible for overseeing the conduct of international trade

By facilitating the process of international trade, such developments have encouraged firms to become more active in trade, and thus have added to the impetus towards globalisation.

Deregulation of financial markets

Hand in hand with these developments, there have been moves towards removing restrictions on the movement of financial capital between countries. Many countries have removed capital controls, thereby making it much easier for firms to operate globally. This has been reinforced by developments in technology that enable financial transactions to be undertaken more quickly and efficiently.

The pattern of world trade

In order to provide the context for a discussion of the place of the UK economy in the global economy, it is helpful to examine the pattern of world trade.

Table 16.1 presents some data on this pattern. It shows the size of trade flows between regions. The rows of the table show the exports from each of the regions to each other region, while the columns show the pattern of imports from each region. The numbers on the 'diagonal' of the table (in bold type) show the trade flows *within* regions. One remarkable feature of the table is the high involvement of Western Europe in world trade, accounting for 40.6% of imports and 42.4% of the exports. Of course, this includes substantial flows within Europe. In contrast, Africa shows very little involvement in world trade, in spite of the fact that, in population terms, it is far larger.

Indeed, trade flows between the developed countries — and with the more advanced developing countries — have tended to dominate world trade, with the flows between developing countries being relatively minor. This is not surprising, given that by definition the richer countries have greater purchasing power. However, the degree of openness to trade of economies around the world varies also as a result of conscious policy decisions. Some countries, especially in East Asia, have adopted very open policies towards trade, promoting exports in order to achieve export-led growth. In contrast, countries such as India and a number of Latin American countries have been much more reluctant to become dependent on international trade, and have adopted a more closed attitude towards trade.

		Destination						
Origin	**North America**	**South & Central America**	**Europe**	**CIS**	**Africa**	**Middle East**	**Asia**	**World**
North America	**905**	107	279	8	22	42	314	1,677
S & C America	135	**112**	86	6	11	8	62	420
Europe	431	67	**3,652**	142	120	129	366	4,907
CIS	24	8	247	**80**	6	13	46	424
Africa	80	11	148	1	**33**	6	73	352
Middle East	72	4	103	3	21	**72**	340	615
Asia	708	70	604	50	70	111	**1,639**	3,252
World	2,355	379	5,119	290	283	381	2,840	11,647

Table 16.1 *Intra- and interregional merchandise trade, 2006 (US$bn)*
Note: world totals have been calculated from the table. Data for China are included in the Asia total.
Source: World Trade Organization.

The pattern of UK trade

Figures 16.5(a) and (b) show the destination of UK exports of goods and services to major regional groupings in the world. The most striking feature of this graph is the extent to which the UK relies on Europe and the USA for more than three-quarters of its exports. Figures 16.6(a) and (b) reveal a similar pattern for the UK's imports of goods and services.

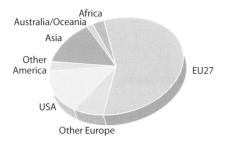

Figure 16.5(a) *Destination of UK exports of goods, 2006*

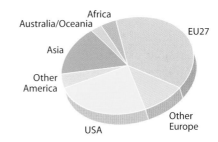

Figure 16.5(b) *Destination of UK exports of services, 2006*

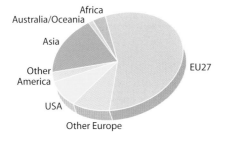

Figure 16.6(a) *Source of UK imports of goods, 2006*

Source: ONS.

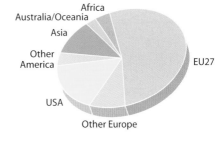

Figure 16.6(b) *Source of UK imports of services, 2006*

The proportion of UK trade (both exports and imports) that is with Europe has undergone substantial change over the past 40 years. This can be seen in Figures 16.7(a) and (b). In 1960, when the Commonwealth was still thriving and the UK was ambivalent about the idea of European integration, less than a quarter of UK exports went to other European countries. However, this has changed as the UK has grown closer to Europe, and now more than half of the UK's exports go to other members of the European Union.

Table 16.2 shows the top 10 countries that made up the UK's export markets and import sources in 2006. This again shows the importance of UK trade with European countries in the twenty-first century, although the USA remains an important trading partner, ranked first among the UK's individual export markets, and the third largest source of imports into the UK. Notice that 62.8% of UK exports go to the European Union, and 58.2% of imports come from the European Union.

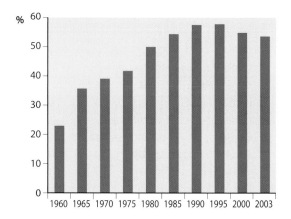

Figure 16.7(a) *UK exports of goods to EU15 (%)*

Note: 'EU15' refers to the 15 countries that were members of the European Union prior to the most recent expansion in May 2004.

Source: calculated from data in Europa: *EU Economy Annual Review 2004*.

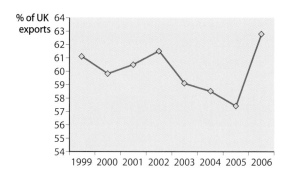

Figure 16.7(b) *UK exports to the enlarged EU*
Source: ONS.

Export markets			Import sources			
Rank	Country	% of total UK exports	Rank	Country	% of total UK exports	
1	USA	13.1	1	Germany	13.0	
2	France	12.0	2	France	9.3	
3	Germany	11.2	3	USA	7.9	
4	Irish Republic	7.2	4	Netherlands	7.2	
5	Netherlands	6.8	5	Belgium–Lux.	5.7	
6	Belgium–Lux.	6.1	6	China	4.7	
7	Spain	5.2	7	Norway	4.4	
8	Italy	3.9	8	Spain	4.2	
9	Sweden	2.1	9	Italy	4.0	
10	Japan	1.7	10	Irish Republic	3.3	

Table 16.2
The UK's top 10 export markets and sources of imports, by country, 2006

Source: ONS.

A substantial share of exports of goods from the UK consists of manufactured goods, especially road vehicles together with machinery and equipment of various types, and pharmaceuticals — and oil, of course. Many of these commodities are also imported in large volumes. In part, this reflects the way in which commodity groups are defined. For example, there are many different types of road vehicle or pharmaceutical product, and specialisation may mean that firms in particular countries focus on particular types of vehicle or drug. By specialising in this way, they may be able to tap economies of scale that would otherwise not be available within the domestic market.

Exercise 16.3

a Using the data provided in Table 16.1, calculate the share of each region in world exports and imports. Think about the factors that might influence the contrasting performance of Western Europe and Africa. In addition, for each region calculate the share of exports and imports that are within the region and comment on any significant differences that you find.

b Using Table 16.2, calculate the cumulative percentage of exports and imports in the UK's top 10 export markets and import sources. Discuss the extent to which this suggests that the UK concentrates on trading with a relatively small number of partners.

c Are there any aspects of the pattern of world trade that took you by surprise? Can you find reasons for these?

Summary

➤ Globalisation has taken place as countries and peoples of the world have become more closely integrated.

➤ Factors contributing to this process have been the rapid advances in the technology of transportation and communications, the reduction of trade barriers and the deregulation of financial markets.

➤ There are substantial differences in the degree to which countries trade: trade with and within Western Europe accounts for an appreciable proportion of world trade, whereas Africa shows very little involvement.

➤ More than three-quarters of UK exports go to Europe and the USA.

➤ The share of UK trade with the rest of Europe has increased substantially since 1960.

The benefits from specialisation revisited

It has been argued that countries can gain from engaging in international trade by specialising in the production of goods and services in which they have a lower opportunity cost of production. This helps to explain some of the patterns in world trade that are shown in the data.

When you think about the global economy, it should be clear that relative opportunity costs will vary according to the very different balance of conditions around the world, not only in terms of climate (which may be important in agricultural production), but also in terms of the relative balance of factors of production (labour, capital, land, entrepreneurship etc.) and the skills of the workforce. This helps to explain why MNCs may choose to locate capital-intensive parts of their production process in one location and labour-intensive activities elsewhere, reflecting different relative prices in different countries.

It may also help to explain some of the patterns of trade. At first glance, it may seem curious that the UK both exports and imports cars, as initially this may seem to contradict the notion of specialisation. However, if UK and (say) German cars have different characteristics, then each country may choose to specialise in certain segments of the market, taking advantage of the economies of scale that are so crucial in car production. Consumers benefit from this, as they then have a wider range of products to choose from.

Trade liberalisation or protectionism?

In spite of the well-known gains from trade, countries often seem reluctant to open their economies fully to international trade, and tend to intervene in various ways to protect their domestic producers.

Tariffs

A policy instrument commonly used in the past to give protection to domestic producers is the imposition of a **tariff**. Tariff rates in developed countries have been considerably reduced in the period since the Second World War, but nonetheless are still in place.

Key term

tariff: a tax imposed on imported goods

Figure 16.8 shows how a tariff is expected to operate. D represents the domestic demand for a commodity, and S_{dom} shows how much domestic producers are prepared to supply at any given price. The price at which the good can be imported from world markets is given by P_w. If dealing with a global market, it is reasonable to assume that the supply at the world price is perfectly elastic. So, in the absence of a tariff, domestic demand is given by D_0, of which S_0 is supplied within the domestic economy and the remainder $(D_0 - S_0)$ is imported. If the government wishes to protect this industry within the domestic economy, it needs to find a way of restricting imports and encouraging home producers to expand their capacity.

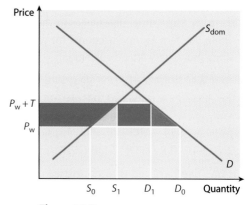

Figure 16.8
The effects of a tariff

By imposing a tariff, the domestic price rises to $P_w + T$, where T is the amount of the tariff. This has two key effects. One is to reduce the demand for the good from D_0 to D_1; the second is to encourage domestic producers to expand their output of this good from S_0 to S_1. As a consequence, imports fall substantially $(D_1 - S_1)$. On the face of it, the policy has achieved its objective. Furthermore, the government has been able to raise some tax revenue (given by the green rectangle).

However, not all the effects of the tariff are favourable for the economy. Consumers are certainly worse off, as they have to pay a higher price for the good; they therefore consume less, and there is a loss of consumer surplus. Some of what was formerly consumer surplus has been redistributed to others in society. The government has gained the tariff revenue, as mentioned. In addition, producers gain some additional producer surplus, shown by the dark-blue area. There is also a deadweight loss to society, represented by the red and pale-blue triangles. In other words, overall society is worse off as a result of the imposition of the tariff.

Effectively, the government is subsidising inefficient local producers, and forcing domestic consumers to pay a price that is above that of similar goods imported from abroad.

Some would try to defend this policy on the grounds that it allows the country to protect an industry, thus saving jobs that would otherwise be lost. However, this involves sacrificing the benefits of specialisation. In the longer term it may delay structural change. For an economy to develop new specialisations, there needs to be a transitional process in which old industries contract and new ones emerge. Although this process may be painful, it is necessary in the long run if the economy is to remain competitive. Furthermore, the protection that firms enjoy that allows them to reap extra producer surplus from the tariff may foster complacency and an inward-looking attitude. This is likely to lead to X-inefficiency, and an inability to compete in the global market.

Even worse is the situation that develops where nations respond to tariffs raised by competitors by putting up tariffs of their own. This has the effect of further reducing the trade between countries, and everyone ends up worse off, as the gains from trade and specialisation are sacrificed.

Quotas

An alternative policy that a country may adopt is to limit the imports of a commodity to a given volume. For example, a country may come to an agreement with another country that only a certain quantity of imports will be accepted by the importing country. Such arrangements are sometimes known as **voluntary export restraints** (VERs).

 Key term

voluntary export restraint: an agreement by a country to limit its exports to another country to a given quantity (quota)

Figure 16.9 illustrates the effects of a quota. D represents the domestic demand for this commodity, and S_{dom} is the quantity that domestic producers are prepared to supply at any given price. Suppose that, without any agreement, producers from

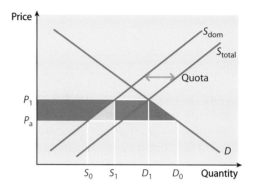

country A would be prepared to supply any amount of the product at a price P_a. If the product is sold at this price, D_0 represents domestic demand, of which S_0 is supplied by domestic producers and the remainder ($D_0 - S_0$) is imported from country A.

By imposing a quota, total supply is now given by S_{total}, which is domestic supply plus the quota of imports allowed into the economy from country A. The market equilibrium price rises to P_1 and demand falls to D_1, of which S_1 is supplied by domestic producers and the remainder is the agreed quota of imports.

Figure 16.9 *The effects of a quota*

Figure 16.9 shows who gains and who loses by this policy. Domestic producers gain by being able to sell at the higher price, so (as in the case of the tariff) they receive additional surplus given by the dark-blue area. Furthermore, the producers exporting from country A also gain, receiving the green rectangle (which, in the case of the tariff, was tax revenue received by the government). As in the case of the tariff, the two triangles (red and pale blue) represent the loss of welfare suffered by the importing country.

Such an arrangement effectively subsidises the foreign producers by allowing them to charge a higher price than they would have been prepared to accept. Furthermore, although domestic producers are encouraged to produce more, the protection offered to them is likely to lead to X-inefficiency and weak attitudes towards competition.

There are a number of examples of such agreements, especially in the textile industry. For example, the USA and China have had long-standing agreements on quotas for a range of textile products. Ninety-one such quotas expired at the end of 2004 as part of China's accession to the World Trade Organization. As you might expect, this led to extensive lobbying by producers in the USA, especially during the run-up to the 2004 presidential election. Trade unions in the USA supported the producers, arguing that 350,000 jobs had been lost since the expiry of earlier quota agreements in 2002. In the case of three of these earlier agreements, some restraint had been reinstated for bras, dressing

The removal of textile quotas contributed to a surge in Chinese exports in 2005

gowns and knitted fabrics. Producers in other countries, such as Sri Lanka, Bangladesh, Nepal, Indonesia, Morocco, Tunisia and Turkey, were lobbying for the quotas to remain, regarding China as a major potential competitor. However, for the USA at least, it can be argued that the removal of the quotas would allow domestic consumers to benefit from lower prices, and would allow US textile workers to be released for employment in higher-productivity sectors, where the USA maintains a competitive advantage.

Similar problems arose in connection with the dismantling of quotas for Chinese textile products being imported into Europe. This led to problems in 2005 when warehouses full of fashion products were prohibited from entry into the EU following a late agreement to delay the dismantling of the quotas.

Non-tariff barriers

There are other ways in which trade can be hampered, one example being the use of what are known as **non-tariff barriers**. These often comprise rules and regulations that control the standard of products that can be sold in a country.

This is a grey area, as some of the rules and regulations may seem entirely sensible and apply equally to domestic and foreign producers. For example, laws that prohibit the sale of refrigerators that contain CFCs are designed to protect the ozone layer, and may be seen to be wholly appropriate. In this case, the regulation is for purposes other than trade restriction.

 Key term

non-tariff barrier: an obstacle to free trade other than a tariff — for example, quality standards imposed on imported products

However, there may be other situations in which a regulation is more clearly designed to limit trade. For example, the USA specifies a larger minimum size for vine-ripened tomatoes than for green tomatoes, thereby raising costs for the former. This has to do with trade because vine-ripened tomatoes are mainly imported from Mexico, but green tomatoes are mainly grown in Florida. Thus, the regulation gives Florida producers an advantage.

Such rules and regulations may operate against producers in less developed countries, who may find it especially difficult to meet demanding standards of production. This applies in particular where such countries are trying to develop new skills and specialisations to enable them to diversify their exports and engage more actively in international trade.

Trade liberalisation and protectionism evaluated

Although the theory of comparative advantage outlined above seems to suggest that there are potential gains from specialisation and trade, there must be some explanation for the widespread use of tariff and non-tariff barriers. The reasons may be partly political: for example, it may be that the people responsible for running protected sectors may have accumulated political power and influence. They will be keen to try to avoid incurring the costs that emerge when protection is removed. However, there are some important economic issues as well.

One issue concerns the relative market power of trading partners. Although two partners may be jointly better off as the result of trade, the theory does not spell out how those gains are likely to be shared between the countries engaging in trade. If one partner has market power, it may be able to appropriate a large share of the potential gains.

It may also be the case that the gains from more openness in international trade arise where low productivity sectors are able to release resources that can be redeployed in an expanding export sector. These gains will be the greatest when the economy is in full employment, so that the export sector before liberalisation is unable to obtain the resources needed for expansion. However, for many less developed countries this is not the situation, as there is high unemployment and underemployment. The danger then is that by opening up to international competition, the low-productivity sectors merely release resources that then become unemployed, leaving the overall economy worse off than before the liberalisation of trade. In addition, it may be that the sort of resources (such as skilled labour) that are needed for the expansion of exports are not available in some countries.

These arguments suggest that the arguments for and against trade liberalisation are not as straightforward as the simple theory predicts, and careful consideration needs to be given to the arguments on both sides, to figure out under what conditions a country will benefit from a process of trade liberalisation.

Summary

- Countries can gain from international trade by specialising in the production of goods or services in which they have a lower opportunity cost of production.
- In spite of these possible gains, countries have often introduced protectionist measures to restrict trade, including tariffs, quotas and non-tariff barriers.
- There may be political and economic reasons for doubting that trade liberalisation is always good in all circumstances.

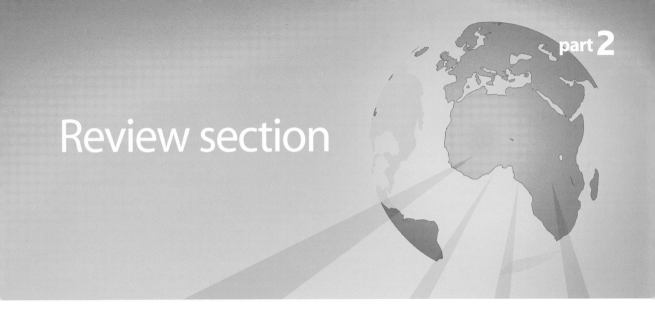

part **2**

Review section

The second module of the AS programme introduces you to macroeconomics — the study of the economy as a whole. This brief review is intended to remind you of the key concepts that have been discussed in each chapter and to provide an overview of the material. This may be especially helpful when you come to the end of the module and want to look back over what has been covered, or when you come to revise in preparation for the examination.

Chapter 9 Measuring economic performance

As **macroeconomics** deals with the interaction between economic variables operating at the aggregate level (that is at the level of the economy as a whole), an important first step is to be able to identify the main variables of importance to the economy and ways in which these can be measured so that performance can be monitored.

For many macroeconomic variables, it is necessary to use measurements based on monetary values. This creates an immediate problem, as the fact that prices change through time means that an adjustment is needed to identify the underlying changes taking place in the economy. The value of an economic variable in current prices is the **nominal value**, which can be misleading when prices are changing. The **real value** is the value measured at constant prices, thus adjusting for the effects of changing prices.

When comparing with a base year, a useful tool is the **index number**. This has wide applications in comparing measurements across time or space. **Inflation** in the UK is measured by changes in the **consumer price index**, which has been used to specify the target for the government's inflation policy since December 2003. Before then, the **retail price index** had been used for this purpose. Yet another price index is the **GDP deflator**, which is an implicit price index formed as the ratio of current price to constant price measures of GDP.

Unemployment is another key variable in seeking to evaluate the performance of the economy. In the UK this is measured by the **ILO unemployment rate** (which is the government's preferred measure) or the **claimant count of unemployment**.

A simple model of the macroeconomy is the **circular flow of income, expenditure and output**. This model suggests that total economic activity in the economy during a period (**GDP**) can be measured in three equivalent ways, although in practice measurement errors prevent the results being absolutely the same. It has been observed that GDP tends to fluctuate around its underlying trend, a process known as the **business cycle**.

Chapter 10 Aggregate demand

The study of macroeconomics begins with an examination of **aggregate demand**, the components of which are consumption, investment, government expenditure and net exports (exports minus imports).

The largest of these components in the UK is **consumption**. John Maynard Keynes argued that the most important influence on consumption is income. Households receive an amount of **disposable income**, which they then choose to allocate between consumption and saving. The **average propensity to consume** is the proportion of disposable income that households devote to consumption, whereas the **marginal propensity to consume** is the proportion of additional income that is devoted to consumption. The relationship between consumption and disposable income is captured in the **consumption function**, the position of which depends upon the other factors that affect how much households spend on consumption rather than saving — such as the rate of interest.

Investment is expenditure undertaken by firms to add to the capital stock; this is important because it affects the overall productive capacity of the economy. **Government expenditure** is assumed to be *autonomous* — in other words, it does not vary with the level of income. Keynes argued that there would be a **multiplier** effect arising from a change in autonomous expenditure.

The **aggregate demand curve** shows the relationship between the level of aggregate demand and the overall price level. This is different in nature from the microeconomic demand curve and shows planned aggregate expenditure at any given possible overall price level.

Chapter 11 Aggregate supply and macroeconomic equilibrium

The **short-run aggregate supply curve** shows how much output firms in an economy would be prepared to supply in the short run at any given overall price level. Together with the aggregate demand curve introduced in the previous chapter, this enables the short-run macroeconomic equilibrium to be identified.

Comparative static analysis can then be used in order to trace the effects of external shocks that affect either aggregate demand or aggregate supply. The distinction between *shifts of AD* and *AS* and *movements along* the curves is again an important one to remember.

Chapter 12 The balance of payments and the exchange rate

The UK is an **open economy** — that is, it engages in international trade by exporting and importing goods, services and assets. The **balance of payments** is a set of accounts that summarises the transactions that are carried out between residents of the UK and the rest of the world. These transactions are separated into three accounts. The **current account of the balance of payments** summarises transactions in goods and services, which in turn distinguishes between **visible trade** (trade in goods) and **invisible trade** (trade in services). The **financial account of the balance of payments** identifies transactions in financial assets. Finally, the **capital account of the balance of payments** sets out transactions in physical capital between the residents of a country and the rest of the world. This last account is much smaller in magnitude than the current and financial accounts.

The overall balance of payments must always be zero and the typical pattern in the UK in recent years has been a deficit on the current account, balanced by a surplus on the financial account.

Closely associated with the balance of payments is the **exchange rate**, the price of one country's currency in terms of another. The exchange rate is important in influencing the relative competitiveness of UK goods and services in international markets. Also important are relative prices and the **real exchange rate** is the nominal exchange rate adjusted for differences in relative inflation rates between countries. Another measure is the **effective exchange rate**, which measures the exchange rate for a country relative to a weighted average of the currencies of its trading partners. The relationship between the exchange rate and the current and financial accounts of the balance of payments is a complex but important one.

Chapter 13 Macroeconomic policy objectives

The policy dimension is an important aspect of studying macroeconomics. This is because a stable macroeconomy is believed to be important for fostering economic growth.

An important aspect of this is the control of **inflation** — remember that this is defined as a rise in the general price level within an economy. In the context of the *AD/AS* model, there are two ways in which inflation can occur. **Cost-push inflation** is initiated on the supply-side of the economy, for example where there is an increase in the costs faced by firms. **Demand-pull inflation**, on the other hand, is where prices increase following an increase in aggregate demand. However, economic analysis suggests that *persistent* inflation can only happen when the **money stock** grows more rapidly than real output. High inflation imposes costs on society — especially when it becomes *hyperinflation*, as has been experienced in some countries.

A second important objective of macroeconomic policy is **full employment**. A society that is operating on the production possibility curve is fully utilising its factors of production, including labour. A high level of unemployment indicates that this is not being reached. Having said that, it is inevitable that there will be some

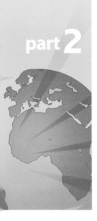
unemployment in an economy. In particular, there will be **frictional unemployment**, which is associated with the process of job search. Changes in the pattern of economic activity in an economy are seen as necessary adjustment to changes in the pattern of consumer demand and comparative advantage. Such changes may lead to **structural unemployment**, whereby workers may need time to retrain for new activities. It is also possible that in some circumstances, the economy will settle at an equilibrium that is below full employment, resulting in some **demand-deficient unemployment** because aggregate demand is at too low a level.

There may be situations in which wages are set above that level that would enable the labour market to be in equilibrium. Furthermore there may be occasions on which wages are slow to adjust downwards following a change in market conditions. Unemployment may then follow from this disequilibrium situation. It then becomes important to distinguish between **voluntary unemployment**, when an individual chooses not to accept a job at the going wage rate, and **involuntary unemployment**, where a worker would like to accept a job at the going wage rate, but is unable to find one.

The balance of payments has also been seen as being of relevance to macro-economic policy. This is not so much in relation to the overall balance, because if the exchange rate is free to find its market level, the overall balance of payments will always be zero. A greater potential problem is where there is an extreme imbalance between the current account and the financial account. In recent years, the typical pattern in the UK (and in the USA) has been a deficit on the current account, offset by a surplus on the financial account. There are concerns that this might not be sustainable in the long run.

Other policy objectives include economic growth (discussed in Chapter 14), environmental issues and the distribution of income. One problem that arises in designing macroeconomic policy is that there may sometimes be conflicts between policy objectives, such that pursuing one target may prevent the achievement of others.

Chapter 14 Economic growth

If the fundamental objective for a society is to improve the well-being of its citizens, then **economic growth** should be viewed as being the most fundamental objective of economic policy. Economic growth enables an increase in the productive capacity of the economy, thus enabling more resources to be made available.

In terms of economic analysis, the process of economic growth can be seen either as an outward shift of the production possibility curve or as a rightward shift in the aggregate supply curve.

There are two major sources of economic growth. Productive capacity may increase either because of an increase in the quantity of the inputs of the factors of production, or it may arise from an improvement in the efficiency with which those factors are employed. **Labour productivity** is a measure of the efficiency of labour, either seen in terms of output per worker or output per hour worked. Similarly, **capital productivity** is a measure of the output per unit of capital, thus reflecting the efficiency of capital. **Total factor productivity** is the average productivity of all factors of production, measured as the total output divided by the total amount of inputs used.

Investment is the process by which the stock of capital in the economy can be increased. Some investment is needed for **depreciation** — replacing physical capital as it is subject to wear and tear. Over and above depreciation, **net investment** adds to the capital stock and thus increases the productive capacity of the economy. Similarly, **human capital** is the stock of skills and expertise that contribute to a worker's productivity. Investment in human capital is anything that improves the skills and expertise of the workforce — for example through education and training.

It is tempting to see increases in GDP as being a measure of the increase in well-being over time, or as a reflection of economic growth. However, Chapter 14 draws attention to a number of problems that arise in trying to use GDP in this way.

It is important to note that although economic growth may be seen as a fundamental objective of economic policy, it cannot be pursued without regard to other important aspects of the economy. Economic growth does bring some costs and there is increasing awareness that countries need to strive for **sustainable development** and growth. In other words, it is not advisable to pursue economic growth for the benefit of the current generation without also being aware of the needs of future generations. This has particular ramifications for the environment.

Chapter 15 Macroeconomic policy instruments

Having discussed the desirable objectives of macroeconomic policy, this chapter examines the instruments that can be used in order to try to achieve those objectives. Macroeconomic equilibrium in the *AD/AS* model can be affected by policies that either operate on aggregate demand or on aggregate supply.

As far as aggregate demand is concerned, there are two main types of policy. **Fiscal policy** involves decisions made by the government on its expenditure, taxation and borrowing. These decisions affect aggregate demand because government expenditure is a component of aggregate demand. The **government budget deficit (surplus)** is the balance between government expenditure and revenue and it is this balance that affects aggregate demand. To some extent, government expenditure adjusts to offset the effects of the business cycle through the operation of **automatic stabilisers** — for example as unemployment rises in a recession, the government budget deficit rises because of increases in payments of unemployment benefits and a reduction in tax revenues. An important aspect of fiscal policy is the way that it affects the balance between the private and public sectors.

Aggregate demand can also be influenced by **monetary policy**, which reflects the decisions made by government regarding monetary variables such as the money supply or the interest rate. Since 1997, the responsibility for monetary policy has

been delegated to the **Monetary Policy Committee (MPC)** of the Bank of England, which is charged with the duty of meeting the government's inflation target. This is accomplished through interest rates — in particular the **bank rate**, which is set monthly by the MPC.

The prime aim of fiscal and monetary policy is to stabilise the macroeconomy. An important reason for this is that it is perceived that firms are more likely to undertake investment when the macroeconomy is stable, as they are able to form expectations about the future more readily.

In seeking to influence the long-term path of the economy, **supply-side policies** are an important tool. These are policies that are intended to affect the position of the aggregate supply curve and thus influence the productive capacity of the economy. Such policies include the encouragement of investment in human capital, measures to promote competition and thus good resource allocation, improving the flexibility of labour markets and ensuring good incentives for economic decision-makers.

Chapter 16 The international economy

The process of **globalisation** is creating an increasingly integrated global economy, so that it is not possible to view the UK economy in isolation. This may enable countries to take advantage of the potential gains to be harnessed from specialisation and international trade. One factor that has fuelled the globalisation process is the rapid technological change in the areas of transport and communications, which has enabled **multinational corporations** to increase the efficiency of their operations by carrying out stages of the production process in different parts of the world.

Deregulation of markets has also affected the globalisation process. The **World Trade Organization (WTO)** replaced the **General Agreement on Tariffs and Trade (GATT)** in 1995. The WTO is a multilateral body with responsibility for overseeing the conduct of international trade, including arbitrating on trade disputes and encouraging the reduction of **tariff** and **non-tariff barriers to trade**. A tariff is a tax on imported goods. Such taxes have been used extensively in the past by countries wanting to protect their domestic industries. However, economic analysis indicates that this may impose costs on society and prevent the gains from specialisation and trade from being fully exploited. Another measure used by countries has been the **voluntary export restraint**, under which a country agrees to limit its exports to another country to a specific quota. This imposes similar costs on society. Both tariffs and quotas have been much reduced under both GATT and the WTO, but barriers to international trade remain, and the balance between trade liberalisation and protectionism continues to be contentious.

Index

Page numbers in **bold** refer to **key term definitions**.

A

AD/AS model 138–41, 156, 169
ad valorem tax 99
aggregate demand 126–35, 138, 139–40
aggregate demand curve **133**–34
aggregate supply curve 136–38
Akerlof, George 90–91
allocative efficiency **55**, 57–58, 61, 193
anti-competitive acts 61
asymmetric information **89**, 90
automatic stabilisers 124, **186**, 188
average propensity to consume **128**
average total cost **56**

B

balance of payments **142**–49, 162–64,
    184, 185
Bank of England 35, 117, 189–91
bank rate **190**
barter economy 13
biodiversity, loss of 71
boom **123**
business cycle **123**–24

C

capital 5, 171–72
capital account of the balance of
    payments **143**, 148
capitalism **59**
capital productivity **170**
capital stock 130, 171
CBI 124
centrally planned economy **4**
ceteris paribus **17**
circular flow model 121, 126–28

circular flow of income, expenditure
    and output 121–23
claimant count of unemployment **119**
Coase, Ronald 80
coincident indicators **124**
comparative static analysis **36**–38,
    139, 140
competition **193**
Competition Commission 61
competitive market **26**
complements **22**
congestion 71, 75–76
conspicuous consumption 19
consumer preferences 23, 50–51
consumer price index (CPI) **115**,
    116–18
consumer surplus 50–**51**
consumption 8–9, 128–30, 138
consumption externality **65**, 66–67,
    68–69
consumption function **129**
Cook, Len 117
cost efficiency **56**
cost-push inflation **156**
costs of production **27**
cross-price elasticity of demand **46**
currency markets 149–50, 162
current account of the balance of
    payments **143**, 144–48, 163–64
customs unions **202**

D

data 111–12, 175
demand **16**–24
demand curve **18**–20, 133

demand-deficient unemployment **160**
demand for money 35
demand-pull inflation **156**
demand-side policies 184–91
demerit goods **87**–89
depreciation **171**
deregulation of financial markets 202
derived demand 33, 34
discount **75**
disposable income **128**
division of labour **11**

E
economic growth **9**, 164–65, *Chapter 14,* 184
economic performance 110–11
economies of scale **56**
education 73, 86–87, 90, 173, 192–93
effective exchange rate **152**
efficiency 54–58
elasticity **40**–48
employment 159–61, 184
entrepreneurship **5**
environment 70–71, 74, 165
equal opportunities legislation 166
equity 86, 92–96
European Common Agricultural Policy 199
European integration 200, 204
European Union 202, 204
excess burden of a sales tax **101**
exchange medium **13**
exchange rates 34, 131, **149**–54, 162, 176–77
excludability **81**
exports 131, 134, 150, 200
external cost **65**
externalities **61**–62, *Chapter 6*

F
factors of production **5**–6, 137, 170
Family Expenditure Survey 115
financial account of the balance of payments **143**, 148, 153

firms **25**–30, 53–54
fiscal policy **185**–88, 195
foreign exchange market 34
free market economy **50**
free-rider problem **82**–84
free trade areas 202
frictional unemployment **159**–60
Friedman, Milton 129
full employment 159–61, 184

G
GDP deflator **123**
General Agreement on Tariffs and Trade (GATT) **202**
geographical immobility 96
Giffen, Sir Robert 21
Giffen good 21
global inequality 93–94
globalisation 148, **201**–2
global warming 70, 79
government budget deficit **186**
government expenditure 131, 132, 185
government failure 62, **96**–102
government intervention 92–102, 166, 186
gross domestic product (GDP) **10**, 121–24, 126–27, 169–70, 174–77
gross fixed capital formation 171, 172
gross national income (GNI) 93, 94

H
healthcare 72, 89, 173
high-income countries (HICs) 93
HIV/AIDS 173
horizontal equity 166
housing market 97–98
human capital **173**, 192
hyperinflation 158

I
ILO unemployment rate **120**
imperfect competition 60–61
imports 131, 134, 150, 200
incentives 4

incidence of a tax **99**

income and demand 20–21

income distribution 62, 93, 94, 95–96, 165–67, 175

income elasticity of demand **45**–46

income inequality 93–94, 175

income redistribution 165–67

index numbers **113**–14

indirect tax **98**

inequality of income 165–67

inferior good **20**

inflation **115**–19, 130, 156–58, 189–91

informal sector 175

information failure 62, 89–91

injections 132

Institute of Fiscal Studies 95

interest rates 129, 130, 131, 134, 189–91

internalising an externality **75**–76, 80

international competitiveness 149–54, 164

international economic growth 178–79

international externality 70, 165

International Labour Organisation (ILO) 120

International Monetary Fund (IMF) 111, 112, 201

international trade 142, 196–200

international transactions 142–54

investment 8–9, **130**–31, 138, 171–72, 192

investment income 147, 148

invisible hand **59**

invisible trade **146**

involuntary unemployment **161**

J

Jobseeker's Allowance (JSA) 119, 120

K

Keynes, John Maynard 128, 132

Krueger, Ann 201

Kyoto World Climate Summit 1997 70, 79

L

labour 5, 137, 173

Labour Force Survey 120

labour market 33, 193

labour productivity **170**

lagging indicators 124

law of demand **18**

leading indicators 124

leakages 132, 133

lemons market 91

life-cycle hypothesis 129

low-income countries (LICs) 93

luxury good **46**

M

macroeconomic equilibrium 138, 139–40

macroeconomic policy instruments *Chapter 15*

macroeconomic policy objectives *Chapter 13*, 183–84

macroeconomics **14**, 110

management 5

marginal consumers 50–51

marginal cost **53**, 57, 66, 67, 69, 77

marginal private benefit (MPB) 67, 69

marginal private cost (MPC) 66, 68

marginal propensity to consume **128**, 129

marginal propensity to withdraw 133

marginal social benefit (MSB) **51**, 66, 67, 68, 69, 77

marginal social cost (MSC) 66, 68

market demand 17

market economy **4**, 59–63

market efficiency 56–58

market equilibrium **32**

market failure **60**–63, 64, *Chapter 7*

markets **13**, 33–35

menu costs of inflation 157

merit goods **85**–87

microeconomics **14**

Microsoft 61

middle-income countries (MICs) 93

migration 148
minimum wage **97**, 160
mixed economy **4**
models **6**–7
Modigliani, Ando 129
monetary policy 188, **189**–91, 195
Monetary Policy Committee (MPC)
    190–91
money 13–14
money market 35
money stock **157**
multinational corporations (MNC)
    201, 206
multiplier **132**–33, 185

N
natural resources 5
net investment **171**
net present value **75**
NIMBY syndrome **79**
nominal exchange rate 150, 151
nominal values **113**
non-excludability 82, 84
non-renewable resources 5
non-rivalry 82, 84
non-tariff barriers **209**
normal good **20**
normative statements **14**–15, 67, 93

O
occupational immobility 96
Office of Fair Trading (OFT) 61, 89
Office of National Statistics (ONS) 111,
    112, 122
oil prices 140
opportunity cost **3**–4, 7–8, 59, 130,
    197

P
Pareto, Vilfredo 55
Pareto optimum **55**
peak 123
permanent income hypothesis 129
political business cycle 124
polluter pays principle 76

pollution 61–62, 70, 76–78, 180–81
pollution permits 77
positive statements **14**–15, 67
poverty 3, 62
price, overall level 133–34, 136–38
price and demand 17–20
price and supply 28–29
price elasticity of demand **40**–44, 99
price elasticity of supply **47**
price mechanisms 49–53
prices and preferences 50–51
prices and resource allocation 49–50
price stability 156–58, 183–84
private cost **65**
private goods **81**
privatisation 193
produced resources 5
producer surplus **52**–53
production costs 27
production externality **65**–66, 68, 70,
    76
production possibility curve (PPC)
    7–8, 55, 169, 197
productive efficiency **55**, 56–57
productivity **170**
prohibition 101–2
property rights 59, 71, 80
protectionism 206–10
public goods 62, **82**–85
public sector borrowing requirement
    (PSBR) 187
public sector net cash requirement
    (PSNCR) 187
purchasing power parity (PPP) 176–77

Q
quotas 207–9

R
real exchange rate **152**
real income effect of price increase
    18, 21
real values **113**
recession 123
regional inequality 95–96

renewable resources 5
rent controls 97–98
resource allocation 49–50
retail price index (RPI) **116**–18
rivalrous goods 81

S

sales tax 98–101
Samuelson, Paul 6, 60
scarcity **2**–3
shadow price **74**
shoe leather costs of inflation 158
short-run aggregate supply curve **137**
Smith, Adam 11, 59, 60
snob effect on demand 19–20
social cost–benefit analysis **74**–75
specialisation 11–12, 197, 198–99,
    205–6
Stiglitz, Joseph 201
structural unemployment **160**
subsidies **99**–100
substitutes **21**–22
substitution effect of price increase
    18, 21
supply 25–30
supply curve **26**–27, 29
supply shock 140, 141
supply-side policies **192**–95
sustainable development **181**–82

T

tariffs **206**–7
taxation 185–86, 194
taxes and subsidies 28, 88–89
technical efficiency **56**

technology of production 28
Thatcher, Margaret 95, 193
total factor productivity **171**
total revenue 42
tourism 73
trade barriers, reduction of 202
trade in goods and services 131
trade liberalisation 202, 206–10
trade unions 160, 193
traffic congestion 71, 75–76
transport 71, 74
trough 123

U

UK fiscal policy 187–88
UK monetary policy 189–91
UK trade 146–47, 203–5
unemployment **33**, 119–20, 159–61
unemployment benefits 193–94
United Nations 111, 176
unit elasticity 41, 47

V

Veblen, Thornstein 19
visible trade **146**
voluntary export restraint (VER) **207**
voluntary unemployment **161**

W

wages 160–61
wealth 128
withdrawals 132, 133
World Bank 93, 111, 201
world trade 202–3
World Trade Organization (WTO) **202**